Discourses of Development

EXPLORATIONS IN ANTHROPOLOGY
A University College London Series

Series Editors: Barbara Bender, John Gledhill and Bruce Kapferer

Discourses of Development

Anthropological Perspectives

Edited by

R.D. Grillo and R.L. Stirrat

BERG

Oxford • New York

First published in 1997 by
Berg
Editorial offices:
150 Cowley Road, Oxford, OX4 1JJ, UK
70 Washington Square South, New York, NY 10012, USA

Berg is an imprint of Oxford International Publishers Ltd.

Library of Congress Cataloging-in-Publication Data

A catalogue record for this book is available from the Library of
Congress.

British Library Cataloguing-in-Publication Data

A catalogue record for this book is available from the British Library.

ISBN 1 85973 940 7 (Cloth)
       1 85973 945 8 (Paper)

Typeset by JS Typesetting, Wellingborough, Northants.

Contents

Preface

This volume brings together contributors from Britain, the United States, South Asia and Africa, and includes a number of the younger scholars now working in the anthropology of development as well as established authors. The majority have a 'Sussex' connection, having studied or worked at the University of Sussex in either the School of African and Asian Studies or the Institute of Development Studies. By 'anthropology of development' we signal an association with the burgeoning tradition which is concerned with the anthropological analysis of development as a cultural, economic and political process, rather than the use of anthropology in application, important though that might be.

As may be expected, the 'development' investigated by social anthropologists generally involves directed change (social, economic, political) in a contemporary context, especially in what used to be called the 'Third World'. Certainly, this is the context within which all of the contributions to this volume are set. 'Development' is, however, a highly contentious concept, and different views of aims, objectives and practices form our starting point. Several contributors explore indigenous concepts and identify ways in which its subjects define and understand the processes which affect them. Others are concerned with what 'Western' developers (both as individuals and as representatives of agencies and institutions) think development entails. This is not to say that we subscribe to a simple, dualistic view of the world in which there are (Western) perpetrators of development and non-Western victims of it. It is not our purpose to reproduce the Manichean vision found in some of the literature. Nonetheless, our perspective certainly leads us to engage critically with processes of directed change, especially with the way in which development 'discourse', as that word is used in the Foucauldian sense, may construct the object of development. This inevitably leads us towards questions about the nature of politics, power, ideology and rhetoric, and about the relationship between discourse and institutional practice in the development field. It also leads to a concern with what might be called the 'culture of aid', and the 'interface' between development personnel and those whom 'development' is supposed to benefit. By treating development and associated processes (however they are labelled) as problematic, both conceptually and practically, the volume seeks to generate new insights into the relationships between the various parties involved and to bring a greater understanding of the ways in which particular 'discourses of development' (NB plural) are generated. Building on the ethnographic approach exemplified by a number of important contributions in this field, the volume thus offers a critical assessment of what Escobar calls the 'development encounter', emphasizing that 'development' is not always the oppressive, 'top-down', monolithic 'industry' depicted in some accounts, but rather a multi-faceted, multi-vocal process, and a complex site of contestation.

Finally, we would like to thank two Sussex graduate students, Heiko Henkel and Tina Lupton, who did all the really hard work editing copy, reading proofs and compiling the Index.

R.D. Grillo and R.L. Stirrat

Notes on Contributors

Emma Crewe	Formerly of School of African and Asian Studies, University of Sussex
James Fairhead	Queen Elizabeth House, University of Oxford
Katy Gardner	School of African and Asian Studies, University of Sussex
R.D. Grillo	School of African and Asian Studies, University of Sussex
Georgia Kaufmann	United Kingdom Jewish Aid and Development
Melissa Leach	Institute of Development Studies, University of Sussex
David Mosse	Centre for Development Studies, University of Wales, Swansea
David O. Nyamwaya	African Medical and Research Foundation, Nairobi
Johan Pottier	School of Oriental and African Studies, University of London
Alan Rew	Centre for Development Studies, University of Wales, Swansea
Kavita Srivastava	Institute of Development Studies, Jaipur, India
R.L. Stirrat	School of African and Asian Studies, University of Sussex
Maya Unnithan	School of African and Asian Studies, University of Sussex
Michael D. Woost	Hartwick College, New York

Chapter 1

Discourses of Development: The View from Anthropology

R.D. Grillo

The Social Anthropology of Development

After many years in which work on development, indeed on anything which smacked of 'applied' anthropology, was neglected or marginalized by the mainstream, in the 1980s there was a turn towards this area of the discipline (Escobar 1991; Gabriel 1991; Grillo 1985, 1994; Turton 1988). Croll and Parkin record that by the early 1990s many anthropologists had come to accept that 'to some degree, development is as much a fact of everyday life for most peoples of the world as the other kinds of overarching frameworks of assumption and action' (1992a: 8). This would seem inevitable in a country like, say, Nepal (Pigg 1992) or Sri Lanka, where, as Woost writes in this volume: 'Exposure to development discourse is a fact of everyday life. Merely walking through the cities, towns, villages and junctions, one is subjected to a caco-phony of signs and symbols related to development' (pp. 235–6).

The attention paid to development since the early 1980s seems ironic in that during the same period, anthropology in Britain and the United States became increasingly self-absorbed with post-modernism and reflexivity. Several themes come together in post-modernist anthropology in ways which, on the face of it, make it an unlikely bed-fellow for 'applied' work: an assumption that anthropologists 'construct' their data, and that what is to be investigated is the process of construction itself; a focus on the 'how' of gathering what become 'data' (i.e. fieldwork) and the placing of it in the public domain (i.e. ethnography); an emphasis on the anthropologist as 'author', on her or his 'authority' and on the relationship between anthropologist and 'subject'. Nonetheless the two strands converge, if not in 'development anthropology', then in the ideas and practices constituting the 'anthropology *of* development' (Escobar 1995: 15 ff.; Gardner and Lewis 1996; Johannsen 1992 and the papers by Fairhead and Leach, by Gardner and by Pottier in this volume).

A distinction between *development anthropology* and an *anthropology of development* (attributable to Charsley 1982), is not universally accepted: Pathy (1987), for instance, confounds the two. Nor is it always defined in the same way: Gabriel glosses it as the difference between studies which deal with 'what ought to exist in future' and those which deal with 'what exists at present'(1991: 37). This is some distance from the more usual, and useful contrast between two kinds of anthropological practice, one engaged directly in application (for example, evaluating a project or offering policy advice), the other primarily concerned with the socio-scientific analysis of development as a cultural, economic and political process. The authors of the papers included here are, on this occasion, contributing to an 'anthropology of development', though in other situations some would undoubtedly wish to describe themselves as practising 'development anthropology.'

The 'development' investigated by social anthropologists generally involves directed social and economic change in a contemporary context, especially in the 'Third World', and indeed, that is the context within which all the papers in this volume are set. Since 1980 there has been a number of significant contributions by scholars in North America, Europe (especially Britain, Holland, France and Scandinavia) and Asia (especially India) to this field of social anthropology. In Britain, for example, there appeared during the early 1990s a series of volumes which emerged from conferences and workshops sponsored by the European Inter-University Development Opportunities Study-Group (EIDOS), created in 1985 to bring together anthropologists from Britain and certain other countries, notably Holland and Germany. The EIDOS volumes included Croll and Parkin (eds) 1992, which explored anthropological contributions to our understanding of the inter-connection between culture, development and the environment, stressing in particular: 'The anthropological emphasis on people's local knowledge and use of their environments, based often on years of painstaking observation carried out in the people's language, provides a perspective that few other disciplines can match' (Croll and Parkin 1992a: 3–4). The papers by Drinkwater (1992), Leach (1992) and Pottier and Nkundabashaka (1992), each of which deal in different ways with the multiplicity of voices present in the development process, have been especially important from the point of view of themes discussed in the present volume.

The Croll-Parkin collection was followed by one edited by Pottier (1993), which examined the anthropological contribution to project appraisal and assessment (Fairhead 1993; Gatter 1993; Griffith 1993; Pottier 1993a, 1993b; Seddon 1993). A third, edited by Hobart (1993), studied the part played by Western scientific knowledge in development and development projects, arguing: 'Not only are indigenous knowledges ignored or dismissed, but the nature of the problem of underdevelopment and its solution are defined by reference to this world-ordering knowledge' (Hobart 1993: 1). It included pertinent contributions by Burghart (1993), Croll (1993), Quarles van Ufford (1993), and van Beek (1993).

Other Dutch (and British) research on development was explored in an important collection edited by Long and Long (1992) covering work by scholars based mainly in the Development Sociology Department of Wageningen Agricultural University (see also van Donge and Long 1992). The Wageningen perspective emphasized the continuing value of 'actor-oriented' approaches to the study of development, arguing that 'an actor-oriented perspective entails recognizing the "multiple realities" and diverse social practices of various actors, and requires working out methodologically how to get to grips with these different and often incompatible worlds' (Long 1992: 5). The Wageningen approach – not surprisingly, given Long's intellectual heritage – met Marcus's demand for 'strategically situated ethnography' (Marcus 1986: 172), which would integrate 'political economy and interpretative concerns' (ibid.: 84). As Marcus and Fischer (1986: 39) put it: 'Ethnography must be able to capture more accurately the historic context of its subjects, and to register the constitutive workings of impersonal international political and economic systems on the local level where fieldwork usually takes place'. Marcus found this in the so-called Manchester School of British Social Anthropology (Marcus and Fischer 1986: 56 ff.) with which Long had been associated: the papers by Arce and Long (1993) and de Vries (1992) admirably exemplify this heritage. Preston, who locates the perspective in a wider, European hermeneutic-critical tradition, praises it for 'getting at the detail of the processes of political life of agents in the Third World' (1994: 184).

The anthropology of development is particularly strong in Britain and Holland, as these four volumes testify, but almost all countries in which the social anthropological tradition is established on the eastern side of the Atlantic have contributed to work in this field. A special issue of the journal *Development Anthropology Network*, published in 1992, contained numerous papers in which the very wide range of work encompassed by the anthropology of development in various European countries is described: see Brokensha's overview (1992). Among other things, the papers reveal that there are different European traditions within the anthropology of development. In Spain, for example, there has long been a connection between development anthropology and Catholic missionary activity (Gammella 1992) which has shaped work in that country. France, too, is, as always, another country, and Baré's edited volume (1995) pulls together a very valuable account of Francophone work in the anthropology of development, and indeed in applied anthropology generally: see especially the papers by Baré himself (1995a, 1995b), and *inter alia* those by Gruénais (1995) and Lenclud (1995). These volumes and others (for example, those discussed below, which have emanated from the United States) raise issues about national traditions of anthropology and its application which have yet to be explored.

Although often apparently speaking for, or at any rate claiming to speak for, 'local' people, the citizens of developing countries, or at least those to which development policies and practices have been applied, developing country anthropologists and other social scientists are notably absent from these volumes. In the several dozen papers in the six collections cited above, the only exceptions appear to be Nkundabashaka, with a paper on Rwanda written jointly with Pottier (Pottier and Nkundabashaka 1992), and Villareal (1992). Nkundabashaka was at the National University of Rwanda; Villareal, although at the time of writing based in Holland, had previously worked for a Mexican NGO (Long 1992: 14). This is an important omission as in South Asia in particular the anthropology of development has a long and important history which needs to be recognized by Western anthropologists (for India, see *inter alia* Kalla and Singh eds 1987; Mathur 1989, 1991; Pathy 1987).

This survey has omitted the considerable volume of work that has appeared in North America throughout the period, though important contributions by Escobar (1991, 1995) and Ferguson (1994) are discussed below. What emerges from the studies considered so far?

Emergent Trends

First, though not especially important in the context of this volume, is the continuing diffidence of anthropologists in the face of other social scientists working in the development field. There is an ongoing defensiveness about what their discipline can and cannot contribute to the theory and practice of development, and indeed to the theory and practice of anthropology (Grillo 1994). Consequently, anthropologists in development and other applied fields often still feel obliged to 'sell' anthropology (Charsley 1995: 20; Escobar 1991: 666–7; Nyamwaya in this volume). The British journal *Anthropology in Action* was partly created in order to provide a forum in which applied anthropologists could present their wares. Although it now offers much more than this, in important respects it remains precisely what it set out to be. Baré's account of applied anthropology in France (1995) is also *inter alia* intended to suggest why anthropology can be useful and should be used. Many 'mainstream' anthropologists, of course, remain extremely sceptical about the contribution that their discipline can supposedly make in the applied field (e.g. Grillo 1994; Lewis 1988), which partly accounts for the continuing defensiveness of those engaged in applied research or in the anthropology of application. Charsley's description (1995: 9) of the way in which anthropological material (and the anthropologist) were incorporated into thinking about the development of sericulture in India in the 1980s shows that such defensiveness may no longer be necessary (see also Gabriel 1991).

Secondly, and again demonstrating continuity, there are the claims that anthropology illuminates those aspects of development which other disciplines ignore. When describing the benefits of an applied anthropology, practitioners still emphasize the most general attributes of the subject, especially its methodology. This is a tune which anthropologists have played for many years, at least since the heyday of Malinowski in the 1920s (Grillo 1985).

Nonetheless, there is now much greater sophistication in demonstrating what anthropologists can and do say about development, and the sense of what anthropologists can contribute has become more focused, even if still defined in terms of methodology in the broadest sense. Inevitably this focus is on ideas about the social and cultural components of change and transformation which in turn stem from anthropology's *raison d'être* as *the* science of culture. This point too has a lengthy history stretching back to the early years of the discipline. It was reiterated by Cochrane (1979), when he was concerned to inject a social and cultural dimension into the work of the World Bank. Wright (1994a) discusses a parallel movement in organizational and management studies towards a concern with 'culture'. Rew's paper in this volume constitutes an analysis of the way in which cultural and social factors appear (or do not appear) in documents concerned with project evaluation and appraisal, and examines 'how project planners and evaluation specialists themselves wrote about issues of cultural identity' (p. 88). He found a 'combination of the consciousness of culture and society with an arbitrary treatment of it' (p. 91). Usually, the conception of projects 'starts from an engineering or economistic discourse that makes issues of social agency and cultural identity only incidental to the project design and implementation' (p. 91). The justification of anthropology cannot and should not, of course, be confined to its methodology. For example, the great volume of work since 1970 concerned with gender, or more recently the environment, has not simply 'illuminated' the cultural dimensions of development, but transformed ways of thinking about social, economic and political relations (Leach's paper, 1992, which incorporates a concern with gender relations in environmental impact, brings several of these strands together). Nonetheless, it is now common practice for institutions concerned with evaluating development project proposals routinely to inquire about their gender implications and environmental impact, and anthropologists, along with many others, can claim some success for both their methodology and the substantive results of their research (though see Crewe's paper in this volume).

Thirdly, the stress on the social and cultural dimension of development is combined with an insistence on the importance of a subjective dimension and the need not just to 'take into account', but to ground analyses in a thoroughgoing incorporation of indigenous perspectives. Earlier I cited Croll and Parkin's remarking on 'the anthropological emphasis on people's local knowledge and use of their environments'. They go on to refer to 'an increasingly important body of work which draws attention to the management of ecosystems, especially agro-ecosystems, by those immediately dependent on their environmental resources – and the disregard, devaluation or ignorance of this experience and local knowledge by those practising environmental management in the name of development' (1992a: 7). Throughout much of the anthropology of development one finds contrasts of a similar kind. For example, Pottier and Nkundabashaka (1992), in the Croll and Parkin volume, discuss an opposition between *vulgarisateurs* (agricultural extension workers) and local cultivators in Rwanda. During the colonial period, these workers operated with the belief that 'indigenous agriculture had nothing to offer as it was the domain of women' (ibid.: 152), and this view persisted way beyond the end of the colonial era. Thus:

> Extension workers still cling to textbook notions of 'modern' farming at the expense of serious enquiry into the viability of local methods . . .. Cultivator-*vulgarisateurs* interactions are mostly sporadic [in Rwanda] where *vulgarisateurs* ('who know') are not interested in wasting time on people 'who do not know'. Interaction boils down to a one-way, dogmatic delivery of textbook instructions (ibid.: 151–2).

The contrast is one between 'modern', 'Western', 'scientific', 'bureaucratic' systems of knowledge and practice and those which are 'local' or 'indigenous' (further below). Crewe's paper in this volume is concerned with the way in which such indigenous knowledge is marginalized in a development context. In her example, the views of stove-users (the 'cooks', i.e. the women) 'continue to be considered "backward" and distorted by exotic beliefs' because they are represented as 'perceptions' in contrast with the 'findings' of Western scientific and technological investigations (p. 68).

To counter such marginalization – and following the pioneering work of Brokensha, Warren and Werner (eds 1980; see also Warren, Brokensha and Slikkerveer eds 1991) – anthropologists often stress the value and importance of the 'indigenous'. In some cases this leads to a privileging of 'local knowledge', causing Richards to reflect that, 'To technologically-minded improvers . . . local knowledge is often or mainly outmoded, and something to be replaced. Anthropological romantics, by contrast, in establishing their credentials as priests of humanistic plurality, are apt to celebrate it' (Richards 1993: 61). But there is a danger, he warns, of assuming that 'small-scale cultivators necessarily abound in agro-ecological wisdom'.

This leads to a fourth theme: a keen interest in 'bottom-up' solutions and mechanisms of empowerment. The focus on the local and the indigenous, widespread in anthropology, chimes with shifts in development thinking which emphasize putting local people and local knowledge first (Cernea ed. 1991; Chambers 1983; papers by Pottier and Rew in this volume). Charsley (1995: 10), for example, draws attention to what he believes was the successful application of the procedure known as 'beneficiary assessment' in the development of sericulture in India. 'Beneficiary assessment' is, he explains, a scheme for 'listening to the people', a slogan taken from the title of a book by Larry Salmen (1987), an anthropologist influential in the World Bank. This orientation is also consistent with (some) conceptions of 'sustainable' development and strategies to foster 'sustainable livelihoods' (Chambers and Conway 1992), and in accord with theories of participation (Nelson and Wright 1995; Wright 1994b).

Several papers in this volume explore this shift, examining the difficulties which some anthropologists have had with this (often populist) orientation. Croll's thought-provoking account (1993) of top-down state controlled development in Maoist China, which purported to draw on, and be based on, local knowledges and cadres, helps focus attention on what Mosse (this volume, p. 264) calls 'the development contradiction of state-directed community self-help'. Woost's paper (this volume) deals with the incorporation of participatory discourse into mainstream (international) development where currently, 'the vocabulary of alternative development . . . has been adopted at nearly all levels of the global development hierarchy' (p. 231). He also draws attention to the way in which, in the 1980s and 1990s, the longstanding discourse about 'community' in Sri Lankan development was complemented by a discourse of 'people's participation . . . everyone . . . has begun to speak the language of "participation"'(p. 229). But, he goes on to argue, 'the mainstream use of participatory rhetoric in Sri Lanka offers little in the way of alternative development. Rather, the notion of participation has been laundered and reshaped in official discourse to fit the mold of an increasingly ruthless drive to . . . turn Sri Lanka into a Newly Industrialized Country' (p. 230).

Although using the rhetoric of participation and empowerment, the way in which development has been constructed in Sri Lanka 'sets definite limits on people's participation. It does not give them the power to define development for themselves' (Woost, this volume, pp. 238). Nyamwaya, too (this volume), writing about health projects in Kenya, argues that support for 'development from below' is largely 'rhetorical': 'Development is still effected in a top-down manner, and there is always the implicit assumption that communities can only develop once they have assimilated specialized technical and material inputs from the outside' (p. 192). He adds: 'while in theory communities are supposed to play a leading role in the health-development process, the process is still largely controlled by government and NGO development "experts" who do not allow communities to play major roles' (p. 184). This and related issues are also explored in the papers by Pottier, and Unnithan and Srivastava. Pottier's analysis of participatory development in action shows that despite the endeavours of PRA (Participatory Rural Appraisal) facilitators, 'dominant discourses are difficult to quell, and . . . even the most "open" workshops remain to some extent *formal and political in character*' (p. 220 original emphases). He concludes that 'Whatever the PRA pundits say about relaxed settings, participatory workshops are structured encounters marked by hidden agendas and strategic manoeuvres' (p. 221). Unnithan and Srivastava, in this volume, extend the theme by looking closely at feminist perspectives on empowerment questions in Indian development, arguing that, 'until the language and idioms of empowerment are shared across communities and the concept of empowerment is continuously re-addressed in the local context and at the level of the state – outside the context defined by development – development programmes themselves will remain only partially effective' (p. 180).

Richard's phrase 'priests of humanistic plurality', cited above, is highly apt. The compassion for the 'people' which runs through the work of anthropologists stems in part from the natural sympathies engendered by living at close quarters with the members of the communities they study, learning the local language and so on. It comes with the fieldwork and is often associated – and this is a fifth point – with cynicism about the aims, objectives and practices of development. In the anthropologists' experience, many development projects of which they have knowledge and with which they have direct contact (because they happened to be located in their area of field research, for example) appear misconceived and misdirected. In the developing world, says Hobart, things are getting worse, and 'development projects often contribute to the deterioration' (1993: 1). 'Most development projects', he adds, 'fall seriously short' (ibid.: 3). This may or may not be an exaggeration, but certainly there is a sufficient number of abject failures of the kind described by Morris (1993) in North Yemen, an almost perfect example of bad development illustrating almost all the criticisms one can make, to justify the anthropologist's scepticism.

This means, almost inevitably, that an important component of the anthropology *of* development is, sixthly, an engagement with critical perspectives on development and the development process. Hence the way in which, in much anthropological writing, development is termed 'development', that is, placed in inverted commas (Ferguson 1994). A good example of this approach is to be found in the work of Escobar (1991; his 1995 book, discussed below, is another matter). In his 1991 paper, whose title, 'Anthropology and the development encounter', obviously recalls Asad's influential collection (1973) on the 'colonial encounter', Escobar skilfully dissects the role of 'development anthropologists' – that is, anthropologists actively engaged with development and development institutions – and points to various ways in which the dilemma faced by such anthropologists has been represented. For example, he cites Bennett as follows: 'Because development has become a historical and national necessity, anthropologists are drawn into participation even as they protest its means and ends . . . Still, to do so is to facilitate development, and such facilitation may seem to violate the anthropologist's credo of self-determination of local populations' (Bennett 1988: 2, cited in Escobar 1991: 669). This in turn leads to a search for alternative ways of doing both development and anthropology, and Escobar himself calls for 'a type of anthropological practice that distances itself from mainstream development institutions and conceptions, even when working within the "development" field' (ibid.: 677). This type of practice should, he argues, be:

> sensitive to the remaking of social analysis that critical anthropologists seem to be working toward; a type of practice that is less

concerned with standard anthropological problems and more concerned with, for instance, social movements, political struggles, and
the reconstitution of identities through development technologies and
resistance to them (ibid.).

To summarize thus far, seven themes emerge from this survey of
recent work in the anthropology of development: (1) A continuing
diffidence on the part of anthropologists working in the development field; (2) an increasingly focused sense of the anthropological
contribution defined in terms of what anthropologists say about
culture and social relations; (3) opposition to the marginalization
of indigenous peoples and their knowledge; (4) a keen interest in
bottom-up solutions and in mechanisms of empowerment; (5)
cynicism about the aims and practices of development; (6) the
emergence of critical views of development and the development
process; (7) the advocacy by some of alternative ways of doing
both development and anthropology.

Development Discourse

A crucial element in Escobar's programme for a new type of
practice is a concern with 'discourse', and anthropological studies
of development discourse are among the most important contributions to work in the anthropology of development. Inevitably
this calls for some discussion of the meaning of 'discourse'.

The term is employed in a variety of senses, which for convenience may be reduced to two (Grillo 1989). In conventional
linguistics, discourse refers to verbal exchanges, the flow of speech
in conversations. This is what 'discourse analysis' in linguistics
actually studies. But discourse may also refer to a wide range of
higher-order linguistic practices (i.e. above the level of the phrase),
of which conversation is but one instance. For example, it may be
used almost as a synonym for what is called 'register' (a style of
language used in defined situations or the property of a social
group, e.g. 'bureaucratic register'/'bureaucratic discourse'). This
leads to a second major sense in which the term is employed. In
the work of Escobar and others who write about development,
'discourse' is associated principally with the work of a number of
French scholars, among whom Michel Foucault has been especially
influential, and it is the Foucauldian version of discourse (see

especially Foucault 1972) which is pertinent here, though in this
sense discourse also bears a family resemblance to the concept of
'paradigm' (Kuhn 1970: 182 ff.).

For Foucault, a discourse consists of a group of statements
linked to a 'referential', itself consisting of 'laws of possibility, rules
of existence for the objects that are named, designated or described
within it, and for the relations that are affirmed or denied in it'
(1972: 91). Discourse thus includes language, but also what is
represented though language. A discourse (e.g. of development)
identifies appropriate and legitimate ways of practising development as well as speaking and thinking about it. A discursive
perspective, however, also embraces a totalizing conception of how
society constitutes its members (or 'subjects'), and of the role of
language in that process. Thus in writing about development
discourse, Croll and Parkin, echoing a phrase of Foucault's, refer
to the 'development gaze' (cf. the 'clinical gaze' or the 'patriarchal
gaze' in critical theory) which *inter alia* 'sets up statements about
the construction of and competition between human and non-
human agents, and the environment and human perceptions of
the environment' (1992b: 33, see also Escobar 1995: 155). Fairhead
and Leach (this volume), adopting a different term, speak of 'off-
the-shelf "narratives", current in development institutions, which
come to define development problems and justify interventions'
(p. 35). As Sherzer has suggested: 'It is discourse which creates,
recreates, modifies, and fine tunes both culture and language and
their intersection' (1987: 296). Thus discourse analysis has to
cover all that is socially and culturally worked through language.
Yet this must involve a detailed process of *contextualization*, as
well as a strong sense that, as Seidel has put it: 'Discourse is a
site of struggle. It is a terrain, a dynamic linguistic and, above
all, semantic space in which social meanings are produced *or
challenged*' (1985: 44, my emphasis).

An important early contribution to the anthropological study
of the discourse of development was the work of Raymond
Apthorpe (1985, 1986, and more recently Apthorpe and Gasper
eds 1996) which has not always received its due recognition.
Arguing that 'the semiotic avenue into cultural analysis of policy
has an original contribution to make to the study of development'
(1985: 88), Apthorpe explored this avenue through a case study of
the model of 'small farmer' rural development policy in Taiwan.
He claimed that the representation of Taiwan's rural economy

within development discourse as an instance (indeed an exemplar) of 'small farmer' development is in numerous ways misleading. Farms are, on average, indeed small, but they are embedded in an infrastructure of communication and irrigation systems which are island-wide. Moreover, the small farm model of Taiwanese society omits all 'statery' (ibid.: 97), and conveniently forgets that a significant proportion of rural incomes come from outside agriculture. Some of the key themes taken up in later writing on development discourse are already present in Apthorpe's paper, not least his insistence that 'for anthropology, semiotics has as much to do with institutions as with discourses and communication' (ibid.: 91; cf. Nuijten 1992: 205). The following section looks at three such studies.

The first of the three, the EIDOS collection edited by Hobart (1993), is also probably the earliest (although published after Ferguson's book appeared in 1990, the Hobart collection was actually based on a conference held in 1986, and the only contributor to refer to Ferguson's work is Quarles van Ufford, 1993: 158). The title of the volume (*An anthropological critique of development*) is somewhat misleading. Except for the paper by Quarles von Ufford, the book is not really about critiques of development at all. The main thread is to do with indigenous knowledge or knowledges (Richards 1993: 75), and Hobart's 'Introduction' in fact points to two kinds of knowledge. In line with the trend identified earlier (and indeed contributing to it), Hobart and some of his contributors conceive of a world with, on the one hand, a series of relatively discrete 'local' or 'indigenous' knowledges (plural), in Indonesia, say, or in Africa (for example among the Dogon; van Beek 1993), or perhaps in the Shetland Islands (Cohen 1993). On the other hand, there is 'western scientific knowledge' (singular), which consistently underestimates the value of these local knowledges. Moreover, the failures of development are seen as the 'limitations of a paradigm, which combines an idealist theory of rationality and a naturalist epistemology' (Hobart 1993: 3). There is thus, in Hobart's view, a thoroughgoing opposition between this Western paradigm and the local knowledges which it oppresses, suppresses, and finally destroys. The Western paradigm has, for example, 'proven ill-suited to explain, let alone deal with, processes which are non-natural and involve reflexivity on the part of human beings concerned. A prime example is the difficulties of coping with unintended consequences, the nemesis of so much elegant theorizing, when it encounters practice' (ibid.). Moreover, while 'local knowledges often constitute people as potential agents . . . by contrast, scientific knowledge as observed in development practice generally represents the superior knowing expert as agent and the people being developed as ignorant passive recipients or objects of this knowledge' (ibid.: 5).

Hobart further attacks the view that the gap between these systems of knowledge can be seen as one which may be overcome by improved communication (see also Gatter 1993: 178–9). This view, he claims, 'rests upon a model of knowledge as communicable propositions and presumes rationality to be shared' (Hobart 1993: 11), as well as on a 'mirage of perfect communication'. Reading Hobart, one cannot help thinking that ideally he would prefer to omit 'perfect' from that phrase. He does not go quite so far as to say so in this paper, but his thinking implies cultural solipsism: 'local' knowledges are grounded in such different philosophical foundations from 'Western' knowledge that communication between them is in fact impossible; rationalities are not shared or share-able. The lack of common ground leads him to argue that within the development process there are 'several co-existent discourses of development' (ibid.: 12), of which he identifies three: 'the professional discourse of developers' (whose underlying rationality 'has been in no small part constituted and justified by academic writings', ibid.: 3; cf. de Vries, 1992: 84, Ferguson 1994: 28, 67 ff.); 'the discourse of the local people'; and that of 'the national government and its local officials'. Then, in line with his earlier proposition, he argues: 'Just how separate and indeed *incommensurable* are the respective discourses of developers, developed and governments is a striking feature of many of the essays in this volume' (ibid.: 12, my emphasis).

If Hobart tackles the question of discourse (and discursive gaps: 'separate and incommensurable') from the point of view of philosophy, the second study, Escobar's *Encountering Development: The Making and Unmaking of the Third World* (1995), treats discourse from an avowedly political stance. Although squarely concerned with discourse and development, the book is something of a disappointment when compared with his 1991 paper which anticipated it. It is rambling, often overheated in its language, and sometimes plain wrong in its interpretation of world historical events, for example, his discussion of post-war US policy towards the colonial powers (ibid.: 31), or his account of the development of ideas about economic and social planning (ibid.: 85). He betrays a lack of understanding of the nature of the environmentalist movement and of the concept of sustainable development (portrayed as 'the last attempt to articulate modernity and capitalism before the advent of cyberculture'; ibid.: 202), and considers that the 'Bruntland report' (*sic*) 'inaugurated a period of unprecedented gluttony in the history of vision and knowledge with the concomitant rise of a global "ecocracy"'. Generally, this is a badly written, curiously ethnocentric book. Nonetheless there is more than a grain of truth in much of what Escobar writes, and his views on development and discourse are important, not least because they are likely to be widely shared by anthropologists.

Escobar is concerned with 'how the "Third World" has been produced by the discourse and practices of development since their inception in the early post-World War II period' (ibid.: 4). He draws extensively on Foucault and on Said (1978), but with 'closer attention to the deployment of the discourse through practices' (ibid.: 11) and claims that 'thinking of development in terms of discourse makes it possible to maintain the focus on domination . . . and at the same time explore more fruitfully the conditions of possibility and the most pervasive effects of development' (ibid.: 5–6). In the years following World War II, he argues, the application of science and technology, and the encouragement of public (state) intervention in the economy, even within the capitalist economies of what was later called the 'North', formed the conditions under which a particular discursive formation ('development') took shape. The emergence of this discursive formation was closely connected with the professionalization and institutionalisation of the field of development (ibid.: 46) and 'created an extremely efficient apparatus for producing knowledge about, and the exercise of power over, the Third World' (ibid.: 9). 'Development was – and continues to be for the most part – a top-down, ethnocentric, and technocratic approach, which treated peoples and cultures as abstract concepts, statistical figures to be moved up and down in the charts of "progress"' (ibid.: 44). Moreover:

> The development economist played a special role in the new universe of discourse. To him (he was almost invariably a male) belonged the expertise that was most avidly sought; it was he who knew what was needed, he who decided on the most efficient way to allocate scarce resources, he who presided over the table at which – as if they

were his personal entourage – demographers, educators, urban planners, nutritionists, agricultural experts, and so many other practitioners sat in order to mend the world (ibid.: 85).

Under 'the development gaze', 'peasants are socially constructed prior to the agent's . . . interaction with them' (ibid.: 155, 107). By 'socially constructed', Escobar means that 'the relation between client and agent is structured by bureaucratic and textual mechanisms that are anterior to their interaction', adding 'this does not deter the agent or institution from presenting the results of the interaction as "facts"'. For Escobar, as for Ferguson (see below), the World Bank provides the paradigmatic example of development discourse in action (ibid.: 167).

Escobar, then, appears to envision a set of ideas and practices which have emerged in the North and are applied willy-nilly in and to the South, in Northern economic and political interests. Like Hobart, Escobar also appears to identify three parties involved in this process, albeit different ones: the developers, those who are developed, and those who resist development. He himself joins with those calling for 'an end to development' (ibid.: vii–viii), and would seek alternatives in local resistance movements which articulate difference (ibid.: 222). As for anthropologists: 'The purpose of institutional ethnography is to unpack the work of institutions and bureaucracies, to train ourselves to see what culturally we have been taught to overlook, namely, the participation of institutional practices in the making of the world' (ibid.: 113).

The third study is Ferguson's *The anti-politics machine: 'Development', depoliticization, and bureaucratic power in Lesotho* (1994, originally 1990). Like Escobar and Hobart, his account of development discourse has been influenced by Foucault, but it stems directly from research in Southern Africa and attempts to understand the course run by development and development projects in Lesotho, especially those associated with the World Bank. For Ferguson, 'development' (always in inverted commas) constitutes a 'dominant problematic': it is 'an interpretative grid through which the impoverished regions of the world are known to us' (ibid.: xiii). Like Escobar, he believes that

The thoughts and actions of 'development' bureaucrats are powerfully shaped by the world of acceptable statements and utterances within which they live; and what they do and do not do is a product not only of the interests of various nations, classes or international agencies, but also, and at the same time, of a working out of this complex structure of knowledge (ibid.: 18).

At the same time, and like Apthorpe, Ferguson accepts the necessity of connecting 'development' discourse with 'non-discursive practices and institutions' (ibid.: 67). Moreover, one of the key analytical questions he addresses is how this 'dominant problematic' works in practice, how it is manifested in the day-to-day world of plans and projects.

This emphasis leads Ferguson to argue that his own approach departs from that of earlier radical critics of 'development' such as the neo-Marxists and dependency theorists of the 1960s and 1970s. He claims to move beyond the kind of critique which simply assumed that 'development' was always and inevitably an expression of imperialist and neo-colonialist interests, whose stated motives of alleviating poverty etc. were surely suspect, to a form of analysis which shows precisely how 'development' works in specific historical circumstances (ibid.: 11). Likewise, he is not concerned to demonstrate that 'development' in Lesotho is necessarily wrong, or based on mistaken ideas and false premises. It may well be, but his own objective is to 'show that the institutionalized production of certain kinds of ideas about Lesotho has important effects' (ibid.: xv). Thus although he provides an extensive list of failed projects, he is not especially interested in determining whether or not this or that scheme failed, or whether it was a 'good' or 'bad' project. The emphasis is rather on analysis which reveals 'characteristic sorts of encounters and frustrations, and significant kinds of outcomes' (ibid.: 228).

His chosen case study is the small southern African country of Lesotho where, during the early 1980s, some eighty international organizations engaged in 'development' work (ibid.: 6–7). Much of this work was set within the framework of an influential World Bank Report of 1975 which, 'like all "development" discourse on Lesotho, tends toward a picture in which the colonial past is a blank, economic stagnation is due to government inaction, and "development" results from "development" projects' (ibid.: 37). Lesotho in the 1960s (shortly before independence) was represented in the Report as 'an aboriginal economy, that is a "traditional" society somehow untouched by the modern world' (ibid.: 32), a picture that, as Ferguson shows, was completely at variance with almost all academic (including anthropological) writing on that region. In this way development discourse was 'constituting the complex reality of Lesotho as . . . an "LDC"' (ibid.: 28). That is, it identified Lesotho as a developing country in terms of the premises of development discourse: that it was an aboriginal society, an agricultural society located within the bounds of a 'national' economic unit, and a society which was 'governable', i.e. 'responsive to planners' blueprints' (ibid.: 72).

Ferguson analyses in some detail the various phases of the so-called Thaba-Tseka integrated rural development project for mountain development, which was inaugurated at about the time the World Bank Report appeared and which must be understood against the background of the Report's premises and conclusions. This project consisted of a large number of supposedly linked schemes (Ferguson lists 64 in operation in 1980; ibid.: 88–100) which together constituted 'almost a mini-state' (ibid.: 81) covering health and education as well as major areas of agriculture in a central part of Lesotho. Many of these projects offered what were apparently technical solutions to what were not intrinsically technical problems (ibid.: 87). For example, Ferguson argues (ibid.: 235–6) that the agricultural 'development' which was proposed could in fact only achieve any kind of success if the problem of land tenure was tackled. But no one seriously advocated doing this because the logic of the scheme demanded the privatization of land, and this would tend to create a landless peasantry who would flock to the cities. For political reasons this was something that neither the then South African government nor that of Lesotho wanted (more charitably it could be argued that the governments did not actually wish to see people driven off the land). The 'anti-politics machine' refers to the way in which development projects take over the role of government and attempt to provide 'technical' solutions.

Ferguson looks more closely at some of these projects, especially those concerned with livestock, investigating 'what happened when the plans produced by the "development" problematic . . . encountered the elaborately structured local livestock system' ibid.: 170), or, as it might be put, when 'rationality' meets 'culture' (e.g. in a rangeland project; ibid.: 173). Once again what appeared to be at stake, as Hobart would argue, was the interaction of two distinct systems of knowledge (and practice) with opposition to the official system being taken to mean ignorance or lack of understanding (ibid.: 186). In fact, by advocating a particular form of livestock management, those responsible for the projects had stumbled into a long-running local dispute:

> The . . . officials who lectured so long and hard at the village meetings were, without particularly intending it, entering into a long-established ideological dispute over the privileges and protections granted livestock as a category of property. And, again without particularly intending to, these officials, all men, entered this dispute on the side of the women (ibid.: 186–7).

In an 'Epilogue' entitled 'What is to be done' (grandiosely echoing Lenin), that question in fact becomes, 'what should we scholars and intellectuals working in or concerned with the Third World do?' (ibid.: 282). His answer: at home, political involvement; in the field, alignment with 'counter hegemonic alternative points of engagement' (ibid.: 287). Thus Ferguson, like Escobar, ends with an appeal for a rather feeble and restricted form of politically correct anthropology.

The Discourse of Development?

What emerges from this survey (apart from the spoken and unspoken assumptions of the superiority of the anthropological vision) are a number of insights which are borne out by other work, but also a number of problems which need to be addressed.

In many contexts there does indeed seem to be present a 'development gaze', or, to change the metaphor, an authoritative voice, which constructs problems and their solution by reference to a priori criteria, for example to ' broad themes which buzz around developmental agencies: malnutrition, labour bottlenecks, soil degradation and so forth' (Gatter 1993: 168–9). In the case Gatter studied, he found that policy recommendations 'implicitly address a farmer who is an individual decision maker choosing freely between a limited array of options. In actuality, most people in Mabumba live in social units in which more than one person makes decisions about farming activities' (ibid.: 170). Three detailed examples of this 'development gaze', illustrating ways in which development discourse constructs the object of development, are examined in this volume in the papers by

Fairhead and Leach, by Crewe, and by Nyamwaya (all three papers also deal with 'Western' versus 'indigenous' knowledge). Fairhead and Leach are concerned with 'readings' of the environment in Guinea, where they find what they call a 'degradation vision' of people-forest relations which has been 'incorporated not only into Guinea environmental institutions, but also into formal sector education and the popular consciousness of state functionaries' (p. 43). This vision is, moreover, 'maintained in policy circles, producing knowledge which excludes considerable counter-evidence' (p. 54). It is a vision which has roots deep in the colonial history of the country (see also Mosse, this volume, for an Indian example of discourse of similar longevity). Crewe refers to the emergence during the 1980s of what was then perceived to be a 'woodfuel crisis'. This was a very influential idea among staff in development agencies engaged in the energy sector, with important practical consequences for their views of appropriate technological solutions (types of stove for cooking). Nyamwaya also contributes to discussion of this theme, referring to the tendency of 'agencies and the government to create objects of development from social categories' (p. 187), and then apply 'standardized package solutions to problems' (p. 194). He adds that the 'project "groups"' thus constructed are 'largely artificial' and concludes that this process assists in their control.

While not denying the validity of the idea of a 'development gaze', we should note its limits. Mosse (this volume, p. 280) says, 'I am not suggesting that development institutions (irrigation bureaucracies or donor agencies) are the creators of social theory, merely that they constrain and select theory [and] nudge the thinking of their members in particular directions . . ..' There is a tendency – illustrated, for example, by Hobart, Escobar and to a lesser degree Ferguson – to see development as a monolithic enterprise, heavily controlled from the top, convinced of the superiority of its own wisdom and impervious to local knowledge, or indeed common-sense experience, a single gaze or voice which is all-powerful and beyond influence. This underpins what I would call the 'myth of development' which pervades much critical writing in this field. It might also be called the *Development Dictionary* perspective, as echoed throughout the book of that name (Sachs ed. 1992). The perspective is shared by Escobar, and to a lesser extent Ferguson and in a different way Hobart. Like most myths it is based on poor or partial history, betraying a lack of knowledge of both colonialism and decolonization, and throughout it reflects a surprising ethnocentrism: it is very much the view from North America. Ill-informed about the history of government, it has a Jacobinist conviction of the state's power to achieve miraculous things: the title of Ferguson's book, *The Anti-Politics Machine*, is an eloquent expression of this. It is also grounded in the 'victim culture'. Rather as those engaged in anti-racist training sometimes argued that there are 'racists' and there are 'victims of racism' (Donald and Rattansi eds 1992; Gilroy 1993), the development myth proposes that there are 'developers' and 'victims of development' (see the unfortunate souls portrayed on the dust-cover of Crush's edited collection, 1995). Escobar adds 'resisters of development', but there is no other way. Thus the myth would, for example, have great difficulty in encompassing the wide range of responses and agendas found among Indian women working in and for development whose work is documented in this volume in the paper by Unnithan and Srivastava.

Drinkwater (1992: 169) points to the 'danger of oversimplifying and setting up a dominant position as an easy target'. Although development is sometimes guided by authoritative, monocular visions, Unnithan and Srivastava's paper (this volume), along with Gardner's discussion of a major project in a country in South Asia, underline the point that development knowledge is not usually a single set of ideas and assumptions. Gardner observes correctly (this volume, p. 134) that

> while our understanding of 'indigenous knowledge' is growing increasingly sophisticated, that of developmental knowledge often remains frustratingly simplistic. This is generally presented as homogeneous and rooted in 'scientific rationalism' . . . [but there is a] need to understand how development knowledge is not one single set of ideas and assumptions. While . . . it may function hegemonically, it is also created and recreated by multiple agents, who often have very different understandings of their work.

To think of *the* discourse of development is far too limiting. To that extent, Hobart is correct to refer to 'several co-existent discourses of development' (1993: 12). But there is as much diversity *within* the community of 'professional developers' (one of the parties identified by Hobart), as between them and other stakeholders or 'players' (in Hobart's account, 'local people' and 'national government'). Within development there is and has always been a multiplicity of voices, 'a multiplicity of "know-ledges"' (Cohen 1993: 32), even if some are more powerful than others: as Pottier, this volume, points out, 'a simple recording of the plurality of voices' is never enough. Preston, who has written extensively on development, provides an interesting way into this subject. *Discourses of Development: State, Market and Polity in the Analysis of Complex Change* (1994) is an exercise in political theory written largely from outside anthropology which places the study of discourse less in the work of Foucault than in a wider hermeneutic-critical tradition. However, in broader agreement with Foucauldian perspectives than he might allow, Preston argues that development discourse is both 'institutionally extensive [and] comprises a stock of ideas that informs the praxis of many groups' (ibid.: 4). It is not, however, singular. He identifies three discourses of development, each located in the changing political economy of the second half of the twentieth century. Each 'find their vehicles in particular institutional locations, and of course are disposed to particular political projects' (ibid.: 222).

First there is (or was) a discourse of 'state engendered order', and of the intervention of experts, located in UN agencies and embodied in multilateral and bilateral aid agencies. This was the discourse of the post-WWII settlement (the Keynsian consensus), which elsewhere he calls an 'elaborated, authoritative, inter-ventionist ideology' (ibid.: 135), incorporating a neo-evolutionary theory of change, derived from Durkheim; an ethnocentric affirmation of the West as a scientific, ethical and political model; a concern with order and with markets; and a vision of elites as the principle agents of change. Secondly, following the collapse of that settlement in the 1970s, the prevailing discourse became that of 'market-engendered spontaneous order', institutionally located in the World Bank and IMF. Third is what he calls 'the discourse of the public sphere' constructed 'on the affirmation of the idea-set of modernity' and 'the optimistic, reason-informed pursuit of formal and substantive democracy' (ibid.: 223). This perspective, which is more or less where Preston himself stands, may be found, he believes, in university research institutes, NGOs and charities.

Marsden (1994a: 36) also presents a much more nuanced view of the current development process and of the range of issues being addressed, and of a much more variegated discourse of development:

It is now commonplace to hear that there are many paths to development, each built on a different cultural base, and using different tools, techniques and organizations. The assumptions underlying the view that it would be sufficient to transfer western technology and expertise no longer hold. It is not the 'native' who is backward, nor is it a failure to incorporate the 'human factor' which is at fault, but the essential inappropriateness of the western package that was on offer (Marsden 1994b: 41).

Likewise:

The arrogance with which policy makers and planners assumed that they were writing on a *tabula rasa* as they intervened in the Third World in the name of development, is being replaced by a reflexive understanding of the partiality of their own knowledge and a heightened appreciation of the value of other ways of perceiving the development task (ibid.: 46).

As Gardner (this volume, p. 143) notes: 'Income generation, participation and "the grassroots" were, by the late 1980s, key buzz words . . .. Gender too was now very definitely on the agenda.' This emerges from Kaufmann's 'partial ethnography', as she calls it, of the different ways in which British practitioners conceptualize the development process. In interviews with her informants:

The various positions of the developers were reflected in their use of different discourses . . .. Words such as 'empowering', 'enabling', 'choice' and 'sustainability' reflect the dominant paradigm operating in development in the early 1990s and would not have been dominant ten or fifteen years ago. The terms are one aspect of the so-called New Poverty Agenda . . .. This discourse contrasts strikingly with the reference to standards of living, measures of economic performance and wealth more often used by the civil servants in general and economists in particular (this vol., p. 117).

'The different discourses are not trivial,' she adds: 'The choice of words reflects different ideological positions [and] different goals' . . . (ibid.; p. 117).

The variegated and multi-vocal nature of the development process described by Gardner is illustrated in Seddon's account (1993: 81) of the complex and carefully constructed composition of teams put together by organizations such the International Fund for Agricultural Development (IFAD). The account shows that the

assumption made by Ferguson, Escobar and Hobart (especially
the latter), that projects are devised by, and in the hands of,
'Western' (scientifically oriented) experts, incapable of communi-
cating with 'locals' and taking 'their' knowledge into account,
needs re-evaluating. For example, the acting leader of one project
in Mali was 'a Malian, a Touareg, a native of Kidal *cercle*, and a
socio-linguist' (Seddon 1993: 99). Such details do not square readily
with Hobart's inclination to interpret development as a Manichean
struggle of epistemologies between which communication is
difficult if not impossible. The 'Other' is constructed as if, behind
an impermeable barrier of epistemology, 'we' can never understand 'them'.

Although Seddon accepts that 'all too often development
projects designed and implemented by international aid agencies
lack that crucial appreciation and understanding of the dynamics
of local economy and society that derives from what I call the
"anthropological approach"' (1993: 71), he believes that Canadian
and Scandinavian agencies, and organizations like IFAD, are more
sympathetic to 'grassroots approaches' (anthropological methods
on the one hand, participative methods on the other). Moreover,
IFAD's approach 'has changed over the last decade, from a more
technical "top-down" form of intervention designed essentially
to improve livestock productivity to one more concerned with the
encouragement of herders' associations to undertake their own
economic development and environmental management' (ibid.:
76). It is often suggested that the NGO sector allows a greater
variety of views of development, and greater sensitivity and
responsiveness to local needs and opinions (see, for example,
Garber and Jenden's account, 1993, of working with Band Aid).
Both Northern and Southern NGOs are, it is argued, able to foster
alternative visions and discourses in ways which sometimes place
their organisers in a difficult position *vis-à-vis* dominant groups.
Woost's paper (this volume) in fact shows that NGO interpretations
of alternative development strategies vary very widely, some being
quite close to the orthodox and mainstream. Others and those who
run them – often the most radical – are indeed politically in a
difficult situation and subject to severe harassment from the
government. The experience of the Sarvodaya Shramadana
Movement (which promotes a Buddhist vision of development)
is salutary in this respect (Woost, this volume).

None of this suggests, as is sometimes implied, an imperviousness to experience, an invincible ignorance, an inability to change on the part of developers (one change, though not necessarily for the better, is that nowadays the guru of development is more likely to be the management expert than the economist; cf. Marsden 1994b: 41). Despite what Hobart says about distancing himself from 'romantic fantasies' about indigenous knowledge (1993: 5), there is a real danger of assuming that ignorance is one-sided; that is, it is 'we' who are only and always ignorant. The danger is that indigenous knowledge is seen as complete, accomplished, and hence static and unchanging. Neither side has a monopoly of knowledge or ignorance, neither party is impervious to argument. Drinkwater (1992: 184), for example, shows how having been 'fixated' on certain policies and practices regarding cattle-grazing in Zimbabwe for forty-five years (both before and after independence), 'growing counter-evidence is forcing certain justifications of the old policies to be declared the shibboleths they are'. His account of his attempts to influence the dominant discourse, with help from a friendly ecologist, is illuminating in this regard (ibid.: 175 ff.).

There often remains, of course, a significant distance between the ideas and practices of development agencies and those of 'local' people. Arce and Long's account (1992) of 'knowledge interfaces' in bureaucrat-peasant interaction in Jalisco (Mexico) is especially valuable for the way in which it reveals 'the types of discontinuities that exist and the dynamic and emergent character of the struggles and interactions that take place, showing how actors' goals, perceptions, values, interests and relationships are reinforced or reshaped by this process' (ibid.: 214). In this instance, certain ideas about technological change (specifically concerning the use of tractors) which emanated from development agencies had been 'processed through a body of local knowledge' (ibid.: 230), thus making them incompatible with the favoured development model. Roberto (*el grilloso*, 'troublemaker'), the extension worker anti-hero of their account, was fully aware of this and other discrepancies between peasant and official views, though the politics of the situation left him almost powerless to act. His case showed 'the enormous gap in communication and in power differentials in Mexico between peasants and state development agencies' (ibid.: 243; a reading of this paper alongside Ferguson is a salutary experience). An important theme, not discussed here, is the way in which anthropologists themselves become caught up in the development process as 'experts' who can bridge discursive gaps (e.g. Gatter 1993: 169–70).

At the same time it should be pointed out that the concept 'local' needs to be handled with care (see, for example, Marsden's thoughtful discussion, 1994a, 1994b, of the problems posed by the notion of 'indigenous' people, 'indigenous' knowledge etc.). Crewe, whose paper (this volume) is concerned *inter alia* with 'evolutionist' and 'androcentric' assumptions in the development process, is worried by the way in which, in expatriate development-speak, 'local' or 'locals' = 'native', as that term was used in the colonial period. She comments: 'Expatriate experts give authority to policy and planning decisions, authority which seems to slip away from national experts.' 'Is it racism?' she asks (p. 72). Certainly it is highly pertinent to wonder what 'local' or 'indigenous' might mean in a country such as India. How is the presence in a development project of Professor M.N. Srinivas, the doyen of Indian anthropology, to be viewed (Charsley 1995), or the feminist activists described by Unnithan and Srivastava (this volume)? Such notions are increasingly inadequate in a globalized world. Pigg's account of *bikas*, the Nepali term usually glossed as 'development', is unusual for the sophisticated way in which it shows how an 'indigenous' concept provides a way of expressing the relationship between various parts of Nepali society (town and country, for instance), and also 'the term through which Nepalis understand their relationship to other parts of the world' (1992: 497). It thus 'connects villagers, urban Nepalese elites, national political institutions, international development, and represent-ations of the third world in the West' (ibid.: 511) (see also Unnithan and Srivastava, this volume, for discussion of the related term *vikas*).

This suggests that if the anthropology of development must be increasingly 'multi-vocal', it must also be increasingly 'multi-sited' (Marcus 1995). Harrison's doctoral thesis (1995) on aquaculture in Africa, based on extensive field research, is an example of the multi-focused, multi-level ethnography that will be needed. Influenced by the work of Ferguson, it goes beyond it by following an FAO aquaculture programme at a number of different levels (from Rome, to Harare (Zimbabwe), to the capital of Luapula Province in Zambia, and to the villages), revealing a greater awareness of the complexity of the processes involved and the multiplicity of voices within it. The thesis moves, disconcertingly at times, from a discussion of development discourse to detailed village-level studies, and then back to the aid organizations. It was manifestly not straightforward to write, and there is no easy, obvious and accepted method for moving between levels and representing different voices in the way that Harrison attempts: indeed, to claim otherwise might well exacerbate the tendency to represent participants as 'them' and 'us' which Harrison rightly deplores.

Studies such as Pigg's, which seek to explore indigenous concepts of development and identify ways in which its subjects define and understand the processes which affect them, or Harrison's essay in multi-sited ethnography, reveal the richness and maturity of the current anthropology of development. For Long, one of the advantages of the actor-oriented approach that he advocates is precisely that it obliges the researcher to acknowledge these 'multiple realities' (1992: 5) and provides a method for examining the coexistence of World Bank officials, 'technical experts', ministers and civil servants, councillors and functionaries, NGOs (from North and South), local people (women and men), a 'radical peasant leader' (de Vries 1992: 61 ff.), and perhaps an anthropologist or two.

Note

1. A number of colleagues commented on earlier versions of this chapter. In particular, I would like to thank Emma Crewe, Buzz Harrison, Jock Stirrat, Anne Whitehead and Maya Unnithan.

References

Apthorpe, R. (1985), 'Pleading and Reading Agricultural Development Policy: Small Farm, Big State and the "Case of Taiwan"', in R. Grillo and A. Rew (eds), *Social Anthropology and Development Policy*, London: Tavistock.

Apthorpe, R. (1986), 'Development Policy Discourse', *Public Administration and Development*, 6: 377–89.

—— and D. Gasper (eds) (1996), *Arguing Development Policy: Frames and Discourses*, London: Frank Cass.

Arce, A. and N. Long (1993), 'Bridging Two Worlds: An Ethnography of Bureaucrat-peasant Relations in Western Mexico', in M. Hobart (ed.), *An Anthropological Critique of Development: The Growth of Ignorance*, London: Routledge.

Asad, T. (ed.) (1973), *Anthropology and the Colonial Encounter*, London: Ithaca Press.

Baré, J.-F. (1995), 'En quoi que bien consister une anthropologie appliquée au développement?', in J.-F.Baré (ed.), *Les applications de l'anthropologie*, Paris: Karthala.

—— (1995a), 'La question des applications de l'anthropologie en France', in J.-F.Baré (ed.), *Les applications de l'anthropologie*, Paris: Karthala.

—— (ed.) (1995b), *Les applications de l'anthropologie: un essai de réflexion collective depuis la France*, Paris: Editions Karthala.

Bennett, J.W. (1988), 'Introductory Essay', in J.W. Bennett and J. Bowen (eds), *Production and Autonomy: Anthropological Studies and Critiques of Development*, Lanham, MD: University Press of America.

Brokensha, D. (1992), 'Development Anthropology in Europe: An Introduction', *Development Anthropology Network*, 10, no. 1: 1–5.

——, D.M. Warren and O. Werner (eds) (1980), *Indigenous Knowledge Systems and Development*, Lanham: University Press of America.

Burghart, R. (1993), 'His Lordship at the Cobbler's Well', in M. Hobart (ed.), *An Anthropological Critique of Development: The Growth of Ignorance*, London: Routledge.

Cernea, M. (ed.) (1991), *Putting People First: Sociological Variables in Rural Development*, Oxford: Oxford University Press for The World Bank (2nd edn).

Chambers, R. (1983), *Rural Development: Putting the Last First*, London: Longman.

—— and G. Conway (1992), *Sustainable Rural Livelihoods: Practical Concepts for the 21st Century*, IDS Discussion Paper, 296, University of Sussex: Institute of Development Studies.

Charsley, S. (1982), *Culture and Sericulture: Social Anthropology and Development in a South Indian Livestock Industry*, London: Academic Press.

—— (1995), 'Anthropology and the South Indian Silk Industry', unpublished paper.

Cochrane, G. (1979), *The Cultural Appraisal of Development Projects*, New York: Praeger Special Studies.

Cohen, A.P. (1993), 'Segmentary Knowledge: A Whalsay Sketch', in M. Hobart (ed.), *An Anthropological Critique of Development: The Growth of Ignorance*, London: Routledge.

Croll, E. (1993), 'The Negotiation of Knowledge and Ignorance in China's Development Strategy', in M. Hobart (ed.), *An Anthropological Critique of Development: The Growth of Ignorance*, London: Routledge.

—— and D. Parkin (1992a), 'Anthropology, the Environment and Development', in E. Croll, and D. Parkin (eds), *Bush Base, Forest Farm: Culture, Environment and Development*, London: Routledge.

—— (1992b), 'Cultural Understandings of the Environment', in E. Croll and D. Parkin (eds), *Bush Base, Forest Farm: Culture, Environment and Development*, London: Routledge.

—— and D.J. Parkin (eds) (1992), *Bush Base, Forest Farm: Culture, Environment and Development*, London: Routledge.

Crush, J. (ed.) (1995), *Power of Development*, Routledge: London.

Development Anthropology Network (1992), Special Issue on Development Anthropology in Europe, *Development Anthropology Network*, 10, Spring 1992.

de Vries, P. (1992), 'A Research Journey', in N Long and A. Long (eds), *Battlefields of Knowledge: The Interlocking of Theory and Practice in Social Research and Development*, London: Routledge.

Donald, J. and A. Rattansi (eds) (1992), *'Race', Culture and Difference*, London: Sage.

Drinkwater, M. (1992), 'Cows eat grass don't they? Evaluating Conflict over Pastoral Management in Zimbabwe', in E. Croll and D. Parkin (eds), *Bush Base, Forest Farm: Culture, Environment and Development*, London: Routledge.

Escobar, A. (1991), 'Anthropology and the Development Encounter', *American Ethnologist*, 18/4: 658–82.

—— (1995), *Encountering Development: The Making and Unmaking of the Third World*, Princeton: Princeton University Press.

Fairhead, J. (1993), 'Representing Knowledge: The "New Farmer" in Research Fashions', in J. Pottier (ed.), *Practising Development*, London: Routledge.

Ferguson, J. (1994 [1990]), *The Anti-Politics Machine: 'Development'*,

Depolitization, and Bureaucratic Power in Lesotho, Minneapolis: University of Minnesota Press.

Foucault, M. (1972), *The Archaeology of Knowledge* (trans. A.M. Sheridan Smith), London: Tavistock Publications.

Gabriel, T. (1991), *The Human Factor in Rural Development*, London: Belhaven Press.

Gammella, J.F. (1992), 'Development Aid and Development Anthropology in Spain', *Development Anthropology Network*, 10/1: 20–3.

Garber, B. and P. Jenden (1993), 'Anthropologists or Anthropology? The Band Aid Perspective on Development Projects', in J. Pottier (ed.), *Practising Development*, London: Routledge.

Gardner, K. and D. Lewis (1996), *Anthropology, Development and the Post-modern Challenge*, London: Pluto Press.

Gatter, P. (1993), 'Anthropology in Farming Systems Research: A Participant Observer in Zambia', in J. Pottier (ed.), *Practising Development*, London: Routledge.

Gilroy, P. (1993), *Small Acts: Thoughts on the Politics of Black Culture*, London: Serpent's Tail.

Griffith, G. (1993), 'Project Appraisals: The Need for Methodological Guidelines', in J. Pottier (ed.), *Practising Development*, London: Routledge.

Grillo, R.D. (1985), 'Applied Anthropology in the 1980s: Retrospect and Prospect', in R.D. Grillo and A. Rew (eds), *Social Anthropology and Development Policy*, London: Tavistock.

—— (1989), *Dominant Languages*, Cambridge: Cambridge University Press.

—— (1994), 'The Application of Anthropology in Britain, 1983–1993', in C. Hann (ed.), *When History Accelerates*, London: Athlone Press.

—— and A. Rew (eds) (1985), *Social Anthropology and Development Policy*, London: Routledge (ASA Monographs 25).

Gruénais, Marc-E. (1995), 'Anthropologie médicale appliquée', in J.-F. Baré (ed.), *Les applications de l'anthropologie*, Paris: Karthala.

Harrison, E. (1995), *Big Fish and Small Ponds: Aquaculture Development from the FAO, Rome, to Luapula Province, Zambia*. University of Sussex, D.Phil. thesis.

Hobart, M. (1993), 'Introduction: The Growth of Ignorance?', in M. Hobart (ed.), *An Anthropological Critique of Development: The Growth of Ignorance*, London: Routledge.

—— (ed.) (1993), *An Anthropological Critique of Development: The Growth of Ignorance*, London: Routledge.

Johannsen, A.M. (1992), 'Applied Anthropology and Post-modernist Ethnography', *Human Organization*, 51: 71–81.

Kalla, A.K. and K.S. Singh (eds) (1987), *Anthropology, Development, and Nation Building*, New Delhi: Concept Publishing.

Kuhn, T.S. (1970), *The Structure of Scientific Revolutions*, Chicago and London: The University of Chicago Press (2nd enlarged edn).

Leach, M. (1992), 'Women's Crops in Women's Spaces: Gender Relations in Mende Rice Farming', in E. Croll and D. Parkin (eds), *Bush Base, Forest Farm: Culture, Environment and Development*, London: Routledge.

Lenclud, G. (1995), 'La question de l'application dans la tradition anthropologique française', in J.-F. Baré (ed.), *Les applications de l'anthropologie*, Paris: Karthala.

Lewis, I.M. (1988), 'Anthropologists for Sale?', *LSE Quarterly*, 2: 49–63.

Long, N. (1992), 'Introduction', in N. Long and A. Long (eds), *Battlefields of Knowledge: The Interlocking of Theory and Practice in Social Research and Development*, London: Routledge.

—— and A. Long (eds) (1992), *Battlefields of Knowledge: The Interlocking of Theory and Practice in Social Research and Development*, London: Routledge.

Marcus, G. (1986), 'Contemporary Problems of Ethnography in the Modern World System', in J. Clifford and G. Marcus (eds), *Writing Culture*, Berkeley: University of California Press.

—— (1995), 'Ethnography in/of the World System: The Emergence of Multi-sited Ethnography', *Annual Review of Anthropology*, 24: 95–117.

—— and M. Fischer (1986), *Anthropology as Cultural Critique*, Chicago: The University of Chicago Press.

Marsden, D. (1994a), 'Indigenous Management: Introduction', in S. Wright (ed.), *Anthropology of Organizations*, London: Routledge.

—— (1994b), 'Indigenous Management and the Management of Indigenous Knowledge', in S. Wright (ed.), *Anthropology of Organizations*, London: Routledge.

Mathur, H.M. (1989), *Anthropology and Development in Traditional Societies*, New Delhi: Vikas Publishing House.

—— (1991), *The Human Dimension of Development*, New Delhi: Concept Publishing.

Morris, T. (1993), ''Eze-vu' – Success through Evaluation: Lessons from a Primary Health-care Project in North Yemen', in J. Pottier (ed.), *Practising Development*, London: Routledge.

Nelson, N. and S. Wright (eds) (1995), *Power and Participatory Development: Theory and Practice*, London: Intermediate Technology Publications.

Nuijten, M. (1992), 'Local Organization as Organizing Practices', in N. Long and A. Long (eds), *Battlefields of Knowledge: The Interlocking of Theory and Practice in Social Research and Development*, London: Routledge.

Pathy, J. (1987), *Anthropology of Development: Demystifications and Relevance*, New Delhi: Gian Publishing House.

Pigg, S.L. (1992), 'Constructing Social Categories through Place: Social Representation and Development in Nepal', *Comparative Studies in Society and History*, 34/3: 491–513.

Pottier, J. (1993a), 'Introduction: Development in Practice: Assessing Social Science Perspectives', in J. Pottier (ed.), *Practising Development*, London: Routledge.

—— (1993b), 'The Role of Ethnography in Project Appraisal', in J. Pottier (ed.), *Practising Development*, London: Routledge.

—— and A. Nkundabashaka (1992), 'Intolerable Environments: Towards a Cultural Reading of Agrarian Practice and Policy in Rwanda', in E. Croll and D. Parkin (eds), *Bush Base, Forest Farm: Culture, Environment and Development*, London: Routledge.

Pottier, J. (ed.) (1993), *Practising Development*, London: Routledge.

Preston, P.W. (1994), *Discourses of Development: State, Market and Polity in the Analysis of Complex Change*, Aldershot: Avebury.

Quarles van Ufford, P. (1993), 'Knowledge and Ignorance in the Practices of Development', in M. Hobart (ed.), *An Anthropological Critique of Development: The Growth of Ignorance*, London: Routledge.

Richards, P. (1993), 'Cultivation: Knowledge or Performance?', in M. Hobart (ed.), *An Anthropological Critique of Development: The Growth of Ignorance*, London: Routledge.

Sachs, W. (ed.) (1992), *The Development Dictionary: A Guide to Knowledge and Power*, London: Zed Books.

Said, E. (1978), *Orientalism*, London: Routledge.

Salmen, L.F. (1987), *Listen to the People: Participant-observer Evaluation of Development Projects*, New York: Oxford University Press for World Bank.

Seddon, D. (1993), 'Anthropology and Appraisal: The Preparation of two IFAD Pastoral Development Projects in Niger and Mali', in J. Pottier (ed.), *Practising Development*, London: Routledge.

Seidel, G. (1985), 'Political Discourse Analysis', in T. van Dijk (ed.), *Handbook of Discourse Analysis, Vol. 4*, London: Academic Press, pp. 43-60.

Sherzer, J. (1987), 'Language, Culture and Discourse', *American Anthropologist*, 89: 295–309.

Turton, D. (1988), 'Anthropology and Development', in P.F. Leeson and M.M. Minogue (eds), *Perspectives on Development*, Manchester: Manchester University Press.

van Beek, W.E.A. (1993), 'Processes and Limitations of Dogon Agricultural Knowledge', in M. Hobart (ed.), *An Anthropological Critique of Development: The Growth of Ignorance*, London: Routledge.

van Donge, J.K. and N. Long (1992), 'Development Anthropology in the Netherlands: Commitment, Crisis and Outlook', *Development Anthropology Network*, 10/1: 15–19.

Villareal, M. (1992), 'The Poverty of Practice', in N. Long and A. Long (eds), *Battlefields of Knowledge: The Interlocking of Theory and Practice in Social Research and Development*, London: Routledge.

Warren, M., D. Brokensha and L.J. Slikkerveer (eds) (1991), *Indigenous Knowledge Systems: The Cultural Dimension of Development*, London and New York: Kegan Paul International.

Wright, S. (1994a), 'Culture in Anthropology and Organizational Studies', in S. Wright (ed.), *Anthropology of Organizations*, London: Routledge.

—— (1994b), 'Introduction: Clients and Empowerment', in S. Wright (ed.), *Anthropology of Organizations*, London: Routledge.

Chapter 2

Webs of Power and the Construction of Environmental Policy Problems: Forest Loss in Guinea

James Fairhead and *Melissa Leach*

Introduction

This chapter examines the contrast between the formulation of problems in development policy and the perspectives of villagers whose views have been subjugated, and everyday activities criminalized, within this formulation.[1] We attempt to identify the conditions in which certain demonstrably false ideas about environmental change have come to acquire validity in policy circles, while others, more correct and espoused by inhabitants, have been excluded from consideration and investigation.

Several authors have recently spotlighted the presence of particular off-the-shelf 'narratives', current in development institutions, which come to define development problems and justify interventions, particularly in conditions where data are poor, time is short, national agendas are overruled and local consultation impossible (Hoben 1993; Roe 1991, 1995). Narrative construction is the stuff of synthesis overview writing within development agencies and policy research institutes, and of inter-agency analytical alignment in development approaches. Narratives help decision-makers confidently fill the gap between ignorance and expediency.

With the spotlight on the narrative, less attention has been given to the ways in which the discursive processes which condition narrative construction also condition knowledge produced about development problems, including the generation of credible 'data'

– often in large amounts. Adherents to the environmental-degradation view explored in this chapter think that there is abundant evidence to support their conviction. Focusing on these narratives also encourages analysis to treat the relationship between international and local agendas as one of dislocation, divided by a gulf which the increasing use of development-institutionally acceptable research methods, apparently responsive to local concerns, might help bridge. Less attention is given to ways in which different sections of local society become involved in the discursive processes in which development-policy knowledge is produced. Such involvement may have developed over long periods, given that present development concerns frequently build on old debates which have already been incorporated into local political processes.

Environmental issues are pertinent in this respect because of the degree to which the environment has become a dominant development concern. They particularly invite critical analysis because of the clarity with which global issues and constituencies as well as local ones are involved in defining and responding to the development problem. The analysis summarised in this chapter (for a detailed treatment, see Fairhead and Leach 1996a) adds to a number of recent historical and social anthropological analyses which have questioned the readings of environmental change which have been driving development policies, revealing major contrasts between external perspectives and locally experienced realities. Contrasting definitions of the environmental problem contain particular images of local practices and justify contrasting development paradigms, commonly amounting to repression of, as opposed to support for, local techniques and institutions (e.g. Behnke and Scoones 1991; Leach and Mearns 1996; Thompson, Hatley and Warburton 1986; Tiffen, Mortimore and Gichuki 1993). The case considered in this chapter concerns ongoing 'savannization' of tropical forest which is not, in fact, taking place.

Forest Loss Perceived

The vegetation of Guinea's Kissidougou prefecture reflects its position in West Africa's forest-savannah transition zone, consisting of patches of dense, high, semi-deciduous rainforest dispersed in savannah. For at least a century, environmental policy-makers have considered the forest patches, which surround old and new village sites, as the last endangered relics of a once extensive natural-forest cover now destroyed by local farming and fire-setting, a destruction they have continually sought to redress. But the experiences of most of Kissidougou's Kissi and Kuranko inhabitants, as well as archival and air photographic comparisons, do not support this view. Instead, they show forest islands to be the result of human management, created around villages in savannah by their inhabitants. They also show the woody vegetation cover of savannahs to have been increasing during the period when policy-makers have believed the opposite (Fairhead and Leach 1996a, 1996b).

West African vegetation maps, which show vegetation zones in more or less horizontal bands, easily lend themselves to interpretation as temporal as well as spatial transitions (Figure 2.1). Whether from desertification, sahelianization or savannization of forest, observers have been tempted to see each zone as the anthropogenically degraded derivate of a prior vegetation type. On many maps, the forest-savannah transition zone is marked explicitly as a 'derived savannah', or ex-forest, zone. And in Guinea, policy-makers since the turn of the century have been convinced of this southwards shift, with the conflation of spatial and temporal transitions incorporated into the scientific canon informing national and regional environmental policy. The first forest reserves established in Kissidougou in 1932 were conceived of as a protective 'curtain' to halt the southwards spread of fire- and farming-induced savannization. In 1993, the same conflation of spatial with temporal zones provided the logic for a major donor-funded environmental rehabilitation project to take forty Kissidougou farmers on a journey to northern Mali, to see the future of their own landscape should protective measures not be undertaken.

Within each vegetation zone, the iconography of spatio-temporal shifts on the vegetation map is complemented by the iconography of 'divergence from a climax vegetation type', the notional maximum vegetation which could exist given climatic conditions. This contains the idea of the previous existence of a 'bigger' and 'better' vegetation type 'prior to human disturbance', and closer to the 'Eden' which Africa's environment so often represented in colonial imaginations. In this way, present conditions in each vegetation zone may be envisaged as the

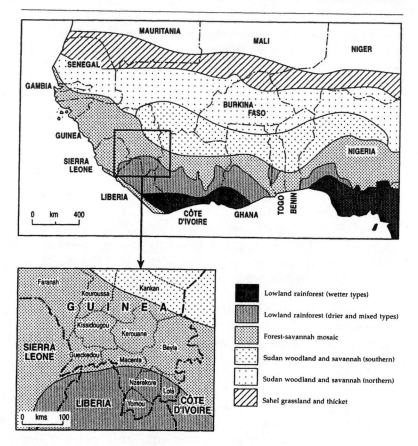

Figure 2.1. Kissidougou Prefecture in the forest-savannah mosaic zone of West Africa (Based on the UNESCO/AEFTAT/UNSO vegetation map of Africa)

anthropogenically degraded derivate of their predecessor (Figure 2.2). And so in Kissidougou, climate (e.g. annual rainfall levels over 1600 mm) and the presence of humid forest species and patches are taken as indicative of high forest potential and hence of its past existence.

The assumption of anthropogenic degradation of a prior natural forest formation was integral to the first delineation of West African vegetation zones in the early colonial period by the botanist Chevalier. This analysis was transferred directly into contemporary policy, since Chevalier was, at the time, the most senior advisor to the French West African colonial administrations responsible for

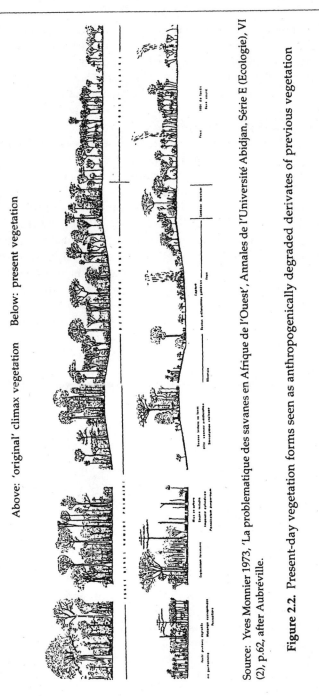

Above: 'original' climax vegetation   Below: present vegetation

Source: Yves Monnier 1973, 'La problematique des savanes en Afrique de l'Ouest', Annales de l'Université Abidjan, Série E (Ecologie), VI (2), p.62, after Aubréville.

Figure 2.2. Present-day vegetation forms seen as anthropogenically degraded derivates of previous vegetation

environmental concerns. Subsequently, deductions made from analysis of the botanical composition ('phytosociology') of vegetation forms in these zones by botanists such as Aubréville, Adam and Schnell reinforced the hypothesis that the forest-savannah mosaic was in temporal transition. Observing the tree species characteristic of forest patch boundaries, for instance, botanists deduced that they indicated savannized forest (e.g. Adam 1948, 1968). They did not consider other possibilities: that this 'transition woodland' could represent a stable intermediate form, the establishment of forest in savannah, or the complex outcome of inhabitants' management strategies.

As Aubréville and Adam in turn became senior figures in French West Africa's forestry administrations, so their phytosociology, interpreted within the degradation logic, became institutionalized as the principle methodology for assessing regional vegetation change, and their publications became key texts in comprehending West African environmental history more generally (e.g. Aubré-ville 1949). Characteristically, these botanists directly observed landscape features and deduced history and people's impact from them. Their disciplinary position and the social conditions of their fieldwork reinforced their pejorative visions of local farming and fire-management practices, rendering it both difficult and seemingly unnecessary to verify change with local people themselves.

It has remained 'scientifically' acceptable to interpret vegetation history and anthropogenic impact from snapshot landscape observations, with deductions from plant and other indicators, vegetation surveys and remotely sensed imagery now adding to the repertoire. For example, modern observers of Kissidougou often take the presence of oil palms to indicate that forest has retreated from the area, while the team preparing Guinea's forestry action plan (République de Guinée 1988) deduced from their air photographic 'snapshots' and vegetation surveys that southern Kissidougou was a 'post-forest' zone. Similar social distance and pre-conviction as characterized the colonial botanists enables today's analysts too to overlook both local people's environmental experiences and management, and historical methods (e.g. oral histories and archive consultation) in comprehending environmental influences and trends.

Historical data sets are nevertheless available today, and their examination produces a very different picture of vegetation change. We compiled a picture of Kissidougou's vegetation dynamics through elderly people's oral recollections concerning vegetation use and management, and conducted comparative analysis of 1952, 1982 and 1991 air photographs and 1989/92 SPOT satellite data, and landscape descriptions found in archives dating from 1893. Social-anthropological fieldwork in Kissi and Kuranko villages throughout 1992 and 1993 provided an understanding of inhabitants' agro-ecological concepts and techniques and the social conditions of their application in the present, enabling closer enquiry into land-use change.

Far from being relics, Kissidougou's forest islands prove to have been created by local populations. In the majority of villages, elders describe how their ancestors encouraged forest-patch formation around settlements which had been founded either in savannah or beside gallery forests. The formation and growth of forest islands around recently established village sites is often visible when 1952 and modern air photographs are compared. Villagers also suggest that woody cover on the upland slopes and plateaux between the forest islands has generally increased during this century, and not declined as has been thought. In the north and east of the prefecture, grass savannahs have become more densely wooded with relatively fire-resistant savannah trees and oil palms. Indeed, the fact that oil palms have spread north into savannahs, encouraged by villagers, suggests that they may be better seen as outposts of anthropogenic forest advance than as relic indicators of forest retreat. Even more strikingly, in the south and south-east, large expanses of grass and sparse shrub savannah have ceded entirely to forest fallow vegetation: the area is actually a 'post-savannah', not a 'post-forest' zone. These southerly savannah-forest transitions are not only evident in air-photograph comparison but are strongly indicated by changes in everyday resource use: for example, the introduction of tree-felling in agricultural operations, greater availability of preferred fuelwood species, changes in roofing and thatching materials, and changes in termite species associated with particular edible fungi. These demonstrable changes, which reflect long-term interactions between the populations of Kissidougou and their forest-savannah vegetation (Fairhead and Leach 1996a, b) strongly challenge the view of a continuing shift of vegetation zones to the south.

Equally, evaluating 'degradation' in terms of a vegetation climax is revealed as inadequate when one takes the impact of long-term climate history into account. Given that West Africa has experienced both long-period, deep climatic fluctuations and changes in climatic variability (Brooks 1986), the history of vegetation form begins to appear as a history of continual transition rather than of divergence from a single, once extant climax. Recent ecological analysis suggests that such ceaseless transitions depend on multi-factor complexes rather than trends in one particular variable: if a transition-causing factor reverts to its pre-transition level, vegetation may move to another state, but it need not return to its original one (Behnke and Scoones 1991; Dublin, Sinclair and McGlade 1990; Sprugel 1991). The various forest and savannah forms in the transition zone can be seen as such multiply-determined states dependent on fire, soil, water, seed availability, animal-related and other conditions. Deflection from one state to another may depend upon a particular, possibly even unique historical conjuncture of ecological and management factors. By altering the balance of interacting factors, people can initiate shifts between states which might be unattainable, or much less likely, through 'natural' ecological processes alone. The shifts from savannah to forest in Kissidoguou could be seen in this way (Fairhead and Leach 1996b).

Yet within Guinea, environmental services have been so convinced of the degradation they are combating that they find it unnecessary to compare their commissioned aerial and satellite images with those from 1952, let alone question their interpretative framework. Even when comparative interpretations are carried out, they are frequently not independent of preconceived ideas of vegetation change. In Kissidougou, the incredulous reactions of forestry staff when presented with 1952 and 1990 air photographs showing increased woody vegetation led them to a sceptical search for ways to render the comparison invalid (the photographs were taken in a-typical years, or incomparable seasons). In other parts of West Africa, similarly surprising results have simply been disbelieved and dismissed: 'Apparent increases in biomass from pre-disturbance [vegetation] to present were labelled "discrepancy" and such discrepancies were omitted from further analysis . . . there seems little possibility that biomass has increased as a result of land use' (Houghton, Unruh and Lefebre 1993). In contrast, justifiable scepticism was cast aside when a comparison of eastern Guinea satellite images taken ten years apart seemed to show significant vegetation degradation, on which basis major donor funds for a regional environmental rehabilitation programme were secured (Grégoire, Flasse and Malingreau 1988). The images of environmental change derived from these 'scientific' analyses have been incorporated not only into Guinean environmental institutions, but also into formal sector education and the popular consciousness of state functionaries. They are regularly reproduced in school geography lessons and national university curricula and theses. For those educated within this vision, casual readings of the landscape come to serve as confirmatory evidence; dry season bush fire is taken as proof of a worsening problem, and the conversion to farmland of a few forest islands near the town for urban market-gardening is taken to suggest forest-island diminution everywhere. Such casual landscape readings are often made during the dry season, when external consultants, forestry agents and urban nationals' visits to villages are concentrated. This is the destructive part of villagers' normal seasonal cycle, when bush is cleared for farming, fires sweep the savannah and trees are cut for construction or sale. Regeneration during the rainy season, anyway more subtle to observe, escapes attention within this seasonal bias (Chambers 1983).

Interpretations of vegetation degradation are reinforced not only by local observation, but also by the global and regional level analyses with which they are in keeping, and which carry the weight of international authority. Given FAO figures concerning rapid forest loss in West Africa (FAO 1990), for example, it appears inconceivable that Kissidougou should be experiencing anything else. Such figures, so frequently publicized in the more glossy development literature and on the radio, are far more accessible to the environmental administrations and urban public concerned with Kissidougou than are analyses of the locality itself. Equally the rhetoric of shared environmental crisis, made so apparent in the 1992 UNCED conference in Rio, appeals far more powerfully to local officials than the statements of the villagers who are supposedly experiencing these problems. This was made evident in the 1993 'Journées de l'Environnement' conference designed to raise awareness of Kissidougou prefecture's environmental problems, where both the Prefect and Kissidougou's urban-based environmental NGO framed their speeches in terms of global concern with biodiversity loss and the common West African struggle against desertification. The projection of global and regional concerns on to Kissidougou's environment has recently increased, but it is not new; it has informed administrative perceptions since the early colonial period. A concern that deforestation in Kissidougou would damage regional climate and hydrology was apparent in the earliest writings of Chevalier (e.g. 1909) and underlay a major watershed rehabilitation programme first outlined in the 1930s, funded in the 1950s following the 1948 Goma inter-African soil conference, and launched again in 1991.

This analysis of environmental change which informs local policy cannot be separated from the financial context in which environmental institutions operate. In Guinea, early colonial administrations first became concerned with the perceived destructiveness of African environmental management because the colonial economy was heavily dependent on 'threatened' natural resources: initially wild rubber, and then, in Kissidougou, oil-palm products and tree crops grown in forest patches (Fairhead and Leach 1995). In the later colonial and post-colonial periods, more regional and global economic imperatives joined these national ones. In the 1950s, new funding envelopes for regional soil, climate and hydrological conservation became available following the heightened Africa-wide environmental concern epitomized by the 1948 Goma conference. More recently, administrative solvency and development activities have come to rely even more heavily on foreign aid and thus become subject to various forms of 'green conditionality' (Davies 1992; Davies and Leach 1991). This greening of aid, and the specific forms it takes, reflects donors' need to satisfy home political constituencies heavily influenced by media images and northern environmental NGOs, as well as their own institutional assessments of African environmental problems.

In Guinea, a large proportion of foreign assistance is now allocated, sectorally and by region, directly to environmental rehabilitation. A new generation of heavily funded environmental projects has emerged, including, in Kissidougou, two component projects of the internationally funded Niger river protection programme. In agricultural and other development activities too, overt environmental sustainability components are important in attracting future funds. Kissidougou's prefecture administration, agriculture and forestry services are well aware of the packages which satisfy the donors in this respect: agroforestry programmes, forest conservation and improvement, bush-fire control, and rationalization and reduction of shifting cultivation in favour of intensive wetland rice. During Kissidougou's 'Journées de l'Environnement', the prefecture's number-two administrator stated explicitly: 'Donors are interested principally in environmental projects, so we must solicit their aid to ensure the development of the prefecture.' He suggested that other localities learn from the example of the Niger protection project zones, where schools, water and other infrastructural developments were provided in exchange for local participation in environmental protection. The emergence of local, urban-based environmental NGOs such as Kissidougou's 'Friends of Nature' society has also been encouraged by recent donor interest, not only in environmental issues but also in the claimed capacity of NGOs to achieve 'participatory' development. In short, presenting a degrading or threatened environment has become an imperative to gain access to donors' funds. In this respect, our own findings were often considered subversive, threatening to the prefecture's future financial and development interests, and to the continued employment and material privileges of environmental project administrators and extension workers.

Considering the environment as degrading and threatened is equally crucial to the solvency of state environmental institutions when they do not receive donor support. Since their inception, francophone West African forestry services have derived revenues from the sale of permits and licences for timber and wildlife exploitation, and from fines for what became environmental crimes in breaking state environmental laws. In Guinea, setting bush fires actually carried the death penalty during the 1970s (Law 08/AN/72 of 14 September 1972). Environmental services have been able to gain such revenues only by taking control of the management of natural resources (e.g. fire and trees), and this through deeming villagers to be incapable and destructive resource custodians. Revenues are thus ensured by a reading of the landscape as degraded and degrading, of forest islands as disappearing relics in an increasingly grassy savannah, not as created in an increasingly woody one. The importance to forestry staff of informal receipts gained while applying policies of repression only accentuates the imperative for this environmental reading, while the antagonistic relationship thus engendered between forestry agents and villagers bars communication about villagers' own environmental experiences. Thus at local and national as well as international levels, the economic structures within which environmental agencies operate frame the ways that information is derived.

The attitudes of forestry staff depend not only on their financial and educational status as forestry service members, but also on their socio-cultural positions. They share with many other formally educated, urban-based Guineans a particular vision of villagers' resource management capabilities. This image of the rural farmer as environmental destroyer and of rural farming and forestry techniques as backward, in need of modernization, conforms with and helps justify urban intellectuals' self-definition as modern and progressive. Such distinctions were reinforced under Sekou Touré's regime (1958–84), when the urbanized were politically and economically privileged, and their vision of a highly mechanized, capital-intensive, technical future dominated rural development approaches (Rivière 1976). As greater attention has come to be paid to environmental than to agricultural issues, the environmental component of this degrading view of village capabilities has become dominant. Generalized notions about 'man's destructive impact on the environment', projected locally, have entered the numerous processes through which urban-educated people understand themselves as relatively more 'civilized' or 'globalized' (Bledsoe 1990). And just as urban circles benefited from the agricultural modernization which wrested resource control from villagers, so they have become the main beneficiaries of environmental control, keeping the moral high ground, while gaining from policies such as those removing timber-cutting rights from 'irresponsible' villagers.

Images of forest loss in Kissidougou are also reinforced as part of processes of ethnic distinction, which depend on colonial portrayals and their subsequent incorporation into local political discourse. From the outset, colonial constructions of ethnic difference among Kissidougou's populations rested partly on stereotypes concerning their environmental behaviour. The Kissia were seen as 'forest people', like other groups further south (Toma, Guerze), with cultural proclivities towards forest conservation. They were seen as more forest-loving largely because of the centrality to local life of the *forêt sacrée* (or 'secret society') initiation ceremonies which they held in their forest islands. Kissi 'sacred' forests were upheld as veritable islands of nature conservation amid the secular destruction all around them (Aubréville 1939), just as they are by today's policy-makers. This was despite the reality that only part of a forest island would be devoted to the 'sacred' forest institution, medicines and powers, and that the 'sacred' technologies would usually be installed only after the forest island had itself been formed.

As 'forest people', the Kissia were contrasted ethnically with the more northerly 'savannah people' of Maninka origin, including Kissidougou's Kuranko populations. In the context of historical and ongoing southwards Maninka migration, their fire-setting in savannah farming, honey-collecting and hunting was considered responsible for southwards savannization (Adam 1948). Where the Kuranko lived within forest islands, this was perceived as having been learnt from the Kissia (Administrateur de Cercle 1913), as it is by modern environmental projects. Yet the Kuranko themselves associate prosperity and fortune with inhabiting a forest island (*haraye ye tu le ro*), and where Maninka immigrants have moved into Kissi villages, they have usually been incorporated into Kissi society and land management. That the majority of supposedly 'forest' Kissi families can trace descent from a Maninka family of savannah origin clearly undermines such arguments of ethnically driven environmental degradation.

During the First Republic, Sekou Touré's state regime encouraged villages to move out of the 'mystified obscurity' of their forest islands into 'the open', into the 'clarity' and 'modernity' upheld by the regime's cultural demystification policy, and into the roadside world more accessible to its demands (Rivière 1969). This policy drew on and reinforced ethnic stereotypes, deepening their construction in terms of forest. Maninka self-representations often draw on the ideal of social clarity, of openness and simplicity in language and expression, and make an explicit contrast between their clear 'savannah language' (*kan gbe*) and the secrecy and obscurity of the forest culture and languages, which they find difficult to learn. Many Kissia perceived Sekou Touré's regime as Maninka-biased, and considered the attempts it made to evict them from their forests and suppress 'sacred forest' schools as attempts to disempower the institution which had hitherto defended the Kissia from Maninka domination, whether cultural or military. The political conditions from 1958 to 1984 therefore reinforced the significance of forest symbolism in Kissidougou's local and ethnically charged political discourse.

In this context, both the present privileging of the forest, and the view that it is threatened as portrayed by the forestry service, coincide with the broader politico-ethnic interests of urban Kissia, interests heightened in the run-up to multi-party electoral processes beginning in December 1993. Sharing one forest – where the forest islands of neighbouring villages have come to touch each other – is one of the strongest metaphors of Kissi political solidarity, linked as it used to be to alliance in warfare and forest initiation. Accepting the idea that the Kissi region could (even until recently) have been united in one forest provides a politically appealing vision of unity, as does blaming Maninka immigration for forest loss. These views are most often voiced within the politically influential urban Kissi community, but they can also be heard in villages when rural Kissia use environmental issues to make politico-ethnic points.

Distinctions between urban-institutional and rural villagers' perceptions of environmental change also derive from different valuations of vegetation quality. For urban observers and the forestry service, high value is accorded to large forest trees, whether for recent global reasons or for the commercial gains to be made from timber exploitation, which has recently become big business in Kissidougou. Villagers do not share this valuation, not least because the forestry laws designed to regulate timber exploitation (i.e. to preserve the environment) deny them all but an insignificant royalty from trees cut by outsiders in their forest islands. Their values are conditioned, instead, by the importance of different vegetation types and species in agriculture, gathering, settlement and tree-crop protection and cultural practices, and in which lower bush fallow vegetation is frequently more useful than high forest (Leach and Fairhead 1994). The large trees of forest islands are, in fact, more the 'fortuitous' consequence of villagers' environmental management for other reasons than a deliberately encouraged feature. While the felling of these trees may be of little consequence to villagers (or to forest area in the long term), to urban and official observers it epitomizes, and thus reinforces their conviction of, environmental destruction.

Forest Loss Explained

The image of environmental degradation in Kissidougou is supported by apparently successful explanations for it in terms of local land-use practices and their changing socio-economic, demographic and institutional contexts. Just as the prevalent socio-cultural, institutional and financial structures lead certain readings of and methods for investigating environmental change to dominate while excluding others from consideration, so these same structures influence the methods and theories brought to bear in understanding why the environment has changed.

Policy-makers' thinking has long been dominated by the view that local land use encourages savannization and reduces savannah tree cover and soil quality. These apparent processes of degradation are readily observable in the short term, in, for example, the clearing and burning of wooded lands for farming and the setting of fire by hunters and herders. But less attention is paid to processes of regeneration and the impact of local practices on them. In villagers' experience, their land use has, in the long run, maintained or enhanced woody vegetation cover and soil quality. The logic of local cultivation practices which encourage the advance of forest in this region has been documented in Guinea by ourselves (Fairhead and Leach 1996) and in neighbouring Côte d'Ivoire by Blanc-Pamard and Spichiger (1973). Villagers tend to consider themselves as improving once less-productive lands, rather than reducing the productivity of once 'naturally' productive ones.

Nevertheless, the contrasting external image of local land-use as inevitably degrading is combined with particular theories about the impact of demographic and social change to account for the long-term degradation which policy-makers believe has taken place. Discussions in development circles of the links between population and environment, poverty and environment, and social organization and environmental management have set the terms of debate which guide causal interpretations by development personnel, consultants and national institutions. Given that it is explanations of supposed environmental degradation which are being sought – and given the prevailing intellectual, social and fiscal structures which condition causal analysis – all but the dominant strands of thinking within these debates tend to be suppressed at the project level. Thus it is Malthusian views of the relationship between population and environment, the deduction that impoverishment forces villagers to draw down their natural resources and the notion of a 'tragedy of the commons', which are used to explain increasing environmental degradation in Kissidougou.

Environmental degradation is attributed to assumed demographic trends by policy-makers who believe that, since local land use is degrading, more people must mean more degradation, principally through extra upland use. An image of low pre-colonial population densities is commonly linked to the supposed existence then of extensive forest cover, and rapid population growth during this century (and now refugee settlements) are held to account for forest decline. Short fallows and long cultivation periods on savannah uplands are often taken as evidence of modern population pressure. That local farmers use intensive cultivation practices for positive ecological and economic reasons, unrelated to population pressure, is not considered. Nor does the possibility that population growth could lead to environmental improvement receive attention. Yet in Kissidougou, where there are more villages, there are more forest islands, and more people can mean that there is more intensive, soil- and vegetation-enhancing savannah cultivation and more generalized fire control.

Socio-economic theories to explain supposed recent environmental degradation attribute it partly to modern poverty, forcing villagers to sacrifice sustainable long-term resource management in favour of short-term uses assumed to be degrading. Recent environmental degradation is also explained through the idea that modern resource use is disorganized and individualistic, a vision shared by many local administrators as much as external consultants and university academics. In many versions of this narrative, a picture of people in greater 'harmony' with their forested environment is projected on to the pre-colonial period, a harmony maintained either by efficacious traditional authority (Green 1991; Stiegelitz 1990) or, in more sophisticated terms, by the integration of fire control within intra and inter-village social, cultural and political relationships (Zerouki 1993). An armoury of factors is held to have ruptured this controlled harmony, including socio-economic change, the weakening of traditional authority, new economic and cultural aspirations and social divisions, and the alienation of local resource control to state structures. The logical policy implication is that resource use can be rendered sustainable by improving forms of 'regulation', 'authority' and 'organization', whether by greater state control (e.g. over timber-cutting and fire) or, in recent policy emphasis, by 're-building' community institutions. These dominant social and demographic explanations for degradation and the idea of degradation itself seem to be mutually sustaining. From within this complex, the actual history of people's environmental use and the complex influences on it fail to receive serious attention.

The institutional and financial structures in which social science is applied to environmental problems in Guinea strongly support such uncritical explanations of degradation. Studies are commissioned by donor agencies and projects who need (or at least, must be seen to have sought) socio-economic information to help them tackle the environmental problems integral to their institutional survival in more 'appropriate' and 'participatory' ways. The environmental problem is thus built into the very terms of reference of consultants who have neither the time nor the social position to investigate village natural-resource management and its changes on any other terms. This problem is not necessarily solved when consultants are Guinean, nor even when they are working in their own areas; indeed, it can be compounded by the urban intellectual images which such local consultants bring to bear. Furthermore, as the dominant social and demographic explanations of environmental degradation are the stuff of academic debate, consultancy reports phrased in their terms gain easy acceptance and credibility.

The interface between environmental-development agencies and villagers, which has developed over more than half a century, often in antagonistic ways, renders the communication of local environmental experiences highly problematic. Villagers, faced by questions about deforestation and environmental change, have learned to confirm what they know the questioners expect to hear. This is not only because of fear, politeness and an awareness that the truth will be met with incredulity, but also because of the desire to maintain good relations with authoritative outsiders who may bring as yet unknown benefits – a school, road or advantageous recognition to the village, for example. In such discussions, the historical ecology that villagers portray is as politically inflected as in their oral histories concerning settlement foundation, where images of initial vacancy (high forest, empty savannah, or abundant wild animals) often justify the first-comer status of current residents (Dupré 1991; Hill 1984). Like the prefecture administration, many village authorities realize the benefits which can accompany community participation in environmental rehabilitation, and in this context they may publicly agree to the 'urgent need' to plant trees, establish village environmental management committees and so on. Nevertheless, acceptance is not without anxiety over losing land to 'project' trees, over losing control over management of local ecologies to outsiders ignorant of their specificities, and over the unknown future demands that apparently generous projects of unknown origin and intent, huge financial resources and foreign interests, may later exact. Everyday forms of resistance thus frequently underlie overt participation: letting project tree nurseries and plantations burn in the dry season, for example, and ensuring that necessary fires are set in ways contrary to agreed project procedures.

It has been surprising to us how little the personal lifetime experiences of development workers from the prefecture influence the way that Kissidougou's environment has come to be perceived. This may be because personal environmental histories have too limited a spatial coverage to challenge a generality, or because unbroken personal histories are themselves rare: state officials are frequently transferred and are posted in preference to areas with which they are unfamiliar, so they have frequently been away from their childhood village environments for long periods. Such people almost invariably justify their perceptions of historical deforestation with examples drawn from roadsides and urban peripheries, with which they have more continuous familiarity, but which in Kissidougou are the proverbial exceptions to the rule.

Scientific challenge to the dominant analysis in Guinea is also rare. This is partly because the scientific information and ecological theory which questions the derived savannah model, and which often proves to support the farmers' explanations we have investigated, is dispersed among different disciplines and their specialist academic journals. These are largely inaccessible to policy makers and national academic institutions. Information from each discipline alone (e.g. botany, hydrology, soil science, demography and climate history) is insufficient to shift thinking in a sufficiently fundamental way; lack of inter-disciplinary criticism seems, indeed, to promote consistency. In any case, little such discussion enters the information bulletins of multinational organisations (e.g. FAO), NGOs, development journals or the media, the sources on which most development personnel rely for environmental science information. Fundamentally, the precepts basic to local science which challenge conventional savannization wisdom are not easily apprehended by researchers ill-disposed either to listen or to understand.

Conclusions

This environmental case illustrates in a particularly striking way how development problems and policies are constituted within diverse, seemingly disparate relations. The vision of environmental degradation in Kissidougou, to which so many people are drawn for different reasons, has, for a hundred years now, been sustained within their scientific, social, political, institutional and financial relationships. These relationships have evolved in ways which mean that today the degradation vision is not associated only with donor agencies and their narratives. It is partly the product of a long history of interaction with, and incorporation into, local social and political processes, and is thus today partly sustained within these. This is not to say that villagers' everyday ecological practice is influenced by the deforestation reasoning, but merely that their ecological reasoning is subjugated in much political interaction, development activities included.

Degradation visions have justified external authorities in exerting various forms of control over people and their resources, often compromising villagers' resource management and attracting considerable animosity. As one man from the north of the prefecture explained bitterly:

> During the period of taxes and hunger, which weighed heavily on us during the First Republic, forest guards prevented us from felling trees, from setting fire even in the field, from cutting chewing sticks, from fishing and from hunting even on our own territory. We were worried and disorientated in land management, feeling ourselves to be strangers on our own lands and robbers from the State.

Nevertheless, villagers have needed to continue many of their agro-ecological strategies despite their criminalization, and have therefore adopted assorted strategies of resistance, whether covert fire-setting or tree-felling, or offering largesse to forest guards. As it was once expressed to us: 'We came to judge it best to continue managing our land as before, giving the forest guards money every year, because it is clearly money that is their priority, rather than

any concern with forest protection.' That Kissidougou's farmers
have been able to maintain landscape productivity in the face of
such repression is in part testimony to the effectiveness of such
resistance (Fairhead and Leach 1995; Millimouno 1993). Cognisant
of rural ill-will towards the environmental services, politicians
have found promises to curb their repressive activities to be an
effective electoral campaign strategy, although following elections,
the other imperatives which this chapter documents have generally
taken hold. It is only very recently that, under both internal and
international pressure, Guinea's forest service has begun to
undergo significant reforms, and their outcomes remain to be seen.

To date, villagers' own ecological knowledge and experience
have been unable successfully to challenge the landscape readings
driving policy. This is partly because of the power relations at
the farmers' interface with environmental agencies and urban
intellectuals. But it is also because views of degradation in
Kissidougou are sustained not on the basis of ignorance, but
through the continual production of supportive knowledge. Those
who are convinced of deforestation and savannization do not
lack data to support their convictions, and it is within this
methodologically supported certainty that alternative methods
and data sets have been disqualified as inadequate, naive,
unscientific or simply improbable.

The Kissidougou case highlights a misreading of the forest-
savannah transition landscape which a growing body of evidence
suggests may well be relevant elsewhere in West Africa and
beyond. The capacity of people to enrich such landscapes has, for
instance, been alluded to in Côte d'Ivoire (Blanc-Pamard 1979)
and Sierra Leone (Annalay and Pocknell 1995), and even by
Aubréville himself on the Bateke Plateaux of Gabon and Congo-
Brazzaville (Aubréville 1949). Other examples of erroneous
analysis of recent savannah derivation have also been documented
in Benin (Blanc-Pamard and Peltre 1987) and Nigeria (Moss and
Morgan 1977). These cases and others firmly put into question
received wisdom concerning the nature of anthropogenic vegetation changes in this region of West Africa, and their implications,
whether for climate (Gornitz 1985), soils or regional economies
(see Fairhead and Leach forthcoming). But the case of Kissidougou
is more pertinent still in illustrating how powerfully certain visions
of environmental change and their linked development problems
can arise and be maintained in policy circles, producing knowledge

which excludes considerable counter-evidence. It is becoming clear that similar processes are at work in many African environmental contexts, from drylands through savannah grasslands and highlands to humid rainforests (Leach and Mearns 1996), and that, all too frequently, it is local land users whose perspectives and priorities are thus marginalized.

Note

1. This paper is the result of our joint and equal co-authorship. It draws on research funded by ESCOR of the then Overseas Development Administration (ODA), to whom we are grateful; the opinions represented here are, however, our own and not those of the ODA. Many thanks are also due to our co-researchers in Guinea, Dominique Millimouno and Marie Kamano; to the villagers, administrators and project staff in Kissidougou with whom we worked; and to our Guinean collaborating institutions: DNFC, GTZ and DNRS.

References

Adam, J.G. (1948), 'Les reliques boisées et les essences des savanes dans la zone préforestière en Guinée francaise', *Bull. Soc. Bot. Fr.*, 98: 22–6.

—— (1968), 'Flore et végétation de la lisière de la forêt dense en Guinée, *Bulletin IFAN*, 30/3: 920–52.

Administrateur de Cercle (1913), *Rapport sur Kissidougou 1913*, Guinean National Archives, Conakry, 2D175.

Aubréville, A. (1939), 'Forêts reliques en AOF', *Revue de Botanique Appliqée et Agronomie Tropicale*, 215.

—— (1949), *Climats, forêts et désertification de l'Afrique tropicale*, Paris: Société d'Edition de Géographie Maritime et Coloniale.

Behnke, R. and I. Scoones (1991), 'Rethinking Rangeland Ecology:

Implications for Rangeland Management in Africa', *ODI/IIED Issues Paper*, 33.

Blanc-Pamard, C. and R. Spichiger (1973), 'Contact forêt-savane et recru forestier en Côte d'Ivoire', *L'Espace Géographique*, 3: 199–206.

Bledsoe, C. (1990), '"No Success without Struggle": Social Mobility and Hardship for Foster Children in Sierra Leone', *Man* (n.s.), 25: 70–88.

Chambers, R. (1983), *Rural Development: Putting the Last First*, London: Longman.

Chevalier, A. (1909), *Rapport sur les nouvelles recherches sur les plantes à caoutchouc de la Guinée francaise*, Senegalese National Archives, 1G276.

Davies, S. (1992), 'Green Conditionality and Food Security: Winners and Losers from the Greening of Aid', *Journal of International Development*, 4/2: 151–65.

——— and M. Leach (1991), 'Globalism versus Villagism: Food Security and the Environment at National and International Levels', *IDS Bulletin*, 22/3: 43–50.

Dublin, H., A. Sinclair and J. McGlade (1990), 'Elephants and Fire as Causes of Multiple Stable States in the Serengeti-Mara Woodlands', *Journal of Animal Ecology*, 59: 1147–64.

Dupré, G. (1991), 'Les arbres, le fourré et le jardin: les plantes dans la société de Aribinda, Bukina Faso', in G. Dupré (ed.), *Savoirs paysans et dévéloppeement*, Paris: Karthala-ORSTOM.

FAO (1990), *Interim Report on Forest Resources Assessment*, Committee on Forestry, tenth session, 24–28 September 1990, Rome: United Nations Food Organization.

Fairhead, J. and M. Leach (1995), 'Reading Forest History Backwards: The Interaction of Policy and Local Land Use in Guinea, 1893–1993', *Environment and History*, 1/1.

——— (1996a), *Misreading the African Landscape: Society and Ecology in a Forest-savanna Mosaic*, Cambridge: Cambridge University Press (African Studies Series).

——— (1996b), 'Enriching the Landscape: Social History and the Management of Transition Ecology in the Forest-savannah Mosaic (Republic of Guinea)', *Africa*, 66/1: 14–36.

——— (forthcoming), *Forests of Statistics: Reframing Environmental History in West Africa*, London: Global Environmental Change Series, Routledge.

Green, W. (1991), *Lutte contre les feux de brousse*, Report for project DERIK, Dévéloppement Rural Intégré de Kissidougou.

Grégoire, J.M., S. Flasse and J.P. Malingreau (1988), *Evaluation de l'action des feux de brousse, de novembre 1987 à février 1988, dans la région frontalière Guinée-Sierra Leone*, Projet Régional FED-CILSS-CCR, 'Surveillance des ressources naturelles renouvables au Sahel-Volet Guinée', ISPRA, EEC.

Guinée Service Forestier (1932), *Rapport annuel de fin d'année 1932*, ANS 2G32(70).

Hill, M. (1984), 'Where to Begin? The Place of Hunter Founders in Mende Histories', *Anthropos*, 79: 653–6.

Hoben, A. (1993), 'The Political Economy of Land Tenure and Environmental Policy in Ethiopia', Draft summary of paper presented at African Studies Association meeting, Boston, December 1993.

Houghton, C.S., J.D. Unruh and P.A. Lefebre (1993), 'Current Land Cover in the Tropics and its Potential for Sequestering Carbon', *Global Biogeographical Cycles*, 7/2: 305–20.

Leach, M. and J. Fairhead (1994), The Forest Islands of Kissidougou: Social Dynamics of Environmental Change in West Africa's Forest-savannah Mosaic, Report to ESCOR of the Overseas Development Administration, London.

—— and R. Mearns (eds) (1996), *The Lie of the Land: Challenging Received Wisdom on the African Environment*, London: James Currey Publishers and Heinemann.

République de Guinée (1988), *Politique forestiére et plan d'action*, TFAP 1988, Conakry.

Rivière, C. (1969), 'Fétichisme et démystification: l'exemple guinéen', *Afrique documents*, 102–103: 131–68.

Rivière, C. (1976), 'Bourgeoisies du tracteur', *Revue Francaise d'Etudes Africaines*, 123: 74–101.

Roe, E. (1995), 'Except Africa: Postscript to a Special Section on Development Narratives', *World Development*, 19/4: 287–300.

Stiegelitz, F.V. (1990), *Exploitation forestière rurale et réhabilitation des forêts: premiers résultats d'un project de recherche interdisciplinaire en Haute-Guinée*, Berlin.

Thompson, M., T. Hatley and M. Warburton (1986), *Uncertainty on a Himalayan Scale*, London: Ethnographica.

Tiffen, M., M. Mortimore and F. Gichuki (1993), *More People, Less Erosion: Environmental Recovery in Kenya*, Chichester: Wiley.

Zerouki, B. (1993), *Etude relative au feu auprès des populations des bassins versants types du Haut Niger*, Conakry: Programme d'amenagement des bassins versants types du Haut Niger.

Chapter 3

The Silent Traditions of Developing Cooks

Emma Crewe

> What is essential *goes without saying because it comes without saying*:
> the tradition is silent, not least about itself as a tradition; customary
> law is content to enumerate specific applications of principles which
> remain implicit and unformulated, because unquestioned (Bourdieu
> 1977: 167, original emphasis).

Introduction

Cultural traditions within European development organizations
have been a neglected field, to the frustration of development
personnel elsewhere. Tandon argues that it is difficult for Africans
to fathom the workings of 'Western' Non-Government Organizations (NGOs) 'not only because of their secrecy but also because
their ideological and philosophical orientations are products of
complex historical forces within their own countries which
outsiders cannot fully understand' (1991: 74).[1] Perhaps it is even
harder for European 'insiders' to make sense of these complex
historical forces. Rather than seeing their own ideology as a
product of history, their thinking is oriented by it. Ideology is
automatically imbued with a character of objectivity for insiders
(Bourdieu 1977: 167), while outsiders are constantly reminded that
historical forces behind the foreign ideology are very different from
their own. What appears as secrecy amongst 'Western' development agencies is probably more likely to be the silence of tradition
being taken for granted. It is aspects of the assumptions made by
'developers', part of the development 'industry's' silent traditions,
that I will try to uncloak in this paper. I will illustrate how

unspoken ideologies have affinities with particular social orders, with reference to my ethnographic study of one area of technology development – improved cooking stoves.

In 1988 I began to study the impact of a government-run project in Sri Lanka.[2] Like the many expatriate researchers who have followed this path before me, I embroidered patterned links between project activity and its effect on 'beneficiaries'. As examples, the benefits were highly inequitably distributed: waged labour was introduced to relatively egalitarian communities, and women were marginalized from control over production and profits. I then embarked on more conventional ethnographic fieldwork in a Sri Lankan village to explore these effects in more detail. The fieldwork was interrupted in 1989 when I was recruited by a British development agency. For fifteen months I worked as a social scientist and, at the same time, continued research by compiling a picture of how 'development' processes are embedded within the political relations of various groups of 'developers' as well as supposed 'beneficiaries'.

I was uncomfortable with the whole business of embracing the 'world of development', or more specifically of developing people through technology, despite Escobar's valid claim that among most anthropologists such discomfort has become worryingly allayed by job opportunities (1991: 659) (putting aside crude materialist explanations, it is easy to forget the anthropological relativism once one has been firmly socialized into development discourses). 'Don't be naive', a Kenyan colleague suggested during a seminar in a Sri Lankan beach hotel: 'naturally your country is more developed. Look at your technology, economy, your standard of living, your freedom of speech . . . What more proof do you need? We Africans have to catch up.' This jarred against years of training in anti-evolutionist thinking. Even more disorientating were the assumptions that people were not voicing. The most overarching ones lay behind missionary-like statements, such as 'people in developing countries have problems and the Northern "experts" can help.' In this paper, I am concerned with the process of European developers struggling to help stove users, i.e. cooks, in Africa and Asia.

Cooking stoves were once an important area of appropriate technology development because they brought together several 'sexy' subjects, as fashionable aims are called in colloquial development jargon, such as working with poor women; raising the income of poor artisans, conserving environmental resources (especially saving trees) and reducing pollution. Stoves attracted a great deal of aid and attention, and many development agencies, government and non-government, became involved in their promotion. By the time I became involved in 1988, most of the large agencies had allocated some funds to stove programmes. Among the various personnel working in the area of stoves – the 'stovies', as they call themselves – I will concern myself particularly with the planners and the engineers. Planners in stoves-work tended to be energy experts, often economists, while the technical people were mostly mechanical engineers. Among those on the receiving end of the attention, in this paper I am concerned with the users of stoves rather than the much smaller number of artisans who make them. The most obvious observation to make is that while the cooks were exclusively indigenous, the technical people were a mixture of indigenous and expatriate, and the planners were a mixture in theory but mostly expatriate in practice.

Before we delve into the work of the 'stovies', it is worth commenting on the involvement of expatriates in international development. In foreign aid-funded projects it tends to be the planners in donor agencies who make the important planning decisions in the public domain. And where do they get their information from? They will tell you proudly that they do not read books unless they are extremely brief. So they hire advisers to write very short reports or to tell them what to do verbally. In addition to these advisers, expatriates impart technical, managerial, marketing, business and social-scientific wisdom through assistance and training. This 'indigenous capacity building', it is hoped, guarantees sustainability or raises awareness about various political issues, such as gender, poverty or the environment. The result is that Africa, Asia and South/Central America have over 150,000 expatriate residents or visitors working in development projects. This 'expert' assistance consumes an estimated $7–8 billion of donor money a year in Africa alone, and even a non-government organization (NGO) may spend up to £900 a day on a very expensive consultant. According to Nindi, the highly paid 'experts' have done nothing to prevent Africa plunging into an economic crisis (1990: 59).

These development 'tourists', as Chambers calls them, must surely offer something (1983: 11). They are usually described as having valuable and unique specialist skills capable of sustaining greater objectivity. It may indeed make sense for donors to send their own appraisers or evaluators to look critically at a project they are funding, because they can represent the concerns of the donor. As a regular habit, however, Nindi argues that 'a number of disadvantages either inherent or created by the adoption of outside planning experts outweigh the apparent benefits' (1990: 48). As examples, their reports are often insufficient in scope and depth, their planning is not supported by locally specific information, they tend to over-generalize about problems and solutions, and they exclude local planners (not to mentioned those planned for) from decision-making (ibid.: 49–50). Since foreigner's inputs are not usually monitored or evaluated, guessing at the accumulated value or impact is an exercise fraught with difficulties. Even so, I hope to make a start through a study of the recent development of cooking stoves.

The Story of Stoves

In the history of stoves until the late 1940s, technological development in the 'South' took place either in kitchens, or occasionally in artisan's workshops, largely as a part of commercial enterprise. Improved biomass stoves were first put on the agenda of planned development in the 1950s, and international agencies became involved during the 1970s. I will consider the impact of advice about stoves given by expatriates since that time.

Half the households in the world use stoves to burn biomass fuels,[3] mainly wood and charcoal, and principally for cooking. A series of chronic misunderstandings about household or domestic energy, deforestation and biomass fuel evolved in most international development agencies during the 1970s and 1980s. In the 1970s, the oil price hikes and alarm about the depletion of resources (most influentially spread by Meadows et al. 1972) combined to create the 'woodfuel crisis'. 'Experts' mistakenly thought that people cut trees to obtain fuel for domestic consumption, thus deducing that a decrease in domestic fuelwood consumption would decelerate the rate of deforestation in areas of scarcity. The orthodoxy also stated that domestic fuelwood consumption increases proportionately with population growth and that both are directly related to deforestation (Cline-Cole, Main and Nichol 1990: 514).

The perception that the demand for fuelwood was outstripping supply in 'developing countries' led to the 'gap theory'. All of the sixty or more UNDP/World Bank energy-sector assessments for developing countries relied on gap-theory calculations (Leach and Mearns 1988: 6). Describing estimates of the size of this gap as wild would be greatly understating the case. To measure the gap, an estimate was usually made of the fuelwood consumed, which was then compared to the available tree stocks (allowing for the annual growth of the population and tree resources). Since estimates of consumption nearly always exceed this annual tree growth, apparently by as much as 200 per cent in some Sahelian countries, it was assumed that people overcame the problem by felling the forests. For example, the Food and Agriculture Organization claimed that 'fuelwood supplies have been rapidly depleted and the cutting of firewood has in turn been a major cause of excessive deforestation' (1985: 8).

Some projections into the future assumed that as the gap grows, the tree stocks dwindle until eventually none remain. In 1984 it was predicted that Tanzania would be completely stripped of trees within six years (Leach and Mearns 1988: 7). It wasn't. The reaction to the predictions of catastrophe, mainly by expatriates, was energy-related intervention on an enormous scale. Initially the solution was seen to be large afforestation programmes, but planners hoped that fuel-efficient stoves would avert the immediate crisis by reducing consumption. The underlying rationale of stoves was consistently linked to saving trees. Claims like the following one about Senegal were not uncommon: 'if stoves were used by 60% of the population they would save over half the annual forest deficit, estimated at 3 million cubic metres of wood annually, and reduce the national energy budget by 20%' (Gern and Evans 1981: 2).

The claims about deforestation, although unwarranted, influenced national governments to concentrate on disseminating vast numbers of fuel-efficient stoves very quickly. Quality was often sacrificed on the altar of quantity. The technical performance of stoves related to fuel consumption became critical. Karekezi, of the Foundation for Woodstove Dissemination (FWD) in Nairobi, surmises that 'the socio-economic aspects of stove development and dissemination took a back seat. In the 1970s, technical and scientific parameters were perceived to be as important as (and probably more important than) the needs and aspirations of the stove user' (1989: 23). Unfortunately, the emphasis on fuel-efficiency at the cost of users' priorities frequently led the users to reject the stoves. Expatriate (and national urban-based) technicians told me that lack of education led the cooks to use the new stove incorrectly or that the abandonment of stoves was evidence of a conservative culture. The technical performance of improved stoves was beyond reproach because the engineers, and not the cooks, were apparently the only rational judges of technology.

During the early 1990s it was accepted by some technicians that the cooks were acting rationally in rejecting early designs. In many cases stoves were introduced to solve problems perceived by designers (such as fuel-inefficiency), which were not necessarily considered troublesome by cooks. It has been found in many places (e.g. Senegal, Sri Lanka, Indonesia and Zimbabwe) that cooks value the speed at which a stove functions above all other features (Crewe 1993: 112). In the mountainous areas of Nepal, Fiji and Guatemala, space heating is more important than fuel con-servation, so well-insulated, fuel-efficient stoves are not popular in most households (Gill 1987: 138). Such a diversity of priorities, however, was not reflected in the stove models emerging from engineers' workshops, because their parameters were set by a policy fashion for fuel conservation.

The technical failings were noticed by energy 'experts'. In 1983 two British writers, Foley and Moss, concluded that not only were most improved stoves making very small reductions in fuelwood consumption, but that some were even increasing the amount of fuel burnt. They also pointed out that the policy premise was flawed: woodfuel consumers are the victims but not the root cause of deforestation. Clearing land for agriculture creates by far the greatest pressure on wood resources, and timber logging, charcoal-making and industrial fuel use all account for substantially greater depletion of the forests than domestic consumption (Foley and Moss 1983: 19-21). Since people cut trees primarily to clear land for cultivation or livestock rather than to burn wood in their stoves, deforestation is ultimately a land and not a fuel issue (Foley, Moss and Timberlake 1984: 11).

Years before Foley wrote about domestic fuelwood consump-tion, 'local' researchers had been pointing out that cooks do not cut green trees. For example, when Indian researchers asked residents of Gujarat, India, about felling trees, one of them said, 'Who will cut the green trees? Don't they give us our livelihood?

It is outsiders who cut them' (Nagabrahmam and Sambrani 1980: 14). But it was Foley and other Europeans and Americans following his line who brought about a change in donor policy. It is they, not Indian researchers such as Nagabrahmam, who are remembered for eliminating the enchantment with stoves as a panacea for all energy ills. The expatriates' advice acted as a catalyst and excuse for giving up the tricky business of working with overworked, resource-poor cooks to improve their kitchen technology.

By the end of the 1980s, almost all the multi-lateral and bi-lateral donors, aside from FAO, DGIS (Dutch) and GTZ, had abandoned stove development. It was deemed to be a failure as a solution to the energy crisis and not relevant to any other development area, despite stoves being one of the most important pieces of equipment for household work. There are certainly other institutional causes for the decline in stoves, aside from the influence of advisers, emerging out of the circumstances of the particular agency. For instance, staff within the Energy Strategy Management Assistance Programme (ESMAP), the key energy department within the World Bank, told me during interviews in 1990 and 1993 that the loss of interest in stove programmes was a result of their own poor record at implementation, the low project cost and lack of explicit macro-level objectives. But expatriate advisers undoubtedly gave the Bank and its own donors their rationale for dropping stove programmes. ESMAP's position in turn influenced the United States Agency for International Development (USAID), who, for example, cut funding for stoves in Nepal at least partly (they claimed) because ESMAP had conveyed negative signals about such programmes. Other staff within USAID's Energy Department have explained that negative policy statements (such as Foley's) and failed stove programmes disillusioned staff to the point where, by 1993, the subject had become 'taboo'.

Meanwhile, stove programmes have been blossoming in many African and Asian countries. By 1993 over 165 million stoves had been installed in kitchens worldwide, mainly in China, India, Sri Lanka and Kenya (Crewe 1993: 112–13). In the latter two countries they were purchased – rather than given and financed by subsidies – by fifteen to twenty per cent of the population. Project staff have learnt to do extensive trials to find out which design would be popular with consumers. Consequently, new stoves have been a roaring success from the users' viewpoint, in Kenya because they use less fuel and in Sri Lanka due to time saved in cooking.

Many national planners in the South welcome stove programmes. Two African energy analysts, Davidson and Karekezi,
argue that an environmentally sound strategy for Africa should
focus on more efficient use of energy rather than growth of supply
(1993: 19, 21). On these grounds, they add, the promotion of wood-
and charcoal-burning stoves should be a component of energy
plans in Sub-Saharan Africa. Karekezi established that, unlike
wood stoves, more efficient charcoal stoves do reduce the rate of
deforestation, since they can decrease the amount of trees felled
for charcoal-making (Bhagavan and Karekezi 1992). A more
sophisticated understanding of biomass systems is now emerging
as a result of the work of Asian and African energy experts.
Regional policy research has become highly organized, and in
Africa alone valuable reports are regularly produced by the
Foundation for Woodstove Dissemination, the Regional Wood
Energy Programme for Africa, the African Energy Policy Research
Network, the African Energy Programme of the Commonwealth
Science Council and the SADCC-TAU Energy Programme for
Southern Africa. But do the expatriates donors, planners and
advisers follow their directives? Not so far.

To summarize the stoves story, most planners in donor agencies
listened most attentively to expatriate advisers and promoted
stoves for the wrong reasons in the 1970s and early 1980s. The
reasons were founded on misplaced assumptions because the
advisers did not listen to cooks and energy users, nor even national
energy analysts and researchers. It is clear that a weak understanding of biomass energy supply and use, established as
orthodoxy by expatriate advisers, gave rise to severely mistaken
policies. We have seen that for roughly fifteen years stoves were
heralded as the technology to save forests. Donors enthusiastically
developed them as technical devices and then persuaded southern
governments or NGOs to set themselves enormous dissemination
targets and hawk them fast. As the promised saviour of forests,
stove programmes failed and so donors gave them up, ignoring
the positive value attached to new stoves for those who were using
them. The reduced workload and/or household expenditure on
fuel was invisible to the planners.

Foley was probably only trying to conjure up a more informed
picture of the relationship between biomass use and deforestation.
But the result of his work was the replacement of one pessimistic
generalization about energy problems (fuelwood use causes

deforestation) with another (improved stoves are a failure). The weakness of such a selective, unilinear causality is described by Campbell (1989: 102). He warns against making causal statements where 'one explanation is abstracted from a number of competing ones and emphasized in such a way that it obliterates the others by denying them'. But his warning may fall on deaf ears unless priorities change, because it would make planning too complicated, lengthy and reliant on contextual information, and therefore expensive.

I promised a conclusion on the impact of the work of European expatriates. Although not a conscious strategy, they have reinvented themselves as experts at the cost of the position of national analysts in Africa and Asia. But that is not the only social transformation which can be traced in this story: it also gives rise to a pattern of engineers displacing the cooks as the technical innovators.

Engineers Displacing the Cooks

In rural areas of Africa, Asia and South/Central America technical improvements to stoves were probably carried out by female cooks, until potters became involved in designing ceramic wood-burning stoves, and metal workers began making aluminium or tin charcoal-burning stoves. Since Indian technologists started working on new biomass stove designs in the late 1940s, technical stove development has moved into the domain of almost exclusively male engineers and technicians. Although the national technologists outnumber expatriates involved in designing stoves, it has often been the latter who claim the credit for the more successful models in their project reports. Cooks have not usually been involved in the development of the stove, except to test its 'acceptability' after a bout of technical work was complete. Producers are usually consulted only to see if the manufacturing processes are technically and financially feasible. Thus, the users and producers have been displaced from the centre of the technical innovation process. Goody (1982: 193) points out that in Europe the 'kitchen was the birthplace of many technical operations and apparatus' concerning the preparation and cooking of food, but 'when these processes left the kitchen for specialist control they generally shifted from the hands of women to those of men'. This is also true of stove development in the South.

Why were cooks not leading stove development? Because their views continue to be considered 'backward' and distorted by exotic traditional beliefs, in contrast to the apparently sophisticated, detached technical expertise of engineers and even social scientists. For example, a survey carried out by a national development organization in Kenya in 1990 showed that the only stove satisfying all household demands was probably the 'traditional' fireplace. But are these 'demands' really taken seriously? In a report of the survey, the writer (a social scientist and development worker) warns that 'these comments represent "perceptions" of the users and are not necessarily related to technical performance'. Cooks, despite their daily practice of cooking, apparently have less technical knowledge in their *perceptions*, than designers in laboratories do in their *findings*.

The implication is that while users passively 'perceive' but do not know, the technical experts actively 'find' and 'know', and even develop knowledge within an objective, scientific discourse. Behind this implication is an assumption that 'Western science' is the only path to objective truth. But what makes science true? The fact that it works? And yet, watching cooks at an open cooking fire alerts an observer to the complex technical skill involved in manipulating fire, stones, air, earth and wood, which also works. In both the Gambia and Zimbabwe, fuel-consumption studies have shown that women using fuel-conservation strategies with a three-stone fire have saved more wood than apparently fuel-efficient stoves (Bennett 1990: 20; Howorth 1992: 24). For example, some Zimbabwean cooks build walls around the open fire, lower the grate on which the pot sits, extinguish the fire as soon as the cooking is finished and arrange the sticks so that the most efficient performance is attained. In wood-burning stove-use, the user is a more influential variable on fuel consumption than the equipment. If stoves are promoted for the benefits to cooks rather than designers, then the technical skills and views of the former should surely be central to an assessment. After all, very often the national male designers are not even regular cooks.

Stating the obvious about most men's relatively light cooking workload is no mere jibe – it sheds light on the quality of expertise. Bloch stresses the importance of *practice* in the use of expertise, giving the example of a Malagasy farmer choosing a bit of forest for 'good swidden' (1991: 187). When the farmer decides on a good plot he whizzes through an incredible processing feat in minutes:

he recalls the complex yet flexible mental model of what good swidden is like, takes in the image of forest before him (the vegetation, the slope, the surrounding countryside, the hydrology, the soil), and then compares the two. This could not be achieved through a simple comparison, with the mental processes running down a single line of analysis, but must involve what Bloch calls 'multiple parallel processing' (ibid.: 191). A technician cannot know exactly what mental image the cook has of a 'good' stove. It is only through the 'complex yet familiar task' of cooking that the cook can compare a new stove against an old one, taking in information about what kind and size of wood it needs, how well air is drawn, how much heat and light is provided, how many sparks fly about, how much smoke is released into the room, whether the heat can be easily controlled, and so on. Such familiarity builds up over years which, not surprisingly, makes them the most experienced experts at cooking with wood.

If we take the engineers' conception of technology as being equated with equipment, machines or 'hardware', then cooking and fuel-conserving techniques which involve manipulating materials (the fuel and stones) are merely practices or skills, as if there is no innovation involved. To be more specific, the creative expertise of cooks is demoted to the category of 'cultural cooking practices', whereby culture and technology are opposed. There is no such opposition in the minds of the cooks. Also, such an assumption misses an essential point. The fuel and stones are just materials in one context, that is, when they are not being used for a purpose, but they are transformed into equipment once the cook has arranged them for a task. Innovation can be involved in either developing new equipment or creating new ways of arranging equipment. Thus, Bush is right to distinguish between (1) tools, such as appliances or equipment; (2) techniques, that is methods or skills for using tools; and (3) technology, which is the organization of tools and techniques for the performance of tasks (1983: 155).

The marginalization of indigenous knowledge is well-documented (Brokensha, Warren and Werner 1980; Chambers 1983; Hobart 1993; Warren 1989). Even so, the puzzle surrounding the perceived insignificance of cooks' knowledge is still not quite solved. Undoubtedly, it has something to do with the people themselves. It appears that technical knowledge is not measured and valued according to its utility for users when put into practice:

the value of knowledge is predetermined by the source of knowledge, that is, the identity of the innovator. More accurately, the identity of both the innovator and the evaluator are relevant: the process of evaluating development technology expresses the unequal power relationship between the two. But that is not all. The identity of cooks is, of course, critically shaped by the fact that in the vast majority of the world's households, cooks are female, and cooking has to be understood within the context of gendered social relations. At the household level, and in international aid and development projects, men control key resources and decision-making processes, while women's work and expertise is undervalued.

As is often the case with women's work, it is assumed that cooks are not technically minded. The cooking expertise of women is invisible because, following Chamber's criterion for low status in development projects, their cooking is carried out in rural areas, is women's household work, is not part of the market economy and is considered messy, tradition-bound and dirty (1986: 143). In short, cooks are a marginalized, relatively powerless group of women with relatively low access to, and control over, valued resources. The stove technicians, on the other hand, tend to be men busily devising clever new widgets in laboratories with valuable resources at their fingertips, applying their more visible knowledge and thus propelling development through the traditionally male medium of hardware technology. Men, by reaffirming their control of technology development through inventions, recreate the gender inequity permeating the social order of the development industry. This does not operate on the level of a conscious ploy by men as a group, but the *result* of their combined innovative efforts is plain enough.

This pattern is not peculiar to stove development. Smith claims that appropriate technology in general is written about and promoted by men, who adhere to the same old androcentric values that dictate that 'men have technical skills and make the technical decisions' (1983: 66). Perhaps it is hardly surprising in Europe or America, where there are very few female engineers or acknowledged inventors, and where technology development is seen as highly specialized and centralized, far away from the location of the users. But that does not mean that women have been excluded from inventing or modifying technology in practice in rural Africa, Asia or South/Central America. It may not be easy to demonstrate this from the written record. Stanley points out that 'if researching women's history is like looking for needles in haystacks, and researching women inventors is like looking for needles in haystacks when everyone denies that needles exist, then researching black women inventors is like looking for those non-existent needles in haystacks that have been scattered by the wind' (1983: 55). Though it is difficult to quantify women's innovations, she surmises that women have been inventing tools and processes in the realm of food-gathering and processing, horticulture, agriculture, spinning, weaving, pottery, architecture, medicine, contraception, music and possibly even mining and metallurgy (ibid.: 56). However, until either the definition of technology widens to incorporate these innovations or more women enter more formal technological domains (e.g., enrol in engineering courses), technology will be interpreted as man-made and development will be men making machines for progress.

Expatriate Expertise Invented

We have seen that women are not deemed to be experts in technology development and assessment. I now want to make a link between male-dominated technical innovation and my other theme, expatriate-dominated planning. The roles of technicians and cooks in stove programmes reveal that value attached to knowledge has little to do with its intrinsic value or function. It is more an expression of the power relationship between the knowledge creator and evaluator. In the final section of this chapter, my intention is to comment on the related power relationship between the expatriates and nationals.

The perceived superiority of expatriate expertise is recreated not by their insightful analysis and talent, but by the planners who rationalize decisions with reference to expatriate-derived knowledge. The ink on the stamp of authority held by expatriates is renewed by constant, repetitive reference to their advice. Meanwhile the nationals speak, but are not heard; their reality is mediated through the worldview of expatriates, reaffirming the latter's place as powerful beings within the international social order. People shape power relations partly by action but also by telling tales about the past, which then act as rationalizations. I have argued in the brief story of stoves that the advice of experts is usually used to rationalize decisions after they have been made. Expatriate experts give authority to policy and planning decisions, authority which seems to slip away from national experts. What are the reasons for this? Is it, for example, stark and simple racism? Not necessarily. It is not purely a question of national or racial identity: for instance, Munasinghe, a Sri Lankan, is frequently referred to deferentially by energy planners and policy-makers. But I would argue that this is because his position has been defined by his place as an adviser within the World Bank, plainly a powerful institution. Conversely, being white does not give a person automatic authority. As a female representative of a small British NGO working in the supposedly narrow field of household energy, I had almost none within the World Bank. The influence of whites is contextual and relational; it depends upon their social position in each context and in relation to those listening to them. One anecdote about stoves, related by a white senior economist at the World Bank who had made one brief visit to Mali, had a decisive influence on her manager within ESMAP. She reported that she had seen people using stoves as flowerpots, and blamed the recent legislation which compelled people to purchase stoves, even though, she deduced, they were universally unpopular. Her 'evidence' was quoted informally by senior managers when justifying their decision to cut funding for stove programmes. The evidence is uncertain. Two years earlier a white member of staff of an American NGO conducted a study of the same stoves programme in Mali during one of her many regular visits to the country, and found that over 90% of fifty stove users were mostly happy with their stove (Crouch 1989: 13). The ESMAP senior staff did not mention this study.

Although simple racism is not the defining process, long-established racial stereotyping underpins many assumptions. The propulsion behind development as social evolution is portrayed with all sorts of arbitrary features which apparently indicate social backwardness. For example, it is common for energy analysts to describe energy 'progress' in terms of fuel-use in relation to supply and demand, whereby populations move up the 'energy ladder' as their societies develop (Ausubel 1989: 80–2). In the typical version of energy modernization theory, the poorest and 'least developed countries' are populated mainly by dung-fuel users. As countries become more developed, their households take a step upwards from dung to agricultural residues, wood, biogas, charcoal, kerosene, coal, and finally gas and electricity. In most parts of Africa, South and Central America and Asia, biomass is still the predominant fuel, especially in rural areas. At the same time, biomass fuel-use remains one of the criteria for relegating the countries and their populations within these continents into the category of 'developing' or 'less developed'.

The argument for employing expatriates is partly informed by the evolutionist idea that all 'locals' (urban or rural, irrespective of class or training) are behind the 'Westerners' in terms of education. The apparent consequence is that the 'locals are not yet *ready* to work on their own', according to one British development worker (what does she think the locals were doing before the development project, it makes you wonder?). Ideology within development agencies is still at least partially informed by the evolutionist heritage of modernization theory, with its historical link to explicitly racialist theories prevalent during colonial times. The word 'local' is often used in an equivalent way to the discredited term 'native'. While there is nothing intrinsically evolutionary about the concepts 'local' or 'native', since they imply place, not character, many development personnel tend to characterize urban-based local development workers as relatively incapable, dishonest or incompetent in startlingly similar language to the colonial administrators of the past. Until recently, the perceived technical failings of locals have been most vigorously charted; in the last decade, management has been identified as their key weakness. Through these stereotypes, it is possible to see that 'local' can be a euphemism for thoroughly derogatory words such as 'primitive' or 'backward' or 'simple'.

In the eyes of the expatriates, the ignorance of the 'locals' is confirmed by the fact that 'they' do not seem to 'speak our language', literally and figuratively. Development organizations create their own language, scattered with acronyms, which is only familiar to 'insiders'. Familiarity with the domain of meaning for each word or expression in this language, the limits of which are fought over by individual speakers, plainly gives an agent a more powerful position in a debate. Although the language is not necessarily consciously created with this in mind, unfamiliarity places you in such a weak position that it is difficult to enter into negotiation at all. The first job of new recruits in a development agency is to learn this language fast. The result of this specialized development language is that the local project personnel, and certainly the local stove producers and users, are confirmed as ignorant in the minds of developers until they are equally fluent in the code.

More significant still than the words used in a development agency's lexicon, which are relatively easy to pick up and inject into meetings and reports, are the 'project cycle methodologies'.[4] As a social scientist, I was asked to comment on the work of counterpart social scientists, and even advise and/or train them in 'project cycle methodologies'. This was extremely embarrassing, as they plainly knew far more than I about choosing appropriate methods for the country in which they had been living and working all their lives. My counterparts had *all* had several years of project experience (at least), while I had spent four months working in development when I started 'advising' them in 1989. Project staff in Sri Lanka, India, Kenya and Nepal had no choice but to accept my 'advice', as if it was given by a social scientist with superior expertise.

According to a Nepali social scientist I 'advised', it is particularly young, inexperienced development 'experts' who feel a pressure to prove their professional worth, so that moral and political rhetoric is swallowed up in practice by a need to gain recognition. This certainly rings true in my experience. While acting out the part of a young so-called 'expert', I was not consciously fabricating a special domain of knowledge to vanquish African or Asian colleagues. Rather, I was being socialized within an organization which defined my social position as having a superior knowledge or skills. If I had no specialist skills worth transferring to projects, I would not just have a lowly social position within the department responsible for implementing projects, I would have had no coherent identity or job. Thus, as an inevitable part of being a member of a social order, I took on a body of knowledge, such as 'project cycle methodologies', gender awareness and how to do participatory rural appraisal. This can be contrasted with my behaviour after a year working as a trainer, when I refused to engage in any more assistance, training or advising. By this time advocacy work had expanded in the organization I was working in, and I was established enough to carve out a new identity unofficially as a British-based policy worker.

One African colleague related examples of how expatriate advisers continually used various strategies to assert their perceived superiority over the 'locals'. These may include putting them down by quoting recent foreign publications (which can be difficult to obtain in most countries), contradicting them, capturing as much speaking time in meetings as they can, referring to their own work in other countries and thus providing a contrast to the locals' apparently meagre national experience and using high technology (such as computers). Do the nationals passively internalize the superiority of expatriate expertise? Not necessarily, he concluded. Nationals in their turn invest considerable effort in developing computing skills to make the point that anything the expatriates can do, they can match or do better (he also added that watching European and American expatriates at work was deliciously reassuring, because it shattered the stereotype of whites being essentially efficient, punctual and sharp-witted). Even if the nationals' resistance is often subtle or even disguised, it reveals that the power relationship is not necessarily accepted by the supposed weaker recipients. The secrecy of national experts, their refusal to write reports, attend meetings or accept advice from expatriates, and their 'misuse' of donor funds could all be seen as forms of resistance or 'weapons of the weak', as Scott calls them when employed by Malaysian peasants (1985).

On an institutional level, however, for the social order to be maintained with the objects of development remaining in their rightful position, the excellence of expatriate expertise must be invented through history. Development tales told by expatriate experts about their success with the 'locals' affirm the authors' place in the wider social order of the development industry. Their body of superior knowledge does not exist in any objective sense, but relies on constant reiteration and renewal of development language, methods and rules. This process is silent so that the experts appear neutral in theory, while in practice they reinvent their powerful position. The situation seems to have changed very little since Adams wrote:

> It's not knowledge or skill alone that's wanted of the expert; there would be less costly, more efficient ways of acquiring them. What matters is the halo of impartial prestige his skills lend him, allowing him to neutralize conflict-laden encounters – between governments, between a government and its governed – and disguise political issues, for a time, as technical ones. An expert helps disguise the government of men as the administration of things, thus making it

possible for men to be governed as if they were things. The full title
is 'development expert' . . . . [T]hat which creates and sustains the
function of expert is the idea of 'development' as one and indivisible
(1979: 474).

Conclusions

The recent fierce criticism of aid has led to calls for greater
accountability, especially a more rigorous evaluation of projects.
It is my contention, however, that the contribution of European
and American expatriates to particular projects is usually overlooked. Moreover, their overall impact on aid over time is almost
never scrutinised. I have tried to evaluate the impact of expatriates
on one development sector, cooking stoves and household energy,
within the context of social and political relations between 1980
and 1995. I have argued that they displaced localized knowledge
and expertise by ignoring national energy specialists. They also
contributed to a transfer of technology development out of the
hands of women and into urban-based laboratories and workshops
which mostly employ male technologists. Even if the technical
work is now mostly carried out by nationals in national institutions, the European expatriates who give technical advice and
assistance and funds for urban-based research play an important
part in the marginalization of women's expertise.

I have given prominence to the role of two ideological themes
in the context of social relations within 'development' processes:
evolutionism and androcentrism. Although my observations relate
to my experience of stove programmes, I suspect that they may
be relevant to other development areas. Whether it is modernization theory (relegating developing countries to economic and
technological backwardness) or romantic populist ideas of
indigenous knowledge (characterizing locals as practical
people with fantastic memories but not much theory), equivalent
evolutionist ideas form a current trend. In relation to the theme of
androcentrism, the fashion for 'gender issues' often amounts
to no more than proposing women's presence in technology
development projects, with little regard to their relative control
over innovation, production and distribution.

It is not enough to revere participatory development, to say,
'Listen to the people, consult the poor and let *them* tell us their
needs', as if they all agreed with each other. People disagree and

compete, partly because their interests are differentially defined by, for example, their colour, ethnicity, class, gender and/or caste. Not recognizing conflicts between interest groups leaves control in the hands of the more powerful by default. We need to understand not only the differentiated interests of the cooks – when split by class, for example – but how they relate to other groups within and outside their communities. We need to study the engineers and the planners, the policy specialists, researchers, anthropologists, sociologists, economists, marketing and business specialists, the campaigners, communicators – the enormous team that makes up the development 'industry'. Their practices must be watched within the context of their institutional affiliation, their gender, their nationality, their class and identity, for to sweep all expatriates into one pigeon-hole is as misleading as generalizing about 'locals'. I hope to draw attention to what 'goes without saying' for the developers (Bourdieu 1977: 167). Once they understand the partiality of their own thought and inventions, draw back their false veil of neutrality and recognize that their efforts are resisted, ignored or improved by the 'weak', they may be better disposed to accept the demise of 'development' as evolutionary progress controlled by men.

Notes

1. Thanks are due to Ralph Grillo for suggesting changes to an earlier draft, and to colleagues at Sussex University for commenting on this material when it was presented as a paper in January 1994.
2. This doctoral research was carried out from Edinburgh University, supervised by Anthony Good, and funded by a Collaborative Award for the Social Sciences from the Economic and Social Research Council. I have concealed the identities of all organizations and individuals involved in the research.
3. Biomass is matter derived from recently living organisms, such as wood, charcoal, animal dung and agricultural residues.
4. The cycle includes the phases of the project, which usually cover planning, appraisal, implementation, monitoring and

evaluation. Project cycle methodologies refer to the way these
activities are carried out.

References

Adams, A. (1979), 'An Open Letter to a Young Researcher', *African
    Affairs*, 78/313: 451–80.
Ausubel, J.H. (1989), 'Regularities in Technological Development:
    An Environmental View', in J.H. Ausubel and H.E. Sladovich
    (eds), *Technology and Environment*, Washington: National
    Academic Press.
Bennett, K. (1990), 'Technical Objectives of Donor-funded Biomass
    Energy Programmes', in P.J.G. Pearson (ed.), *Energy Efficiency
    in the Third World*, University of Surrey: Surrey Energy Economics
    Centre.
Bhagavan, M.R. and S. Karekezi (1992), *Energy Management in
    Africa*, London: Zed Books and AFREPREN.
Bloch, M. (1991), 'Language, Anthropology and Cognitive Science',
    Man, 26/2: 183–98.
Bourdieu, P. (1977), *Outline of a Theory of Practice*, Cambridge:
    Cambridge University Press.
Brokensha, D., D.M. Warren and O. Werner (eds) (1980), *Indigenous
    Knowledge Systems and Development*, Lanham: University Press
    of America.
Bush, C.G. (1983), 'Women and the Assessment of Technology: To
    Think, to Be, to Unthink, to Free', in J. Rothshild (ed.), *Machina
    ex dea: Feminist Perspectives on Technology*, New York: Pergamon
    Press.
Campbell, A.T. (1989), *To Square with Genesis*, Edinburgh: Edin-
    burgh University Press.
Chambers, R. (1983), *Rural Development: Putting the Last First*,
    London: Longman.
—— (1986), 'The Crisis of Africa's Rural Poor: Perceptions and
    Priorities', in *The Challenge of Employment and Basic Needs in
    Africa*, Nairobi: International Labour Organization.
Cline-Cole, R.A., H. Main and J.E. Nichol (1990), 'On Fuelwood

Consumption, Population Dynamics and Deforestation in Africa', *World Development*, 18/4: 513–27.

Crewe, E. (1993), Size isn't Everything: An Anthropologist's View of the Cook, the Potter, her Engineer, and his Donor in Appropriate Technology Development in Sri Lanka, Kenya and the UK, University of Edinburgh Ph.D. thesis.

Crouch, M. (1989), *Expansion of Benefits: Fuel Efficient Cookstoves in the Sahel. The VITA Experience*, Arlington: VITA, unpublished report.

Davidson, O. and S. Karekezi (1993), 'A New Environmentally Sound Energy Strategy for the Development of Sub-Saharan Africa', in S. Karekezi and G.A. Mackenzie (eds), *Energy Options for Africa*, London: Zed Books.

Escobar, A. (1991), 'Anthropology and the Development Encounter', *American Ethnologist*, 18/4: 658–82.

Foley, G. and P. Moss (1983), *Improved Stoves in Developing Countries*, London and Washington: Earthscan.

Foley, G., P. Moss and L. Timberlake (1984), *Stoves and Trees: How much wood would a wood stove save if a woodstove could save wood?*, London and Washington: Earthscan.

FAO (1985), *Fuelwood Supplies in the Developing Countries*, Rome: United Nations Food Organization.

Gern, G.A. and I. Evans (1981), *Ban ak suuf Cookstoves in Senega: Evaluation*, Submitted by Aprovecho Institute to USAID, unpublished report.

Gill, J. (1987), 'Improved Stoves in Developing Countries: A Critique', *Energy Policy*, 15/2: 135–43.

Goody, J. (1982), *Cooking, Cuisine and Class: A Study in Comparative Sociology*, Cambridge: Cambridge University Press.

Hobart, M. (ed.) (1993), *An Anthropological Critique of Development: The Growth of Ignorance*, London: Routledge.

Howorth, C. (1992), 'Energy Transitions in Africa', *Boiling Point*, 27: 18, 23–4.

Karekezi, S. (1989), 'Responding to the Global Need for Local Action in Domestic Energy', in E. Viklund (ed.), *Nordic Seminar on Domestic Energy in Developing Countries*, Lund: Lund Publications, Lund Centre for Habitat Studies Publications (Lund University), Seminar Reports, No. 31.

Leach, G. and R. Mearns (1988), *Beyond the Woodfuel Crisis: People, Land, and Trees in Africa*, London: Earthscan.

Meadows, D.H., D.L. Meadows, W.W. Behrens III *et al.* (1972), *Limits of Growth,* New York: Universe Books.

Nagabrahmam, N. and S. Sambrani (1980), To Keep the Home Fires Burning: Women's Drudgery in Firewood Collection, Institute of Rural Management, Anand, unpublished report.

Nindi, B. (1990), 'Experts, Donors, Ruling Elites and the African Poor: Expert Planning, Policy Formulation and Implementation – A Critique', *Journal of Eastern African Research and Development,* 20: 41–67.

Scott, J. (1985), *Weapons of the Weak: Everyday Forms of Resistance,* New Haven and London: Yale University Press.

Smith, J. (1983), 'Women and Appropriate Technology: A Feminist Assessment', in J. Zimmerman (ed.), *The Technological Woman: Interfacing with Tomorrow,* New York: Praeger.

Stanley, A. (1983), 'From Africa to America: Black Women Investors', in J. Zimmerman (ed.), *The Technological Woman: Interfacing with Tomorrow,* New York: Praeger.

Tandon, Y. (1991), 'Foreign NGO's, Uses and Abuses: An African Perspective', *Ifda Dossier,* 81: 67–78.

Warren, D.M. (1989), *Indigenous Knowledge Systems: Implications for Agriculture and International Development,* Iowa: Ames.

Chapter 4

The Donors' Discourse: Official Social Development Knowledge in the 1980s

Alan Rew

> Development institutions are part and parcel of how the world is put together so as to ensure certain processes of ruling. (Arturo Escobar 1991: 674, emphasis added)

> To 'donate' is to give implying an altruistic motive; strictly, and perhaps more neutrally, 'suppliers' should replace 'donors' in the vocabulary of this study. (Richard M. Titmuss 1973: 81)

The Importance of Deconstruction 'From Within'

'Development' is as much a set of currently existing institutions and practices with an international remit and compass as it is sets of concepts containing powerful ideological visions with normative tools of reform on behalf of economic growth and poverty alleviation. Development is therefore at the same time rhetoric, official practice and political theory, while also serving as a framework for descriptions, on a global scale, of human misery and hope. As anthropologists, we know that the drama of human activity and interests ensures that visions, methods, institutions and routine practices are blended and combined into complex social processes that are hard to capture with single theories and metaphors. In a benchmark analysis of development programming in action in Lesotho, Ferguson (1990: 17) recognizes the complex transformations of interest and intentions, and treats the outcome of a development project and programme as 'neither an inexplicable mistake, nor the trace of a yet-undiscovered intention, but as a riddle, a problem to be solved, an anthropological puzzle'.

Intuitively, anthropologists will readily accept this general view of complexity and nuance in development outcomes and decision-making and the need to understand the puzzle that Ferguson identifies. The difficulties come in deciding *how* to research and then to *balance* the richness and layers of the desired account. Within the traditions of development studies, the tools to undertake the first task have been at hand for some time. The need to provide first-hand, nuanced studies of the subtle intertwining of bureaucratic politics, economic interest and local social institutions in development planning was recognized, at least a decade before, by Schaffer (1975) and Apthorpe (1986). The method used ('access' studies) could easily be adapted to allow an emphasis on either the interface with political economy (Lamb 1975), the connection with local social institutions and civil society (Rew 1986), or the prospects for administrative reform (Clay and Schaffer eds 1984). The conundrum that continues, within the separate traditions of both development studies and anthropology, is the degree to which the transformations and complexities of access relationships and allocated outcomes provide the specifics and details of relatively unchanging power relations or the extent to which they challenge these power relations and add further dimensions and voices.

Porter, Allen and Thompson (1991) have contributed an outstanding analysis of a single project which addresses exactly these issues. Their general account of 'control-orientation' is based on what appears to be an unusually badly designed development project. It is certainly not representative of all development projects, but it does serve as an eloquent case-study to highlight the distinct possibility that much development planning is an exercise in wishful thinking about administrative and technical control and management. The authors see this desperate wish to produce the certainties of control – 'control-orientation' – as a distinctive 'development' value and pathology. Perhaps the dominant strand in 'development discourse' theory accepts that variations and transformations are part of the interplay of neo-colonial power and 'development' knowledge. For Escobar (1991) they are part of the detail and 'processes of ruling'. Since development projects often combine national and international capital and administrations, major configurations of power are rarely far from the context of technical aims and activities. Even so, unless these 'processes of ruling' can be given a concrete form and can explain the relative importance of new practices and knowledge, the explanation will remain static and true mainly by definition.

Project practices often do vary greatly in their aims and impact and can introduce new voices or improve professional practice. There is no *certainty* that projects will fail or always consolidate national or international power relations. Admittedly, some projects are naked in their use of power and in the brute reality of their distribution of benefits and poverty. Hydropower development, in all but the very remotest areas, usually produces severe disruption and the loss of homes and employment; but it usually produces widespread even if incomparable social and economic benefits for relatively distant co-nationals. Growing experience with these projects has shown that they need very careful social and institutional assessment and alternative provision if the actual *creation* of impoverishment through engineering development is to be avoided (Cernea 1996; Rew 1996). Yet these do not represent *all* projects. If there are projects which extend the reach of the national state (Ferguson 1990), there are others which weaken it or throw it on the defensive (Wood 1994: chapter 22). And if a large number of projects fail to reach their aims, assuming they were clearly stated in the first place, there are others which succeed and those which even transcend their original purposes because of the development of institutional capacity through training and skill development (Uphoff 1992).

The aims and means of development planning practice have changed with post-Cold War conditions and the dominance of neo-liberal economic thinking. In the early 1980s the focus for strategic analysis was the national government and state institutions. A social analysis was mainly needed to add an extra dimension to investment appraisals that carried through the national government's economic and social policies. In the late 1980s and 1990s, however, there has been an explosion of non-governmental and community-based organizations in both Northern and Southern countries and of their networking and linkages (Clark 1990). This has led to the appreciation that a project's web of stakeholders should include a range of organizations within civil society. At the same time, popular participation has become a necessary part of the agenda and now complements the focus on cultural and social identity that characterized the earlier projects.

Social assessments carried out by the new NGO-influenced social development professionals or by consultants managed by them have proved especially useful to aid agencies when designing projects in the context of 'considerable uncertainty due to a lack of awareness, commitment or capacity' (World Bank 1994). In this respect, social assessments have come to occupy a strategic role, since they have encouraged and allowed the design of 'process projects' that build on experience and are responsive to change. Yet there are risks in this approach for the professionals and in the expansion of social development expertise. Questions that must be asked about the expansion of anthropological and comparable analysis within the aid agencies concern its sustainable impact on development operations and policy and on the parent discipline of anthropology.

Some of the risks concerning the impact on development operations are internal to the aid agencies. They concern the way in which the agencies may wish or need to restrict the impact of social development specialists at policy levels. There are also external factors concerning the changing nature of development aid. Calls for increased foreign development aid to prevent famine, rehabilitate the victims of civil war or assist in the economic restructuring of formerly central-planned economies increase along with the recognition of aid's mistakes. The argument that more investment funds are needed is countered by the argument that the need for self-reliance, existing institutional capacities and social contexts limit the amount of aid that can or should be absorbed. Indeed, there is a series of moral ambiguities and choices in the relationship between foreign development aid and cultural choice within most Third World countries. The demand from some for more aid ('because our country is poor') is countered by worries about the debt burden and by questions of the kind, 'can foreign experts really hope to bring about change in cultures so different from their own?' And why allow 'experts', whether foreign or local, to be the ones to decide which aspects of the society need 'developing'? Griffin (1991) has forcefully restated a longstanding criticism of aid – that long-term foreign assistance, intended to alleviate poverty by promoting economic development, has failed. If it is accepted that foreign development aid is only needed for short-term emergency assistance, then the prospects for all development specialists including social development ones, looks relatively unsustainable. On the other hand, it could be accepted that post-Cold War changes have led to a more diverse institutional context for development and for aid policy, with an increasing stress on civil society, local and community-based organization and NGOs. These changes have created new opportunities for social development professionals: the number of social science advisers in the British Government's Overseas Development Administration has grown exponentially (Rew and Bunting 1992). Terms of reference for social development consultants have also changed, from an emphasis on the interplay of cultural identities and the conservatism of existing social practice to an emphasis on empowerment and participatory planning. These changes have accompanied the growing use of ideas of empowerment and tools for 'participatory assessment'.

The pervasive, hegemonic influence of development discourse in Africa, Asia and Latin America, and now a part of Europe, gives a high priority to 'studying up' and to development agency assessment 'from within'. The neo-liberal and post-Cold War changes in development aid policy and context have only confirmed what practitioners know from their routine contacts with the aid agencies – development practice is complex, diverse and usually contested. The different academic disciplines that contribute to development advice and policy bring contested priorities to the internal-aid supply debate, and so, too, do those with contrasted regional and agency experiences and career potentials. The changing credibility and political constituencies for development aid in the northern countries also affect the level of development aid budgets and the way they have to be justified, which in turn affects knowledge and practice about 'accountability'. The result has frequently been the impasse and post-impasse uncertainty in development analysis brought about by neo-liberalism and post-modernism that has so often been highlighted (Booth ed. 1994: 298–311), rather than a new vitality and set of practical and analytical challenges, especially for the social sciences (Gardner and Lewis 1996: 21). These new directions have been affecting practice in the design and evaluation of the key building blocks of aid policy – development projects.

Development projects are interventions that use human skills and other types of capital to enhance productive assets and stimulate economic activity. The imagery is of rational control and the managed design and implementation of ends and means. An understanding of the scope for 'direct control', 'indirect influence' and 'the appreciation of context'[1] is an essential part of project managers' skills: they need to appreciate the project's setting to manage it better and to influence the impact of hard-to-predict outcomes. The project designers, and then subsequently the project management, attempt to orchestrate the balance of resources and time between direct control, indirect influence and research in order to produce both immediate management and longer-term strategic planing. Whereas many technical and economic factors are usually thought amenable to the sphere of 'direct control', the 'social factors' have often been consigned to the sphere of 'context' together with other non-economic factors, such as ecological and institutional ones. These non-economic factors have so often been conflated at the margins of the development-planning discourse that Meier (1994), in an evaluation of United Kingdom development research, treats them as a single, residual part of his evaluation.

It is increasingly recognized, however, that the 'social' factors are distinctive and that there are disciplines, such as anthropology, which have special interpretations and methods of analysis. Increasingly, 'social' factors are seen to represent the common purpose and skill of the social groups caught up as stakeholders in the project processes and not just residual, non-economic factors. The social skills and capacities of project beneficiaries can contribute substantially to the likelihood of sustainable activities once the initial development investment has been completed. Recent years have seen the growth of techniques of planning which have a consultative and avowedly social bias to them, including, for example, 'stakeholder analysis', 'participatory (rural) appraisal' and 'teamup logical framework analysis'.

While practice is always multivalent, contested and changing at different rates, the legacies of combined past practice, layers of accumulated development knowledge and existing organizational interests and commitments do limit the range of possibilities for the effective use of new knowledge and practice. Following Foucault (1974), we recognize that a discursive formation provides a general framework of thought and text that establishes 'what ideas can appear, what sciences can be constituted, what experiences can be reflected in philosophies, what rationalities can be formed only, perhaps, to dissolve and vanish soon afterwards.' Discourse is 'an epistemological space specific to a particular period' (Miller 1994: 150). One aim when deconstructing the elements of a discursive formation has been to identify the relatively stable isomorphisms that organize the practices, institutions, power relations and theories which constitute the field of experience. The more dynamic use of the method is to identify, through deconstruction, exactly those 'certain processes of ruling' that Escobar highlights and that limit and channel emerging new practices and potential sources of knowledge.

This last application of the method is also one that could be useful to practitioners seeking to alter practice from within a development aid organization. Social development practitioners, like any fieldworker, must tread warily and have regard to both power relations and sensitivities. They are often very aware of the dangers of co-option, but have usually chosen to argue for change 'from within' and so find it difficult (but not impossible[2]) to acknowledge publicly the full range of organizational debate and contests. The relative absence of agency members airing their internal debates in public should not mislead us into thinking that there is a lack of search for new information. On the contrary, critical external and internal evaluations of changing aims, practices and impacts can be important resources within the internal aid debate since they are often used to fuel new organizational ventures and messages or lay to rest old ones. It was mainly to contribute to the debate 'from within' development policy practice that I undertook a survey of a large number of texts concerning development operations in 1992, the results of which are reported here. The aim was to produce one or more statistical indicators about the use of social development methods which could then be used to sharpen the focus of existing practice. Most agencies were prepared to release evaluation documents for our purpose.

The textual survey and the subsequent review of trends reported in the next two sections of this chapter try to assess the internal aid debate and the extent to which social development methods have made an impact on general development knowledge and discourse. The state of the operational art at the end of the 1980s is assessed through an analysis of key development-project texts from a number of aid agencies. The time frame for the investigation, and the fact that the survey period coincided with a change in the development paradigm, was wholly coincidental and not a part of the survey design. Nonetheless, the results do allow us to see new practices and knowledge struggling to move from the outer spheres of the project planner's interest towards the spheres of central management interest and direct control. From a position of providing information 'for mainly context', social development advice increasingly seeks to move to the project manager's sphere of 'important to influence', and, perhaps, towards her/his aim of 'direct control'.

A Survey of Aid Project Documents

The survey concentrated on post-completion evaluation documents accessible in the UK and tried to establish the degree of interest in socio-cultural factors within the text. It was undertaken with the encouragement and support of Curtis Roosevelt and T.S. Epstein in order to advance an understanding of cultural entitlements and human rights.[3] Nonetheless, by the coincidence of its timing the survey does give a picture of the operational art during the 1980s. It allows us to develop a baseline of textual and operational knowledge against which expectations for post-Cold War development activity can be set.

The method for the 'meta-evaluation' was to identify how project planners and evaluation specialists themselves wrote about issues of cultural identity rather than imposing a prior definition of 'social' or 'culture' on the analysis. This inductive way of working would, we felt, allow even poorly articulated views of culture and society to emerge.[4] We accepted that the factors we were interested in might emerge in both implicit and explicit ways and that a generous interpretation should be used. Beyond the initial stages of sifting, in which broad orders of magnitude can be established, the results are therefore interpretative and qualitative.

Two key questions were asked of a database of 386 project evaluation and appraisal documents and a sub-sample of 113 reports from five aid agencies. First, have socio-cultural dimensions been recognized, whether explicitly or implicitly, by project preparation and evaluation teams? Secondly, in the case of the sub-sample of projects only, do they go on to specify a methodology or even to indicate a broad approach that would allow socio-cultural factors to be incorporated and integrated with the economic and technical analysis and the recommendations for the project? We had assumed it might be possible to ask a third question: did the ability to recognize and incorporate socio-cultural dimensions in design or implementation contribute to the project's degree of success or failure? The results of the survey led us to conclude that it was not appropriate to ask it on this occasion.[5]

A total of 386 database records for project texts were first established from lists of over 1000 documents in total. The records were entered partly on the basis of availability (of the documents in Swansea or in UK libraries) and partly by an initial judgement about relevance to the survey. Relevance, it was agreed, would be that the sector or type of project would either be heavily dependent on many people's behaviour patterns and participation (e.g. the adoption of new crops or family planning) or that the project would enforce changes in behaviour patterns (e.g. resettlement from infrastructural development). Types of project that were only concerned with, say, highway improvement and maintenance or the development of trade were not listed. The relevance of the text was established using these criteria through an examination of the tables of content and internal headings. It took a considerable proportion of the total research time of four months to establish the database. It was then decided to take a random sample of 1 in 3 of these documents and to carry out more detailed investigations. In the event, 113 documents were read in full, giving a 30 per cent sample of the initial quantity of documents that had been screened. This subset of documents was then read in full and analysed. The likely relevant sections of the text were entered in full into an unlimited text database and then successively searched on key words.

The type of projects covered by the eventual database are as shown in Table 4.1:

Table 4.1. Project reports studied, by sector

Natural resources	110	
Water and irrigation		72
Agriculture, rural development and environment		38
Roads and public infrastructure	93	
Education and training	91	
Health, population and nutrition	53	
Urban, industrial and other	39	
Total	386	

The survey showed that three-quarters (85) of the 113 full reports in the database referred to socio-cultural factors in one way or another. This had not been expected, despite our initial screening for broad relevance.[6] The initial hypothesis had been that a sizeable minority of the documents would show notable interest and that a majority would essentially ignore socio-cultural considerations. Our hypothesis stemmed in part from our prior view that probably one half to two-thirds of investment projects would avoid much reference to social and cultural variables. These factors, we thought from previous project experience, might be treated as marginal to economic and technical design; and in the search for coherence, project designers would rely on technical or economic design criteria and treat socio-cultural information as largely anecdotal. Only a small but growing proportion of projects would, we hypothesized, have recognized the need for a specialized social-science input. We had simply assumed that any evaluation's willingness to address social and cultural factors would reflect either the involvement of specialized consultants or highly specific topics such as resettlement or irrigation management that explicitly prompted a managerial interest in the social and community context of the operations.

In fact, we had seen the issue as too polarized and had not counted on the more widespread but less specialized awareness of social and cultural context that was evident in the evaluations. Some of this interest may be merely 'lip-service' and contractual: to be on the safe side donors and governments added a 'social' element to collective terms of reference, and consultants responded with a 'social' section to meet these requirements. This does not, however, appear to be the main consideration for mentions of socio-cultural factors: there does seem to be a definite awareness of the need to consider them during project planning and implementation. Problems were identified that could not be explained by wholly technical or microeconomic analyses. However, the interpretation and use of a socio-cultural perspective in design or in implementation strategies is rarely considered in the documents. Rather, the factors are handled in a largely inconsistent and arbitrary manner.

Social and cultural factors were offered as 'catch-all' factors that could be stated as reasons for difficulty in projects but that were not or could not be taken further given the project's design and the state of the operational art. It is clear that an awareness of social context had not permeated the aid agencies' or executive agencies' normal procedures to any extent. Cultural and social considerations are generally viewed as 'outside' the agency and about 'the customs of the locals' rather than as an essential aspect of technical assistance work and design. The inclusion of a non-economic social scientist in the project implementation and evaluation teams was one clear indication that the agencies were explicitly aware of social and cultural factors and could deal with them on an established institutional basis. It was, however, difficult to establish the extent of these specialists' impact on design or implementation. In a little less than ten percent of the projects, it was apparent that separate socio-cultural studies had been commissioned and were usually attached as annexes. Surprisingly, there was no direct indication in the main texts of how these studies had been utilized.

It is necessary to present another result of the survey in order to understand this combination of the consciousness of culture and society with an arbitrary treatment of it. With relatively few exceptions, it is the *projects* that are seen as the fundamental entities. The projects are not viewed as an explicit set of objectives and aims, planning processes and resource flows with respect to the recipient society. They are most often seen in quite mechanistic terms – as discrete economic and even physical entities or as containers of development that have been placed in the local society and economy for its members to open. With rare exceptions, the sponsoring or implementing organization starts from an engineering or economistic discourse that makes issues of social agency and cultural identity only incidental to the project design and implementation.

It is this discursive hiatus and the lack of an apparent methodology for incorporating socio-cultural factors that may explain the inconsistency and dual tendency within the data. On the one hand, there is an evident wish to include culture as an explanation for project outcomes and processes. On the other hand, culture and society are seen as obstacles to the project or, largely implicitly, as factors to be managed reactively if the project is to succeed. In some ninety percent of all reports, management is cited as a problem or shortcoming or as inefficient. In fact, these mentions occur so frequently with all organizations and sectors that we felt it might not be sufficient to treat the finding at face value and decided to see if 'management' was being used as an oblique way of referring to something else. Closer examination of the texts does reveal that 'management' problems often reveal concerns about 'the management capacity' of local officials and entrepreneurs, breakdowns in cross-cultural communication, a subsequent intolerance, a mismatch between local leadership and cultural values and the management structures of the projects, and conflicts between the development community's interests and those of the local staff and beneficiaries. We concluded that 'management difficulties' can often be a proxy indicator of social conflict that invited a fuller, less internalized and coded analysis. What might otherwise appear to be a rather straightforward middle-level management function can, in the context of an externally funded development project, become a point of friction between project personnel and within local community relations, ultimately frustrating top-level management in its ability to reach a solution.

Another proxy indicator of socio-cultural awareness may be gender awareness. In 35 percent of the texts, discussion of social and cultural traditions was intertwined with discussion of customary gender relations. To some extent, this conflation arose through the stereotyped lumping together of two 'difficult' social development areas for ease-of-implementation and evaluation-management purposes. In other cases it arose because 'gender relations' were validly seen as a sub-component of a social and cultural assessment and therefore included without special comment or separation; perhaps in yet other cases heightened awareness of one had led to a heightened awareness of the other.

Underlying the original survey design was a hypothesis that there would be variation according to donor practice and according to the nature of specific sectors. Because of the small numbers involved, the results cannot be considered conclusive. Nonetheless, there were a number of results that challenged our initial guesses about what we would find and that in some cases appeared counter-intuitive and suggestive of further research.

There was considerable variation in the styles of each agency's evaluation reports, emphasizing the differing origins, charters of organization and accountability of the aid agencies, the scale of the projects they tended to organize, and the dominant intellectual traditions of the countries concerned. In keeping with these contrasts, our preliminary expectations had been that the World Bank was probably less ready to recognize socio-cultural factors than the (mainly European) bilateral agencies.[7] The Bank's known emphasis on the necessary economic efficiencies of the markets for labour, land and capital when dealing with welfare issues was assumed to be inimical to the development of social-action methodologies. Equally, it was expected that in the more collective and state welfare traditions of post-World War II, Europe would encourage the planning of projects that were more sensitive to social and cultural factors. However, to judge from the texts, the World Bank appeared as sensitive to socio-cultural factors as any of the bilaterals and in some cases was even more so. The one donor that had most thoroughly incorporated socio-cultural factors was the Swedish International Development Agency, whose evaluation reports showed a general tendency towards greater use of social, cultural and historical interpretations of development. On the whole, however, the variations in agency style and traditions were not thought to be especially important as an explanation of socio-cultural awareness.

There are also contrasts by project type or sector. Of the five major classifications into which the data falls – natural resources and irrigation, roads and infrastructure, education, health and population, and urban and industrial development – the educational and training projects were distinctive in their relative lack of recognition of social and cultural factors. Over thirty percent of the projects in the database made no mention of these. By contrast, the health and population projects all made some mention of these factors and in some cases had the fullest accounts and acceptance of behavioural aspects. It is difficult to see that it is the nature of the sector or its context that could produce these contrasts. Rather, it seems to be because there is relatively little search for the attitudinal and social backgrounds influencing educational outcomes, whereas there is concern to trace beliefs and behaviours related to health-care and disease-prevention.

Two other unexpected sub-sectoral findings concern small-scale industry and environmental conservation. 'Environmental conservation' projects, with eleven projects in the database, and 'small-scale industries', also with eleven projects in the database, had *no* mentions of socio-cultural factors. The result was unexpected for small-scale industries, since these projects need to explore the relevance or otherwise of cultural context for small-scale entrepreneurs and their behaviour. It is also surprising in the case of environmental conservation, since in many cases resource conservation involves the enforcement of state rights over the tenures, livelihoods and customary uses of minority and/or resource-poor groups.

Current Social Development Knowledge and Practice

Although these results of textual analysis are generated from development projects in the 1980s, many of the findings are of continuing importance today. The survey revealed that there was a diffuse interest in social and cultural factors but that this lacked impact through a failure to develop an understandable and acceptable methodology. Lack of impact continues to worry social development specialists working in international aid organizations, even though recent methodological developments concerning participation claim to offer a greater prospect of recognition, effectiveness and sustainability than there was in the early 1980s. The survey results showed that there had been a variable impact on sectors. Variable impact continues to be a tactical and strategic issue and has considerable importance for the careers of social development professionals . Some are unfortunate in having to work with divisions that are suspicious of or antagonistic to the growth of social development expertise, while other cognate professionals forge alliances of mutual benefit. For example, in my experience, the educational development and human resources specialism in donor agencies continues to be dominated by welfare economists rather than sociologists or anthropologists, whereas there is usually continuing liaison between social science and health advisers.

The long-term role of social development specialists is also somewhat uncertain. There is, for example, considerable variation between aid agencies in the ways that they incorporate social development expertise. In some agencies social development expertise lacks critical mass and is dispersed into a range of geographical and technical functions, while in others it is concentrated, and possibly contained, into a single division. Socio-cultural assessment is now very much part of the project's 'furniture', but its practitioners also worry about their impact and effectiveness.

The survey does raise the question of whether or not the analytical paradigm used by the social development analysts could be improved or was even minimally satisfactory for its dual purpose of both capturing local knowledge and realities and allowing their summary and synthesis for use by project planners. The texts we surveyed gave a sense of a static, external analysis. It was dependent on the *professional* expertise of analysts who would provide a social engineering expertise comparable to the civil or irrigation engineering specialists with whom they had to work – they provided 'the people side' of the design. The social experts were largely dependent on their own personal and academic authority when trying to convince other technical specialists. The emphasis was on a special 'folk' or 'indigenous' knowledge to be uncovered and used largely as 'useful context' and 'issues for further investigation'. It gave the social analysts a distinctive field of enquiry and technical authority, but it also expected them to offer a method for controlling the cultural or indigenous elements – thus giving rise to in-built disappointment. The disappointment was not, however, radical. It was widely accepted that human behaviour is difficult to predict and that other technical specialists had comparable problems in predicting risk and uncertainty. All project planners accept that there can be both expected and unexpected results from an intervention. These results can, in turn, be either desirable or undesirable. On the whole, in the project documents, socio-cultural factors were seen to lead to results that were unexpected and undesirable. Both expected and desirable results were attributed to the design of the project, good luck, skill in implementation management and so on. The aim in employing a socio-cultural specialist was to anticipate more of the previously unexpected results and to design out the undesirable factors. These are not easy tasks to accomplish for a lone specialist acting in a technical and outsider's role.

Lessons are learnt over time, and organizations may need years rather than months to change practices and procedures. It is not at all clear what time period is needed for aid agencies to distil new methods from cumulative experience and to adopt recruitment aims, training and procedures that ensure project staff have a better understanding of the influence of socio-cultural factors. Nonetheless, the growing acceptance of the need to incorporate socio-cultural analysis has been especially marked in certain technical fields in the last ten years. There has been a particularly marked acceptance of non-economic social-science contributions in the field of irrigation management, in the design and implementation of water-supply improvement schemes and in farming systems research. The field-based research publications of Korten (1983) and Uphoff (1992) on irrigation management have demonstrated the need for more contextual and experiential accounts of development policy implementation and scheme management. At the same time, social anthropologists may have grown more rather than less sceptical about anthropology's terms of engagement in development work, and this has made the incorporation of its insights even more difficult to realize. There is, for example, Hobart's claim (1993) that there has been a growth of ignorance in development, not a growth of new knowledge based on lessons from experience, as well as Escobar's (1995) strictures on 'compromise'.

Chambers (1992: 48) blames a tyranny of professionals and outsiders for the failure to appreciate the need for new lessons:

> We, the professional outsiders, had a monopoly of powers of analysis. Most outsiders have then either lectured, holding sticks and wagging fingers, or have interviewed, machine-gunning with rapid fire questions, interrupting, and not listening beyond immediate replies. [. . .] Our beliefs, demeanour, behaviour and attitudes have been self-validating. Treated as incapable, rural people have behaved as incapable, hiding their capabilities from us, and even from themselves. Nor have we known how to enable them to express, share and extend their knowledge. The ignorance and inabilities of rural people have been not only an illusion, but an artefact of our own arrogance and ignorance.

To move beyond this impasse, the assimilation of lessons based on the new professionalism of the NGOs and a recognition of past errors and inadequacies was needed. Chambers has done much to undermine the tyranny of the outsider professionals, with their reliance on technical and questionnaire surveys usually administered with insufficient regard for local realities and contexts. After a period of experimentation with quick and dirty *rapid* rural appraisal methods (RRA), the emphasis in alternative appraisal techniques is now on *relaxed* and participatory methods (PRA). Chambers argues (ibid.: 45) that there is a need for a movement from extractive methods of data-gathering and analysis to methods that reverse dominance and that start a process of empowerment. He writes: 'Both the traditional questionnaire survey and the classical social anthropological investigation are extractive, even though their means of extraction differ (ibid.: 44).'

The need is for participatory data-gathering and analysis through which the initiative is passed to the people. 'The time of PRA may have come.'

What is PRA? It is a set of techniques and methods 'intended to enable local people to conduct their own analysis, and often to plan and take action'. There has been a major growth in this activity in recent years. Chambers describes it in some detail (1994: 953–4). It is 'a growing family of approaches and methods to enable local people to share, enhance and analyse their knowledge of life and conditions, to plan and to act.' It flows from and owes much to 'activist participatory research', 'applied anthropology', field research on farming systems, agroecosystem analysis and its parent 'rapid rural appraisal'. Chambers acknowledges that the problem with RRA is that while having the virtues of simplicity of data-collection, cost-efficiency and on-site (even if hurried) investigation, it also has the vices of a lack of quality control and the ever-present danger of an extractive learning by outsiders. It facilitated the rapid production of plans and reports but did not contribute to sustainable local action or institutional development.

Chambers traces the introduction of participation into the standard planning practice of rural development to the 1980s or even before. By 1988, participatory RRAs were listed as one of a number of 'RA' methodologies. Subsequently there was an explosion of innovation in India, especially in the NGO sector. By 1992, Chambers was in a position to take stock and review the developments in techniques and methodology.

The effectiveness of location-specific projects depends on good-quality information about local interests and effective communication between outsiders and community members. PRA has gained popularity as a method of information collection that is held to be more reliable than conventional social research because 'the objective is less to gather data, and much more to start a process . . . the outsider is less extractor and more convenor and catalyst' (Chambers 1994: 960). The approach has gained considerable popularity in natural-resource project-planning, especially in forestry and farming-systems research and in programmes designed to achieve equity for, say, women and in health and nutrition projects. It is used by a variety of agencies, especially NGOs, at project and programme level.

A major recognition of its potential is the adoption of PRA approaches in poverty assessments by the World Bank. Norton,

Owen and Milimo (1994) show how the incorporation of participatory research techniques to discern local-level perceptions of
poverty is able to 'give a voice to the poor' while also enriching
the World Bank's technical poverty profile and filling lacunae in
that institution's understanding of the dimensions of poverty. The
use of participatory research methods was found to have an
important policy relevance and not just anecdotal or illustrative
utility. The data collected showed the variation in the attributes
of poverty and led to more meaningful internal discussion within
the Bank itself. There were also gains identified, from the Bank's
point of view, in the link between governments' poverty-strategy
documents, the Bank's lending strategy and the involvement of
institutional 'stakeholders' within the country concerned. The
forging of these links was thought most promising in the cases of
Morocco and Peru, although 'to be sure, both countries represent
examples where the participatory involvement entailed a strong
"carrot and stick" approach to Bank-government dialogue'
(Norton and Stephens 1994: 22).

This apparently ready acceptance of PRA in the 1990s (and its
in-house advisors and managers) by the aid agencies contrasts with
their far more cautious incorporation of individual social analysts
in the 1980s. The contrast may stem from the cumulation of
incremental lessons learnt from operational experience. It can be
argued that the initial experience of the 1980s led to the adoption
– a decade later and on a larger scale – of the earlier lessons.
Alternatively, it can be argued that the main difference is conceptual. The projects of the 1980s stressed cultural and social
identity considerations; the newer projects have stressed process,
social action and 'empowerment'.

Norton and Stephens (1994), reviewing the use of PRA within
poverty assessments in Africa, note trade-offs between the
immediate duties of the Bank's task managers and the need to
address the institutions of civil society in poverty-alleviation
programmes. They show that the principal analytical tension in
PRA centres on the relationship between the participation of
'primary' and that of 'institutional' stakeholders. This comment
may indicate that more recent social development practice has
encountered a similar difficulty in moving from a generalized
interest in social reporting to the reform of agency rationalities
and methods to that shown in our survey of social development
practice in the 1980s. Norton and Stephens appear to argue that

this is not the case: aid agency practice was illuminated and changed as a result of the participatory assessments.

In order to judge the general potential of these participatory methods, we do need a greater understanding of their reception within executing organizations and major aid agencies. These methods are increasingly mainstream. German aid grants now use their own participatory methods (ZOPP, Zielorientierte Projektplanung, usually translated as Target Oriented Project Planning) extensively, and the British ODA uses them for both project design and review and in the field management of project implementation. Critical reflections on the practice of PRA are also now appearing (e.g. Brown 1994; Gujit and Cornwall 1995; Richards 1995), but with a few exceptions (e.g. Mosse 1994; Rew, Mosse and Farrington, forthcoming) there has been little detailed analysis of the risks, biases and benefits of actual PRA work in organizational and project planning contexts. Chambers (1994) himself notes five dangers in the use of the method. These can be compressed into the potential dangers of ritualism and insincerity, amateurish over-enthusiasm, and hostility from the participating specialisms and disciplines. Perhaps the biggest challenge, Chambers writes, is in the establishment of PRA as a way of operating in large-scale organizations.

An important contribution to the theoretical and critical literature on development planning research methods has been made by David Mosse (1994). He reports the reception, at local community levels, of PRA teams in a rainfed farming-improvement project in western India. Mosse was involved in the PRAs but also maintained a critical stance to the development and use of these methods within the community. It is especially interesting that the case he reports can be perceived by champions of PRA as the *one* case in which it was rejected.[8] This is not true, even for southern India, where it has been pioneered. I am aware of cases in which rural elites have declared their lack of interest in the exercise or in which it is apparent that the exercise misfired and that groups within the rural population could not voice their disquiet or wishes (Rew and Hobley 1994).

Mosse's contribution is not to show that a PRA failed but that at least some of the information collected in a PRA is likely to be difficult to interpret or even suspect. The PRA method emphasizes intensive interrogation and the use of role reversals and visual techniques in public settings. Each of these emphases can be problematic. First, the information is elicited in a social context where the influence of power, authority and gender inequalities are great and highly likely to bias the PRA results. In particular, it is the (self-consciously) *public* nature of PRAs that makes the production of local knowledge an outcome of what Mosse calls 'officializing strategies' and 'muting'. The interaction of insiders with outsiders in a public forum turns the information into action within an 'officializing' context and also mutes and silences the voices of, for example, women. Secondly, there is a heavy bias towards *verbalized* information in PRAs. Since poor, low-status people want to protect their economic and social security (even when offered self-determination!), they will resist, from time to time or frequently, the call to voice their needs. It follows that issues of cultural identity and indigenous knowledge remain: the 'incapacities' or mutedness of some social categories that Chambers and Mosse both note are not reached simply by a change in the role and behaviour of outsiders. Thirdly, an important part of practical cultural knowledge remains encoded in technical routines and everyday experience and cannot easily be elicited verbally. Thus important aspects of practical knowledge are encoded in the culture in ways that make it difficult if not impossible to access by PRA means. The implication of Mosse's account is that knowledge of *both* private and public events is needed, and that exercises in supposed 'public empowerment' should be balanced by the extended study of a culture and by critical observation.

Conclusion

The survey of social development practice in the 1980s reported here shows how difficult it has proved to institutionalize and use critical social reflection within development project planning: social analyses, when commissioned, remained in annexes in their project appraisal and evaluation documents. In the 1990s there has been a significant change and a far greater scope for social analysts to influence project design and implementation. There is far greater use of 'social' planning methods in mainstream project design. The accounts by Mosse (1994) and Norton and Stephens (1994) of actual participatory planning practice, for example, could *only* arise because in-house social appraisal advisors and managers in the UK's Overseas Development Administration and the World Bank had sponsored them and argued for the commissioning of detailed social development consultancy. The academic discipline of anthropology in the United Kingdom does not fully appreciate these more recent developments. First, it is not easy to review the relevant literature sources, which are often in aid agency documents with a limited circulation or in project discussion papers. Secondly, the post-modernist and interpretative turns in anthropology appear indifferent to piecemeal reform or declare it to be futile (Hobart ed. 1993; Rew 1994).

While there have been significant changes in official social development knowledge, and amendments to current development discourse as a consequence, the reforms in favour of social action and 'participation' should not be overstated. The recent emphasis has been more on the development and use of a suite of techniques and methods and less on the critical appraisal of the methods and their use. The selection of techniques is not especially important when compared to the need to vest planning responsibilities in common-purpose groups that are appropriate to the task and aim at issue and to a prior understanding of the social and cultural conditions governing effective participation in planning.

Social development specialists working in the aid agencies have argued strongly for grants or donations of aid with which their agencies could lever agreement on social goals (such as poverty reduction) and ensure that there was room within which to manoeuvre the enhancement of basic and technical human skills and allow the expression of cultural meanings to 'development'. Their efforts have been rewarded with some recent success. At the same time, however, there is increasing pressure on aid budgets and the growth of various critiques, and also fatalism, about the aim of global poverty reduction through aid. Aid administrators are required to demonstrate that the money they are allocated has actually been spent and that it has been spent wisely. They are increasingly subject to indicators of effectiveness, accountability, disbursement and visible impact. These pressures are transmitted into increasing demands for rationality and clarity in the definition of project aims and aid-use. Although the aid project planners always state that aims and means may need to change in response to wider social and economic events, the current emphasis is on the effective supply of aid rather than the donation of enabling grants which are tolerant of long periods of social experimentation and capacity building. The danger is that the pressures on development aid will be turned into pressures on social development specialists for methods which give more and more control over aid supply and over the management of 'popular consultation' by government and other aid agencies.

Notes

1. Cusworth and Franks (1993) provide a good review of these three 'environments' of decreasing control and understanding, represented as three rings spreading out from the central project task of relating inputs to outputs.
2. For example, the Overseas Development Administration and the Foreign Secretary were in open dispute about the latter's decision to allocate investment aid to the controversial Pergau Dam hydropower project in Malaysia because of its uncertain development benefits.
3. The survey originated from an idea of Scarlett Epstein. It was sponsored and funded by Curtis Roosevelt and the Roosevelt Institute. I am especially indebted to them both for their keen personal interest and support and for the extended discussions that led to the research reported here. I was ably assisted by Ikaweba Bunting and Damian Rew, both of whom searched for and then entered the relevant documentary texts. Ikaweba Bunting was responsible for the initial textual analysis and drafted a report on the survey results. Damian Rew was responsible for the initial design and maintenance of the database. The responsibility for the overall design and for the analysis reported here is mine alone.
4. The key words used to identify actual or potential cultural factors were the following: culture, cultural, socio-cultural, socio-economic, socio-political, traditional, local, indigenous, institutional, ethnic social considerations, ethnic patterns, institutional setting, land-tenure, local customs, social structures, indigenous structures, traditional practices, historical settings,

family structure, impact on women, social organization, community-based, historical patterns.

5. The investigation initially aimed to research the precise relationship between cultural sensitivity and project success and to do so with a combination of wide multilateral and bilateral coverage and selected detailed investigations of particular projects. As the research began, it was clear that these aims were too ambitious. The coverage had to be reduced considerably because documents were unobtainable from certain selected multilaterals, and the aim of surveying the contribution of cultural factors to project success had to be amended since the projects never committed themselves to an evaluation of their success or failure. The final aim of the survey was to investigate the degree to which social and cultural factors were recognized and used.

6. The full results are reported in Rew and Bunting (1992).

7. The bilateral agencies were: United States Agency for International Development; United Kingdom Overseas Development Administration; Swedish International Development Agency; Danish International Development Agency. The one multilateral agency was the World Bank. The United National Development Programme and the Food and Agriculture Organization were not able to release evaluation documents.

8. Robert Chambers, personal information.

References

Apthorpe, R. (1986), 'Development Policy Discourse', *Public Administration and Development*, 6: 377–89.

Booth, D. (ed.) (1994), *Rethinking Social Development:Theory, Research and Practice*, London: Longman.

Brown, D. (1994), 'Seeking the Consensus: Populist Tendencies at the Interface between Consultancy and Research', in A. Rew (ed.), *From Consultancy to Research: The Interface Between Consultancy and Research*. Proceedings of a conference held at the Centre for Development Studies, March 1994, Swansea: Centre for Development Studies, University of Wales.

Cernea, M. (1996), 'Understanding and Preventing Impoverishment from Displacement: Reflections on the State of Knowledge', in C. McDowell (ed.), *A Tamil Asylum Diaspora: Sri Lankan Migration, Settlement and Politics in Switzerland*, Oxford: Berghahn.

Chambers, R. (1992), *Rural Appraisal: Rapid, Relaxed and Participatory*, University of Sussex: Institute of Development Studies (IDS Discussion Papers 311).

—— (1994), 'The Origins and Practice of Participatory Rural Appraisal', *World Development*, 22/7: 953–69.

Clark, J. (1990), *Democratising Development: The Role of Voluntary Organisations*, London: Earthscan.

Clay, E. and B. Schaffer (eds) (1984), *Room for Manoeuvre: An Exploration of Public Policy Planning in Agricultural and Rural Development*, London: Heinemann.

Cusworth, J.W. and T.R. Franks (eds) (1993), *Managing Projects in Developing Countries*, London: Longman.

Escobar, A. (1991), 'Anthropology and the Development Encounter', *American Ethnologist*, 18/4: 658–82.

—— (1995), *Encountering Development: The Making and Unmaking of the Third World*, Princeton: Princeton University Press.

Ferguson, J. (1990), *The Anti-politics Machine: 'Development', Depolitization, and Bureaucratic Power in Lesotho*, Minneapolis: University of Minnesota Press.

Foucault, M. (1974), *The Order of Things: An Archaeology of the Human Sciences*, London: Routledge.

Gardner, K. and D. Lewis (1996), *Anthropology, Development and the Post-modern Challenge*, London: Pluto Press.

Griffin, K. (1991), 'Foreign Aid after the Cold War', *Development and Change*, 22/4: 654–85.

Gujit, I. and A. Cornwall (1995), 'Critical Reflections on the Practice of PRA', *PLA Notes*, 24: 2–7.

Hobart, M. (ed.) (1993), *An Anthropological Critique of Development: The Growth of Ignorance*, London: Routledge.

Korton, D.C. (1983), 'Social Development: Putting People First', in D.C. Korton and F.B. Alfonso (eds), *Bureaucracy and the Poor*, West Hartford, Conn.: Kumarian Press.

Lamb, G. (1975), 'Access, Marxism and the State', *Development and Change*, 6/2: 119–35.

Meier, G.M. (1994), 'Review of Development Research in the UK:

Report to the Development Studies Association', *Journal of International Development*, 6/5: 465–512.

Miller, J. (1994), *The Passion of Michel Foucault*, London: Flamingo.

Mosse, D. (1994), 'Authority, Gender and Knowledge: Theoretical Reflections on the Practice of Participatory Rural Appraisal', *Development and Change*, 25/3: 497–525.

Norton, A., D. Owen and J. Milimo (1994), *Zambia Poverty Assessment, Volume 4: Participatory Poverty Assessment*, Washington: The World Bank.

Norton, A. and T. Stephens (1994), *Participation in Poverty Assessments Workshop on Participatory Development*, Washington: The World Bank.

Porter, D., B. Allen and G. Thompson (1991), *Development in Practice: Paved with Good Intentions*, London: Routledge.

Rew, A. (1986), 'Institutional Culture and Persistent Structures in Papua New Guinea', *Public Administration and Development*, 6/4: 391–400.

—— (1994), 'Social Standards and Social Thought', in C. Hann (ed.), *When History Accelerates: Essays on Rapid Social Change, Complexity and Creativity*, London: Athlone.

—— (1996), 'Policy Implications of the Involuntary Ownership of Resettlement Negotiations: Examples from Asia of Resettlement Practice', in C. McDowell (ed.), *A Tamil Asylum Diaspora: Sri Lankan Migration, Settlement and Politics in Switzerland*, Oxford: Berghahn.

—— and I. Bunting (1992), *The Role of Social-cultural Factors in Project Appraisal and Evaluation Reports*, New York: Roosevelt Institute.

—— and M. Hobley (1994), 'Results of the August "JFPM" Visits: Conclusions and Recommendations', *Western Ghats Forestry Discussion Notes*, 3: 1–9.

——, D. Mosse and J. Farrington (eds) (forthcoming), *Process Monitoring and Process Documentation: Evolving Methods for Social Research and Development Practice: Cases and Issues*.

Richards, P. (1995), 'Participatory Rural Appraisal: A Quick and Dirty Critique', *PLA Notes*, 24: 13–16.

Schaffer, B. (1975), 'The Problems of Access to Public Service (theme issue)', *Development and Change*, 6/2.

Titmuss, R. (1973), *The Gift Relationship*, London: Penguin.

Uphoff, N.T. (1992), *Learning from Gal Oya: Possibilities for Partici-*

patory Development and Post-Newtonian Social Science, Ithaca and London: Cornell University Press.

Wood, G.D. (1994), *Bangladesh: Whose Ideas, Whose Interests?*, Dhaka: Dhaka University Press.

World Bank (1994), *Guidelines for the Social Appraisal of World Bank Projects*, Washington, D.C.: World Bank, Environment Department.

Chapter 5

Watching the Developers:
A Partial Ethnography

Georgia Kaufmann

The concept of development suggests a movement from a less to a more evolved state: a process of completion.[1] As Esteva argues: 'Development occupies the centre of an incredibly powerful semantic constellation' (1992: 8). Since the end of the Cold War, the shift from colonialism and the emergence of the international agencies, it has become one of the cognitive binding forces that holds the global system together (Johnston 1991: 164, 168–9). Increasingly it shapes the discourse by which international communication is conducted, the way in which governments and international organizations interrelate. What is curious about the development relationship is the way that it has been transformed over time from its roots in exploitative colonialism (Johnston 1991: 157–9; Larrain 1989: 6–7) to the ethos of international brotherly help and global co-operation in the fight against poverty and the calls to cooperative endeavour against the perceived ecological and demographic threats raised by the UN conferences in Rio de Janeiro and Cairo.

The process of development involves a relationship between the developers – the experts, technocrats, advisors, specialists, volunteers, fieldworkers – and the developed, the recipients of the aid and advice. The developers, whether working at home, 'overseas' or 'in the field', are caught up in the gargantuan task of changing, shaping, homogenizing and, supposedly, improving the lot of the developed. Many developers are wary of the power structures and hierarchies that are bound up in this relationship. Development is at best a dialogue, at worst the imposition of a set of ('our') processes and beliefs on the 'other'.

The analytic study of the development relationship tends to focus on either the grassroots experience of the other or institutional relationships of development. Rather than focusing on the 'other', the developed, this paper turns the lens on the developers. My aim is to consider the manner in which individual developers based in Britain think and conceive of development. As such this paper is but a partial ethnography. The objective was to examine the reasons that led developers as individuals into the development process, and the motives and ideas that guide their professional lives. It was not, however, intended to track what the developers' actual jobs consist of, nor what outcomes result from their actions, and it is in this respect that the view is incomplete. The basis for this investigation was the belief that the rationale and paths of individuals' entry into the professional arena of development effect their aims, objectives and the manner in which they work. As individuals at the empowered end of the development relationship, their own explanations and narratives could be expected to determine, at least in part, the results of their labour.

The research for this chapter was conducted through a series of semi-structured interviews with developers, individuals directly involved in British development, as advocates, policy-makers and technical experts. Locating the developers was the first task. For practical reasons the research was restricted to individuals working in Britain. The intention was to get a broad cross-section of people working in different sectors: government, politics and NGOs. British development agencies, both governmental and non-governmental, are largely shaped by the colonial experience. The Overseas Development Administration (ODA) emerged out of the reconstructed colonial service (Lee 1967; Morgan 1980: 13–32). This government ministry inherited from its parents, the Colonial Office and the Department of Technical Cooperation, a predisposition to bolster government institutions and services in the ex-colonies. British NGOs evolved to fill the gaps that official aid programmes had not targeted. Freer from political constraints, the NGOs have been able to foster small-scale, grassroots development, providing in many respects a complimentary service to the more political, high-profile governmental projects. While cooperation and dialogue between the ODA and NGOs is increasing, in some respects they work towards different goals and follow different blueprints. It seemed probable that the differences in their approaches to development would be reflected in their personnel.

Lastly, I included politicians with a demonstrated commitment to development issues. The ODA is not independent of Parliament, and politicians ultimately play a significant role in shaping the policies that the civil servants in the ODA carry out.

The sample of British developers presented in the following pages is neither random nor statistically significant. I approached the ODA and the major British development NGOs to find out who was working on policy issues, and then asked them as well as politicians in the Houses of Parliament for an interview. Few refused, although some were unavailable and passed me on to colleagues. In nearly all cases I went to the office of the individual in order to conduct the interviews, all of which took place in the summer of 1993. The informants were asked to talk about how they came to be working in development. They were also asked to define development and to talk about their experience and knowledge of it. The aim of the paper is to consider what patterns, if any, there are in the beliefs of the people who become developers and if this effects what they do.

Following the trend in anthropology of allowing the informants' voices to speak, rather than translating for them, this paper uses the interview material directly. The informants were shown a draft of the section(s) relating to their interview and were invited to comment further on their reported remarks. The consequent literary dialogue was an aspect of the research that had been impossible in my previous fieldwork. As a process it raised questions about the authority of the informants and myself to control the text, which reflect some aspects of the power relationship within development *per se*. As I shall show below, the developers were in a far more powerful position regarding what I wrote of them than my previous informants in Brazil. Nevertheless, as a participant observer with direct participation in the development process (i.e. as a then Fellow at the Institute of Development Studies), this paper, my own narrative, cannot be anything other than my own partial perspective.

Watching the Developers

While I was setting up the interviews I had an opportunity to reflect on the nature of participant observation. My professional base at the time was the Institute of Development Studies (IDS).

This institution has an international reputation as one of the leading players in the academic study of development. It also plays no small consultative part in forging and influencing policy. Yet, despite its obvious pertinence, I felt it was too close to home to include in my sample. In many respects this is a serious omission since I thereby neglected the academic component of development, which is not insignificant. My omission is an acknowledgement of how difficult it is to observe if totally submerged in participation.

It was also striking how using the same techniques as I have 'in the field', i.e. doing anthropology in the South, felt so different in this Northern context. My previous experience of fieldwork was in a *favela* (shanty town) in Brazil. There I had conducted demographic interviews with a questionnaire as well as living in the community, gradually building up the trust and confidence of a network of informants who conversed with me. During the demographic interviews, and while arranging them, the respondents were usually polite and intimidated by the mere fact of their interaction with a foreign (white) woman. My attempts to put people at their ease rarely overcame the formality that the respondents adopted. The efforts I made to relax respondents in the interview were not sufficient to overturn the social hierarchy that framed our meetings. Even though the interviews took place in the women's homes, most often in their kitchens, and they had agreed to the interview, I (as proxy for the questionnaire) was in control of the way the time would be spent, the order and themes of the conversation. Although we were occupying their physical space, the control over temporal space was ceded to me. Conversely the informants in the current study were far more participative: sitting in their offices, behind their desks, they entered the exchange of information as equals. Not only was I entering their physical domain, they were in control of how much time to allot me. The sense of empowerment and ownership that the professional developers appeared to experience left little room for their objectification. This owed much to our relative equality on the social scale.

The different responses I encountered in similar processes in the North and South reflect the relative experiences of empowerment and disempowerment in different social settings. This raises questions of hierarchy and ownership about the North–South relationship. Anthropologists pride themselves on their respect for their informants and increasingly concern themselves with the rights of the informants to the knowledge that the anthropologists have gleaned. They nevertheless have to work hard to engage in level relationships with their informants in the South. In the past they appropriated the knowledge as their own. Now they try and return the ownership somehow. Nevertheless, the Brazilian women seemingly gave me the ownership of their stories, whereas in entering into an observer-informant relationship with develop-ment professionals in the North, there was doubt as to who owned what. Informants made their requirements clear. It was frequently requested that the interviews should be 'off the record' and anonymous. Despite the apparent equality in the Northern interviews, the informants were aware that they had much to lose, that their words could be dangerous for them. In Brazil the women had little, could lose little, and used their narratives as a form of exchange, i.e. empowerment. It is almost as if the transfer of words upset the balance of (in)equality in each relationship.

This reflected an understanding of the power of knowledge and words. In the North, people felt free to speak only when they could not be identified. Similarly they were in a position to hide behind jargon (Mueller 1986: 36). This practice emerged in the changes that informants requested to the draft version of the paper I sent them. Their rewritten versions took the form of a shift from an informal and chatty discourse to a formal and jargon-ridden one. Words and knowledge are sources of power and are used to control the social space between observer and observed. Bureaucracies in particular use words to define problems, set agendas and arrest control of process (Mueller 1986; Wood 1985). In contrast, the poor women who gave me their life and fertility histories in Brazil were by and large indifferent as to whether or not the data were anonymous and occasionally insisted that they should be identified. They argued that no one would believe 'my' stories unless they were verifiable. Such poor, ill-educated women could not use language to fend off my prying questions. Although my Portuguese is accented and imperfect, my technical vocabulary often exceeded that of my informants.

Another difference was the attitude to time. In England time was a precious commodity. The interviews were conducted in an allotted period of time, for which I was grateful and conscious of its 'value'. In my previous fieldwork in Brazil, while the timing of the interview was negotiated by both, the duration was rarely curtailed by the informants, who either had more time at their disposal or, despite my efforts, felt that they were in some way beholden to me for making the effort to come and see them and talk to them.

The different responses to the same process of being interviewed, by two groups of people at either end of the development chain has implications for the development relationship *per se*. Put crudely, can these two sets of people ever hope to interact as equals in a relationship? As Escobar comments (1991: 667), 'The encounter between, say, peasants and development experts is socially constructed, that is structured by professional and bureaucratic mechanisms which are anterior to the encounter.' The different ways in which Northern and Southern informants reacted to the same process reveals the profundity of hierarchy.

This is not to suggest that there was a uniform response to the questions I asked in the interviews. On the contrary, the overriding impression I gained during the course of the interviews was of differences in the approach to and motives for working in development. This paper proceeds by presenting informants' responses to the question of what led them into development and what do they think of it? The combination of a desire for anonymity and the stark contrasts between the different informants' views and opinions left me with a dilemma in how to represent these to the reader. The original intention had been to work through each institution, demonstrating the relationship between informant and institution, but this would make it too easy for them to be identified. Consequently, I have attempted to make the informants unidentifiable by naming them in alphabetical order and, following PRA techniques, I have turned them into fruit.

Paths to Development

The question of how individuals came into development seemed to generate a range of responses that fell broadly into two groups, political or professional, with some overlap. Some chose careers in development as a means of pursuing their political interests, NGOs being the perfect forum for such a combination of the professional and the political. Mr Apple, for instance, works for one of the leading development NGOs (in Britain these include Action Aid, Christian Aid, CAFOD, Oxfam and SCF). The youngest of all the informants, his route in was also the most direct. As a student he was left-wing, politically active, but focused on domestic issues. He thought of the Nicaraguan Solidarity activists as 'wishy-washy'. Nevertheless, after travelling around in the Third World for six months, he changed course and took a Masters degree in regional studies. Following this he targeted the NGOs for work and finally secured employment after a spell of voluntary work.

Such a direct path proved to be unusual, the norm being a far more circuitous path. Mr Banana, for example, currently a high-ranking civil servant, traces the roots of his interest in development to studying geography at school. This led him to an interest in societal systems, which he pursued by working for a year as a voluntary social worker. As a student his interests turned to systems beyond Britain. He spent time working with an indigenous American population. Later he joined a major NGO working in Asia Minor on health issues and became convinced that human well-being, including health, was effected by political and economic factors. He then spent several years working in Asia before going back to England and taking up an academic post, later entering the civil service. At an early stage in his career, he had worked out that by mid-life he wanted to be working for one of the major international or national agencies. He has achieved his goal.

Messrs Apple and Banana both targeted development as the professional vehicle for playing out their political beliefs. For others, politics itself was the chosen career, of which development was a special interest rather than a specific goal in itself. It can be hard to separate the two strands, as in the case of Mr Cherry, who is both an established development practitioner and a politician. He began his political life at an early age while still at school, joining the Labour Party and the UN Students Association. His grandfather had been a missionary in India, so that he grew up with a sense of India as part of the family background. In addition to this, his mother ran a course in social administration, as a consequence of which 'home was always full of people from all over the world – African, Malaysian, Arab, Jewish. It was a terrific stimulus, there were always discussions and debates at home.' After studying social administration, doing military service and a stint as the Secretary of the International Union of Students, he went into Parliament for Labour. Once in Parliament he became active in international affairs, sitting on various development-related committees and serving in the FCO and for ODA. After he lost his seat he became involved in development through his political activities and held senior positions with two development NGOs. The interest in the political aspect of development has continued into his current activities in 'creative diplomacy' and global governance.

For Lord Damson the involvement in development has come later as a result of his other interests. As a spokesman on Foreign Affairs in the House of Lords, he has sat on several select committees, the last two of which were on development. His interest in foreign affairs has been a longstanding one, but more particularly with Europe. In his case it was the position he had come to occupy through his political activities that led him to development. He was aware that an interest in development was difficult to maintain and required an investment of time and travel that he could afford.

One of the first points that Mr Elderberry made was that his background was atypical for a developer. He did not come from a middle-class home and had not been exposed to other nationalities and other cultures at an early age, but like other interviewees he had been driven since his youth by politics. In the 1960s he studied social sciences before spending a year as a social worker. He worked with poverty and deprivation. When he turned thirty he changed direction and went to work in the Ministry of Social Affairs of a Latin American Country. He stayed for four years, switching to NGO work during that period. On his return to the UK he continued to work in the NGO sector.

One of the characteristics that Mr Elderberry thought he lacked in contrast to other developers was an early exposure to other cultures. For Ms Fig this was the salient feature of her early life and undoubtedly influenced her. Her father, posted to Latin America, married a local woman. She was brought up in a privileged milieu but was conscious from an early age of the differences in lifestyles and the injustices associated with poverty. The contradictions between her lifestyle and the poverty she saw around her was uncomfortably stark and made her want 'to do something useful'. Following an education in England, she went in pursuit of a 'meaningful' job while working in the City. Finally she obtained an appointment in a major NGO, in research and advocacy, and her interest was in 'tackling the structural causes of injustices'. Only later did she realize that what she wanted to do was 'development' and that her role was in fact 'integral to the agency's development work'. It seems that political motivation, whether clothed in socialist theory or in the naked form of wishing to 'do good', was the impetus that led people on to the development path.

For some the conversion to development as a cause came later in life. In the case of Mr Grape he was in his thirties when he threw in his career in and decided to study. Although he elected to study anthropology, this was more out of curiosity aroused by reading ancient myths and legends than a comparative development perspective. The turning point for him occurred while he was conducting fieldwork in West Africa. Two particular experiences made him reflect on how development operates and question ways in which traditional people come to be integrated into modern society. From this he went to work for a major NGO in West Africa. Afterwards he spent some time doing research and consultancy work before joining one of the major NGOs about four years previously. Despite the slow start, once he had chosen his new path he followed it quite directly. The motivation arose out of a desire to do something, which initially was to write a protest piece on West Africa. Development was something he stumbled on in the course of self-fulfilment and then committed himself to, rather than an idea that dominated him from an early stage in his life.

For others the route into development might be described as a professional accident. They were passive travellers rather than active navigators, and simply ended up in development. Mr Huckleberry could not 'make my mind up what I wanted to do. I wanted adventure.' He is now working as a senior civil servant. Like many of the civil servants he was led into development by his technical skills, in agriculture, but unlike the others, the thirst for new experiences catapulted him overseas: 'growing things is fun. Growing things in difficult places is even more fun.' He started working overseas in Africa, but moved to the Caribbean, Asia, the Pacific and back to Africa before settling into Whitehall.

Such accidents are more characteristic of the civil service than the NGO sector. This is a result both of the nature of a government bureaucracy, and the way in which civil servants are treated like tools that can be applied in different sectors. For example, Mr Juniper started life as a historian but metamorphosed into an economist. He served in other government departments before coming to the development field. Mr Kiwi is also an economist. His service for the government has been peppered with eight years spent overseas. He started out as an economist working in an African country and then went on to work as a consultant before joining the civil service and being stationed in the Pacific and Africa. While he did not express a driving reason for having become a development economist, his skills had been applied in that direction from the beginning of his career.

Ms Lime is also a long-serving civil servant. Her training never implied a future in development. She started her working life in mental health, working for another state authority, but moved over into the civil service administration, working first in other branches of Whitehall. The Ministry that she worked for had ties with the British Aid programme, and she was sent to Africa for project evaluation. 'It was a shock in every sense, seeing the under-development of these countries. Seeing what we did that worked or didn't work.' This impressed her greatly, and she wrote a report 'with obvious sympathy' that her Ministry found 'disturbing'. Later she moved into the development stream and now occupies a high-ranking administrative job within aid administration. She feels that she is not close to development work nor the issues, but that her job as it is now is far more constructive than previous positions. She believes that she is involved in getting good value for government money spent in development.

Unlike the other civil servants, Ms Mandarin's expertise is in the social, not the formal sciences. She works on social development. Significantly she had already been working as a development consultant before she joined the civil service. The need to recruit from outside the ODA rather than use in-house experts for 'social', non-economic development reflects the bias of what development has tended to mean to the Government in the past.

Although there is no clear-cut demarcation separating these individuals into neat categories, they fall into the two loose groupings (somewhat overlapping) of the politically and pro-fessionally motivated. More significantly, this seems to reflect the likelihood of them working for either NGOs or the civil servants. This says less about the NGOs: it is not so surprising to find political beings in the NGO sector. But it signifies a great deal about the civil service's view of expertise. Individuals with little or no knowledge of development find themselves, like Ms Lime, wielding considerable power. Their expertise is sought in their function rather than in their knowledge of the field.

The bureaucracy of government seems to treat development as an extension of economics and financial planning. Economists are brought in from other areas and are applied to the specific problems of development. The more recent emergence of social development within the ODA as something specifically different suggests a weakening of the link between development and economics.

Concepts of Development

A salient feature of the interviews was the language that individual informants employed. The various positions of the developers were reflected in their use of different discourses, as the following extracts demonstrate. Words such as 'empowering', 'enabling', 'choice' and 'sustainability' reflect the dominant paradigm operating in development in the early 1990s and would not have been dominant ten or fifteen years ago. The terms are one aspect of the so-called New Poverty Agenda (although it remains a mystery to me how development could ever have been about anything else). This discourse contrasts strikingly with the reference to standards of living, measures of economic performance and wealth more often used by the civil servants in general and economists in particular. The different discourses are not trivial. The choice of words reflects not only different ideological positions, but also different goals. Institutions and bureaucracies define their goals and courses of action (policy and projects) as a result of their comprehension and definition of what constitutes a problem and its resolution. 'Labels and institutional practices are issues of power; they are invented by institutions as part of an apparently rational process that is fundamentally political in nature' (Escobar 1991: 667). The order that is imposed on the social order by a given development discourse constitutes the framework for a relationship between the developers and the developed: in other words, development is what we (the developers) define it as (Mueller 1986; Wood 1985).

In the following passages, the socially sensitive, political (for this read 'left-wing'), enabling discourse stands in stark contrast to the hard, economistic, apolitical (for this read 'right-wing'), growth discourse. Individual conceptual positions unsurprisingly reflect their location within the development world, as well as individual experience.

Let us return to individual cases. Mr Apple's rapid entry into development provided him with little opportunity to sojourn in the South. His views on development reflect his political leanings in their theoretical tone and lack of grounded example:

> Equity. We live on the earth with finite resources. There is some room for manoeuvre with new technology, but there are gross inequalities. Development is about bringing people in the South to a higher standard of living, and in the North to a lower.

His framework for viewing development was heavily influenced by both his left-wing politics and his training in development economics: 'Development is about getting economics right.' He extended this definition to the social by including individuals' personal responsibilities in the North:

> For many, there is an unwillingness to address their own role and responsibility in these issues. We are rich because other people are poor and vice versa. Many of the causes of poverty in the Third World have their roots here.

The scent of dependency theory in these words is strong. Like Frank (1966), Mr Apple sees the nature of poverty in the South as causally bound up with the wealth of the North. Development for him is a political agenda.

This contrasts with Mr Banana's understanding of development, which emerged from his professional experience in Asia and Africa, watching professional experts arrive and,

> prescribe lifestyles to the poor . . .. Development is about choices. It's about enabling people – in as much as NGOs and the state can enable – enabling people who are disabled in some way to have choices about how they are going to live their lives.

For Mr Banana, development became a career path after coming to understand the importance of political process in determining poverty. His own political agenda, however, seemed to centre far more on the politiking and power-mongering that determine so much policy formulation, as we shall see below.

Mr Cherry's understanding of development is influenced by his political background:

> Development is about people, about enabling more people, men, women and children, to realize their potential . . . . The first reality of life is that we are born into a totally dependent world system, economic, strategical, environmental . . . therefore fulfilling your individual goals can't be done outside the context of the social world.

He talked about the need for checks and balances, and how development had to work within the limits of the impossibility of fulfilling everyone's needs. A current seems to have swept Mr Cherry along for most of his life. He was alerted to and committed to internationalism and took this awareness with him from his childhood into political life.

Lord Damson's view of development – perhaps because he was not steeped in development discourse – was pragmatic. His non-use of professional jargon enabled him to take a relatively fresh and direct approach. He had a clear rationale for why development was necessary:

> Until Mrs Thatcher arrived, it was regarded as axiomatic that extremes of wealth and poverty in a nation were unacceptable and dangerous. By the same token, in the world in which we live, with ever better communications, the same proposition applies. It is dangerous if this gap not merely exists but also increases.

He saw a variety of problems – environmental, demographic, scientific – that were widening the gap. For him the issue was not development *per se*, but finding a resolution:

> Development is not the answer, but maybe *an* answer. What I find unsatisfactory about most discussions about development is how little attention is paid by government to what is effective development and what isn't.

He was sceptical about the agendas and criteria that are used in the real decision-making processes concerning aid, and he regarded development as a political relationship.

Mr Elderberry considered himself an outsider in comparison to the other, middle-class development professionals. This view is manifest in his personalized understanding of development:

> Development is about ordinary poor people and their capacity to
> respond to their needs and fulfil their capacity. It's a process which
> they can pass through . . . it's fulfilment as social beings, emotional,
> intellectual needs . . . .

He held the view that for many development professionals, the
'People' were abstracted (and objectified). Such objectification
leads to either awed respect or denigration. Mr Elderberry, because
of his own background, felt on a level with the poor and tried to
treat the recipients of aid, the poor, as 'ordinary people'.

Messrs Elderberry and Damson's freedom from development
jargon reflects or allows them to identify development as a social
and political relationship. By operating outside the discourse or
paradigm, they are not drawn into the view that development is a
simple relationship of giving aid and assistance. The incestuous
nature of the relationship between discourse and ideology is
exemplified by Ms Fig, who learnt (and formulated) her ideas
about development while engaged in it professionally, as those
discourses were changing:

> A few years ago we talked almost exclusively about empowerment,
> now we're clearer that [we] don't empower people; they empower
> themselves. The poor themselves want more than empowerment, they
> want jobs. Development isn't about only having more but about being
> more.

She later amplified this initial statement by adding:

> the poor want tangible improvements in their lives. The focus of
> development is increasingly on securing sustainable livelihoods and
> basic social and economic rights. Given the feminization of poverty,
> gender issues are increasingly important. ·

Ms Fig's discourse portrays the genealogy of development-
speak. The power of the current discourse is also evident in Mr
Grape's thinking:

> [Development] is enabling people to be more in control of their own
> lives and move from a position where they are constrained from
> influencing their own destiny through poverty, to one in which they
> can be liberated from this poverty trap, and through this process enjoy
> a better quality of life.

The experience that radicalized him in West Africa was seeing people trapped by poverty and marginalized, and this theme has fed in to his work. For him development involves social, political and economic processes.

A radical departure from this use of jargon was exemplified by Mr Huckleberry. Over time he had become increasingly aware of the nexus of social relationships and political manoeuvres that surround any development project. He was one of the few to admit to having completely rethought his views on development over the years:

> I came to realize that *people* is what it's about, not just seeds in the ground. It's what people do with the pips in the ground.

Development is, therefore,

> a desirable and sustainable state of change. Change from what is to what might be. Twenty-five years ago I would have said 'increased productivity per unit area', but things lose clarity over time. Now it's a question of who and what do people want, and I recognize that this changes over time. Then there is the sustainability-environment argument – the more I try to tie it up in a concise, easy, water-tight definition, the harder it is. The more I try to define it the more I realize that it's judgements made at a particular time, in a particular place, for particular reasons. What was sustainable ten years ago is no longer considered so . . .. Sustainability is a value judgement in which ecology plays a part but quality of life also plays a part.

Mr Huckleberry, despite his self-professed, disengaged adventurism, was extremely conscious of the socio-political dynamics that effect the micro-processes of development projects. As he put it, it is not so much a question of new seeds or more money, but what people do with them in the particular circumstances and how this is effected by the wider socio-political framework. He also pinpoints the nature of concepts that are proclaimed as watertight principles yet are in constant flux changing to suit new political situations.

This approach is quite different from the remaining informants, who were mostly transformed into developers on the job. They all work as technical advisors or departmental heads in the civil service, all directly involved in government aid. As I suggested above, development is dominated by economists, a pattern which seems to be replicated in the academic discipline of development studies. Their technical expertise-led approach to development is manifest in the following accounts exemplified by Mr Juniper's. While I described it as 'strictly economic', he considered it 'predominantly economic':

> Development is making people better off, enlarging life opportunities. As an economist I think of it in material terms: standard of living, higher spending power, etc.

In addition to this, he thought much of the social development agenda unclear and unhelpful, clarifying later that it 'should be clearer about objectives and decision criteria and how to adjudicate trade-offs'. Initially he said:

> They want to reduce poverty and improve the status of women. As an economist, if you want people to be better off, then you want them to be better educated and more healthy. They are into taking into account the processes by which people relate to each other. But I regard these as constraints on project design and project implementation. The criteria of projects should be increased standard of living.

Within such a perspective, development can be reduced to economic growth, played out through specifically designed projects, and the social participation throws up 'a conflict of interests'.
Subsequently he reformulated this and wrote:

> Economists are naturally concerned about developing the social sectors – health and education – because they contribute directly to people's perceptions of well-being and because progress in these areas contributes powerfully to material progress. The social anthropologists throw light on the processes by which people and groups relate to each other and have done service in highlighting how women and the poor are affected by development. These aspects are important in understanding the constraints on project design and implementation. However, it is not so clear from them how the benefits of social-process objectives are to be assessed and how they are to be made commensurate with material living-standard improvements. Conflicts of interest are bound to arise in development, with losers as well as gainers. Social groups will be affected by projects. However, in the last analysis there have to be explicit, generally material criteria for deciding which outcomes are acceptable.

Mr Juniper's initial position in the interview and subsequent re-drafting arguably signalled the existence of an ideological debate about the definitions of development. The choice and re-selection of words is significant because it reflects the power of naming (and labelling) in the process of defining problems, policies and projects (Escobar 1991; Mueller 1986; Wood 1985).

Mr Kiwi, another economist, had a more open perspective:

> [Development is] improvement in the quality of life of poor people. Internationally inequalities of income are as unacceptable as national inequalities of income. I find it difficult to get away from the view that the most important thing is improving the economic indicators.

But his time overseas caused him to 'take a broader view of the development process':

> It gave me an appreciation of the institutional and political constraints on development, the close interactions, the importance of a political economy rather than just economics, of bureaucracy and the way it operates . . . .. We, the development community, have not taken enough cognisance of these factors. In Africa, post-independence, the principles of political economy have been running the economies, not economics.

Mr Kiwi's experiences conflict with his formal training, so that although he acknowledges that development should be one thing, he recognizes that it is often something else. He had 'experiences which demonstrate the limitations of my discipline so that although I believe that development is best achieved by the application of sound economic principles, I recognize the import-ance of other factors.' The tension between discourse and words is a manifestation and cause of different practical outcomes, i.e. the application of aid.

The approach of Ms Lime to development closely relates to her professional involvement in it, in as much as it is project specific. Development

> has to be sustainable. It has to be a project that lasts. It has to be a starting point something that builds . . . to raise the countries up to a point where they compete on equal terms.

She has a strong sense of injustice and of the need for a practical, sympathetic approach, and was aware of the conflict of ideas between the straight economists and the social develop(ment)ers, referring to 'economists and people' as if they were mutually exclusive categories. But despite the fact that her work involves development as much as that of anyone in her institution, she did not feel herself to a professional developer and therefore felt it inappropriate to pass judgement on the debate.

This raises the question of what development is. Ms Lime did not feel that she was specifically developing, yet Ms Mandarin, who had been a developer long term, asserted that she had not used a development framework until she arrived in her present position: 'It is not a word I like. I take the word as a word we all use: achieving self-potential.' By adopting a discursive approach to development and rejecting formulaic definitions, she is left with a lack of clarity. She was asked what words she would use instead: 'Not poverty alleviation, something else . . . justice, peace, happiness. The Aid Programme is about making people happy. Perhaps, improved well-being.' The problems for her were how to define this improved well-being, and by whose criteria. The aid donor and the aid recipient might have different notions of well-being, different ideas about how to achieve it. This creates a dilemma for fixed agendas such as projects and plans: 'The whole thing is relational and shifting. Concepts of well-being change over time, history, society and culture.'

This is precisely the form of discourse that straight-laced economists find so baffling. But it targets the central problem. By definition, a development 'project' needs a 'logical framework'. But in the adoption of these terms and frames of reference, they become the property of the developers, not the developed. Yet taking the local cultural context into account can seem like an obscurantist endeavour which 'constrains' the efficiency (as defined by the developers) of a project, rather than augmenting the chances of a successful outcome.

Developers, Mud and Politics

Among the problems involved in doing anthropology with participant informants who will read the 'ethnography' is the knowledge that they may or may not agree with your interpretation and the fear that they may retract their words. As I wrote up the interviews, I had continually to omit the most interesting comments because they were 'off the record'. When, in the past, male anthropologists observed secret male initiation rites and wrote them up for the perusal of male and *female* colleagues, the breaking of the informant-observer trust bond was not at stake. The informant would never have found out. This is quite another context. As I argued above, it reflects the relatively empowered position of the Northern informants.

While I was conducting the interviews, three patterns of difference struck me forcibly: economists versus the others, field experience versus desk experience, and gender. Moreover, these characteristics were not mere superficial attributes but seemed to effect their conception of what it is the developers were doing in a significant way. These variations are discussed in the following section.

Apparently there is no unique route into development. The categories used above distinguish between the different mechanisms and motives that propel or pull individuals along certain career paths. In some cases there is a clear political rationale that drives them. With other individuals their professional expertise is such that they were drawn into it. Of course there are overlaps: Lord Damson, a career politician, finds that his professional interests have led him into development. It will be argued here that the motives and causes of the individual's development career influences the kind of development she tries to do.

The informants were not without ideas of their own on types of developers. Talking of the civil service, Ms Mandarin suggested that following the transition from colonialism to aid, the civil service had inherited ex-colonial administrators and missionary types. These had gradually been replaced by technical staff over the years, who were mainly economists. More recently, in the same way that the idea of development opened up from the narrow conceptions of merely economic growth (Esteva 1992: 13–14; Seers 1969), the professional expertise of developers has extended beyond the economists. However, that economists still dominate development seems unarguable. It would be all too obvious and trite to adopt an 'us' and 'them' attitude to economists, being an anthropologist myself, and not useful.

We can amplify the distinction raised above between those who have experience in the field and those who do not. Mr Kiwi found it 'difficult' to escape his taught view that improved economic indicators were the aim, but experience caused him to extend his criteria. Unlike Messrs Apple and Juniper, he worked for extended periods overseas, and despite sharing with them a predilection for quantitative measures, he was less confined by the limits such measures impose.

Another informant posed a hypothesis concerning the kinds of people that gravitate towards the NGO sector. Mr Elderberry suggested that there was a disproportionate number of middle-class English women, who were in some way culturally 'disassociated'. They had been exposed at an early age to other cultures, either by having been brought up abroad (e.g. Ms Fig), or through other means (e.g. like Mr Cherry). I would argue that rather than cultural disassociation, these individuals had simply had their horizons extended at an earlier age than, for example, Messrs Banana, Grape, Huckleberry and Kiwi.

Nor would experience overseas, in and of itself, necessarily constitute enough for people's conceptual frameworks to be changed. Ms Fig recalled how, as a child, she wanted to know why shanty-town dwellers had raised national flags above the roofs of their shacks. The explanation offered was that they were trying to save their homes from demolition by sporting their nationalism. She remembers this irony and injustice, but it is hard to evaluate whether it is this experience or her reaction to it that propelled her in the pursuit of 'usefulness' in her life. The problem is one of genesis. Does someone become an economist because of a predilection to model the social chaos around them, or does the discipline so alter the way they think that they are transformed into economists?

In either case institutional culture, including academic disciplines, mould the manner of conceptualizing and dealing with the process of development. They provide a discourse for thinking and acting. The palpable tension that exists between the 'scientists' on the one hand and the social developers on the other arises from the potency of a situation in which two ideologies are brought into conflict. Paradigmatic systems of thought tend towards holism. Where two sets of belief that are determined on explaining the same phenomena come into contact, sparks will fly. When the actors are driven by belief and good will, the wagers are high. As Mr Banana argued:

There is a collective delusion, particularly amongst those who have had active experience . . . in government, as colonial officers. Very few have had village experience, they have had ex-pat experience . . .. When you are dealing with people who haven't been right in it, in the mud, you can't keep on saying to them, 'You don't understand the real world', because they'll marginalize me, and I'll be of no use. I need to get alongside them and use their language. I need to get into the paradigms of the system so as to hang on in. People's models of how the world works are based on analyses that don't really stand up to detailed dissection.

The stakes in this ideological battlefield are vertiginous. The different parties want to improve the world, and most want to change it, but to embark upon this endeavour it helps to be sure of the ground. Those who talk about empowerment, enabling, fulfilment and achieving self-potential adopt a set of criteria, assumptions and objectives that share little in common with those whose target is the increase of economic indicators and material wealth. The need for certainty on disputed ground makes for unhappy cohabitation. The result is the adoption of strong defensive ideological positions, and tension around the other position.

The choice of words reflects more than a predilection for vocabulary: it comes from a combination of background, politics and training. More significantly, it reflects the way in which the developer conceptualizes the task in hand. Different theories and different paradigms throw up different discourses and ultimately praxis. The mediator between these competing teams of practitioners is politics. The modes of discourse are a form of power-broking.

It is curious that the individual with the most openly expressed 'boy scout' attitude to development, Mr Huckleberry, was perhaps the most willing to reflect on the ideology in a self-critical way and the one who had literally spent the most time 'in the mud'. If, as Mr Banana suggests, it is not the fact of having spent time overseas but the quality of that experience that counts, then muddiness could be seen as an index of engagement in socio-political reality.

Whether people are driven or led into development, they necessarily confront the problems associated with the conflict between concepts of development and development reality. Messrs

Huckleberry and Kiwi both began with restricted notions of development, and yet were forced by their experiences to reappraise their thinking. Like many of the informants they both pointed to the political framework being the most influential component of development. Mr Kiwi opined that the political process was 'the constraint in which we try and do development'. Mr Huckleberry highlighted the different levels of game-playing that occur, from the political agendas of countries to the grassroots politiking of local big men. The need to understand the power structures that frame development work is essential. This point was illustrated by Mr Banana:

> My starting point is that our work as development technicians at all times requires us to work in environments that are determined by political processes. We need a power map. We can only be effective development technicians if we take note of that power map. The best development work takes place in the context of power shifts . . .. We're not agents of change, but we are operators in a political environment.

This is *the* reality that all the different developers operate in. The discourses that they employ are simply alternative mechanisms for effecting change within the framework. As Johnston points out (1991), the discourse imposes a discipline, a limit on what can be operationalized. The dominant ideology in development is the economic-growth led model. The user-friendly social-development alternative is still somewhere between an illicit bed partner and a subversive. Some of the alternative discourse has been brought into the mainstream by the major international agencies (UNDP 1990; World Bank 1990), but in absorbing the new *paroles* they lose their potency. The old paradigm re-dresses itself, but does not change.

The real battle is not, however, between the developers, but between the developers and the policy-makers, the politicians. At its simplest, aid is about helping poorer countries develop. The choice of countries, the kind of aid, the largesse of resources, all these owe most to a host of political and economic criteria and agendas that have little to do with development.

Development is on the political agenda to the extent that people want to engage in it. A case in point is the recent Pergau Dam scandal, in which the complexities of 'aid' revealed themselves.

As Mr Kiwi wrote in commenting on the early draft of this paper:

There are different constituencies on whom we have to rely for support for aid work. They include those who are altruistically motivated, those who are motivated by UK commercial factors and those who are motivated by the wish to use aid to further UK political ends. Satisfying their needs within a single aid programme inevitably leads to contradictions and tensions.

The relationships that constitute the development process consist not only of North/South polarities, but also North/North and South/South ones. This adds another layer of politiking and hidden agendas to the proceedings. Mr Huckleberry described spending most of one night in Tokyo poring over the minutiae of an international trading agreement he was helping to draft. In the end, he argued, the effort was not about development but about diplomacy and communication. They had to ensure that the signatories *understood* each other. The intended recipients of such trading agreements, the man in the street, the woodcutter in the forest, the farmer in the field, may never feel the effect of that document drafter's concern for detail. But the politicians will. 'Development is all about understanding each other', concluded Mr Huckleberry.

Conclusion

This chapter set out to examine whether or not there was any consistent patterns that could be found to determine what kind of people became developers. The developers who were interviewed did not form discrete groups. Rather, they were vaguely aligned by the virtue of their route into development. Their understanding of development is the result of an interaction between personal experience, political commitment and technical training. These coalesce to form a specific development discourse in which individuals think and set agendas for their operational activities.

In writing this chapter, I have been highly conscious of the 'power map' that shapes development. While I began with cursory remarks about the relatively empowered position of the developers in relation to Southern informants, i.e. the developed, I have been struck by the ironies of this position. They may have desks and large budgets at their disposal, but like the developed they are also bound and disciplined by constraints. The political framework within which they operate is powerful, and often at odds with their professed goals. Their need for anonymity, and the tone of their re-writing of their spoken words, shows how they too are vulnerable.

Note

1. Most of the work for this chapter was undertaken at the Institute of Development Studies at University of Sussex, but it was finished at the Harvard Center for Population and Development Studies during the holding of a Bell Fellowship. Anna Robinson and Ralph Grillo offered me indispensable comments for which I am grateful.

References

Escobar, A. (1991), 'Anthropology and the Development Encounter: The Making and the Marketing of Development', *American Ethnologist*, 18/4: 658–82.

Esteva, G. (1992), 'Development', *The Development Dictionary: A Guide to Knowledge as Power*, London: Zed Books.

Frank, A. G. (1966), 'The Development of UnderDevelopment', *Monthly Review, September 1966*, pp. 17–30.

Johnston, D. S. (1991), 'Constructing the Periphery in Modern Global Politics', in C. Murphy and R. Tooze (eds), *The New International Political Economy (International Political economy Yearbook Vol. 6)*, Boulder: Lynne Rienner.

Larrain, J. (1989), *Theories of Development: Capitalism, Colonialism and Dependency*, Cambridge: Polity Press.

Lee, J. M. (1967), *Colonial Development and Good Government*, Oxford: Clarendon Press.

Morgan, D. J. (1980), *The Official History of Colonial Development: The Origins of British Aid Policy, 1924–1945*, London: MacMillan Press.

Mueller, A. (1986), 'The Bureaucratization of Feminist Knowledge: The Case of Women in Development', *Resources for Feminist Research* 15/1: 36–8.

Seers, D. (1969), *The Meaning of Development*, University of Sussex: Institute for Development Studies (IDS Communication Series 44).

UNDP (1990), *Human Development Report*, Oxford: Oxford University Press.

Wood, G. (1985), 'The Politics of Development Policy Labelling', *Development and Change* 16: 347–73.

World Bank (1990), *World Development Report 1990: Poverty*, Washington: IBRD.

Chapter 6

Mixed Messages: Contested 'Development' and the 'Plantation Rehabilitation Project'

Katy Gardner

Understanding development as a social construct, and thus indefinable in any absolute sense, is by now commonplace among social scientists working in the developmental domain (for a broader discussion, see Gardner and Lewis 1996: 1–8). This is a reflection of the post-modern sensibilities now common within all the social sciences, but on a more immediate level it has resulted from the breakdown of all major paradigms of development and the ensuing uncertainty over how it (whatever 'it' is) might best be studied (Long and Long eds 1992: 22). Though once there may have been developmental absolutes which researchers could measure, comment upon and perhaps even 'fix' with their recommendations, the days of innocent positivism are, for many, long gone.

One alternative which has been gathering momentum in recent years is the analysis of development as discourse. Drawing on the work of Foucault, development is interpreted as a mode of thinking and a source of practices which have been produced and reproduced within particular historical, political and economic contexts (see in particular Escobar 1988, 1991, 1995; Ferguson 1990). Rather than being politically neutral, in these analyses development emerges as historically rooted in colonialism and thus inextricably linked to the exercise of Northern power over the South. Esteva argues, for example (1993: 7), that when the term was first coined in the late 1940s, vast areas of the post-colonial world were suddenly labelled 'underdeveloped'. A new problem was created, and with it the solutions, all of which depended upon the rational-scientific knowledge of the so-called 'developed' powers (Hobart 1993: 2).

Understanding development as a form of knowledge which, like orientalism, functions as a mechanism for ruling the 'Third World' (Escobar 1991: 674) has been a fundamental breakthrough for the anthropology of development. It has helped us focus on the interface between different forms of knowledge within development projects and encouraged a more rigorous assessment of notions of 'indigenous' knowledge (Hobart ed. 1993). By indicating how development thought is deeply structured by Western assumptions of scientific rationalism, we can begin to appreciate how so-called indigenous knowledge may not be as readily systematized and categorized as some may believe (Fairhead 1993; Scoones and Thompson 1993).

However, while our understanding of 'indigenous knowledge' is growing increasingly sophisticated, that of developmental knowledge often remains frustratingly simplistic. This is generally presented as homogeneous and rooted in 'scientific rationalism'. Although writers such as Escobar and Ferguson are right to point out that the development industry largely draws upon a common pool of discourses peculiar to our age (cf. Ferguson 1990: 9), we also need to understand how development knowledge is not one single set of ideas and assumptions. While at one level it may function hegemonically, it is also created and recreated by multiple agents, who often have very different understandings of their work.

In the following account I hope to show how, within one project, 'development' meant various things to different actors, and over time drew on different types of knowledge. These understandings were not discrete and separate but constantly influencing and influenced by each other. They were affected by changing political and inter-personal conditions within the project as well as the wider historical context, and thus were constantly dynamic. My account also indicates the contested nature of development, not simply between 'donors' and 'recipients' – a categorization which, in this case, is of limited use – but at virtually every level, and between every actor in the project. Although potentially these tensions might be a source of creativity, in this case they led to conflict and eventual project breakdown. In particular, I wish to focus on definitions of what 'good' development practice involved, for during the later stages of the project this was constantly changing as different interest groups struggled to gain control. I should add that I too was a player in this process, for as a consultant employed on a short-term basis my task was to provide anthropological knowledge and assist in redesigning the project; I was thus one of the redefiners.

The Plantations Rehabilitation Project (PRP)

For reasons of confidentiality, I have disguised the identity of this project. Like others that have been, in civil service jargon, 'up and running' for more than a few years, the history of the Plantations Rehabilitation Project (PRP) in a small post-colonial state in the tropics provides an excellent mirror to changing developmental paradigms. Indeed, its roots stretch back to the days of colonialism, when plantations were first established by Europeans in the mid-nineteenth century. While generating considerable profit for their owners, these were relatively separate from the rest of the region. Then, as is still the case today, the plantation sector did not affect the majority of local people who live in the plains. Instead, the new plantations were situated in the hillier parts of the country, and labour for clearing the jungle and later cultivating and picking the crop was either drawn from indigenous 'tribal' groups from the surrounding hill areas or imported from other nearby countries.

From the start, plantation labourers have therefore been heterogeneous in language, religion and ethnic background. Although today some estates also use local labour, the majority of workers are hill people or have ancestors across the border, often thousands of miles away. Born on the estates, they have little prospect of leaving; as ethnic minorities, they are socially as well as economically dependent on them for their survival.

When at last the country gained independence from its colonial rulers, many plantations were bought by nationals. These were later confiscated by the government and passed into state ownership. Following subsequent political developments these were again privatized, and financial packages were provided to help the new owners improve the quality of their product and the welfare of their workers. A considerable proportion of estates have, however, remained in European hands. Today, although the majority of the country's one hundred and thirty estates are locally owned, about half the total acreage, employment and production remains in the control of three European companies.

As in colonial days, contemporary plantations have the feel of isolated fiefdoms. The dependency of workers, who rely upon the estates for their economic survival, housing, health care and usually entire social network, gives those that run them vast power. All estates are organized around a feudalistic hierarchy of managers, administrative staff and workers. Owners are not usually involved with their day-to-day running. Managerial control extends to almost every aspect of estate affairs. It is the manager who settles disputes, metes out punishments and even approves marriages between labourers. Boundaries between administrative staff and labourers are strict, both physically and socially. Labourers live in separate areas of the estate (named 'labour lines') and in many estates routinely express their subservience to the manager or other administrative staff by saluting each time they pass.

Between labourers there is further division. Foremen, for example, have substantial power over co-workers, not only at work, but also outside working hours. There are numerous other distinctions between labourers, each affecting their relative status and well-being. Registered workers, for instance, have a right to employment, housing, maternity and sick leave, plus other benefits. In contrast, unregistered labourers have none of these rights and are only employed when labour demands exceed the supply of registered workers. The 'casual' nature of their employment is not just cheap for the estates (wage levels, for example, are considerably lower), but also indispensable for meeting the seasonal fluctuations in labour demand. Not surprisingly, access to registration (which is often passed down between women within a household) is a central issue on most estates.

As an important supplier of export goods and thus foreign revenue, the plantation sector is vital to the country's national economy. In the early 1970s, however, after several decades of political turmoil, various changes of ownership and lack of capital investment, many of the estates were in a bad way. Their potential for improvement, plus continuing European interests in the industry, made the plantation sector a prime target for bilateral aid, and in 1977 the Plantation Rehabilitation Project (PRP) was initiated. This involved an aid package of $22 million, to be spent on improving the estates. The funds were earmarked for European-owned estates as well as some medium-quality national ones.

Rather than being administered directly by the aid agency (which I shall call AID), the project was to be run by a group of expatriate consultants, working for the company which had successfully won the contract. These worked alongside their government counterparts in the Project Management Unit. AID's immediate involvement was therefore limited to annual monitoring visits by teams of advisors and administrators. Ultimately it was these officials who called the shots, for they had the power to recommend to AID that funding should or should not continue, or that the direction of the project should change. Combined with this, like all bilateral aid programmes, the project could only take place with the co-operation of the national government (through the National Plantation Board), plus the owners of estates participating in the project. Power relations between these groups has always been ambivalent. Although the donor government, through AID, holds the purse strings, the recipient government and the plantation owners are 'consumers' of bilateral aid, who may shun a particular project or policy if it appears unpalatable.

From the beginning, then, the project consisted of four distinct interest groups: the consultants based in the Project Management Unit, AID, the recipient government and the plantation owners. None was internally homogenous. A fifth interest group was, of course, the plantation labourers. Although registered labourers are organized into a union which has a considerable reputation for militancy, they have always been excluded from any lobbying or decision-making power within the project. Unsurprisingly, throughout the project's history all four power-holding interest groups have had distinct agendas, and much time has been spent on complex negotiations before decisions can be made. As we shall see, while in earlier phases these negotiations were still viable, as consensus on the meaning of development has decreased, they have grown increasingly difficult.

Although the project's primary objective was to support the plantations through technical changes, $4 million was set aside to improve welfare facilities and working conditions for labourers. This 'social' component was partly a response to public concern in donor countries over the condition of labourers in European-owned estates precipitated by various 'exposes' in the media. The component also dovetailed with recent national legislation, the Plantation Labour Rules (1977), which listed specific obligations of owners to provide satisfactory health care, water supplies, education and housing. Now, for example, plantations were legally obliged to replace mud and thatch huts with brick houses at a rate of 10 percent per year. AID's project, it was hoped, would assist them in this process. Participating estates were to use the funds as an interest-free loan to match their own spending on 'social development.'

The PRP was to run for thirteen years. Like many projects which have spilled into more than one decade, it has spanned various eras of developmental philosophy and is thus easily labelled 'old-fashioned'. By the time I became involved, in 1991, it had acquired a reputation for being a developmental 'white elephant', receiving substantial criticism both within AID and in independent reports.

Phase One of the project began in 1980, after three years of negotiations between the different interest groups. Progress in the first years was slow, and little was achieved under the project's social component. In Phase Two, plantations were offered a loan towards the cost of new houses. By 1985, however, only one-third of estates had taken advantage of the loans. The provision of other facilities for workers, such as tubewells, was also limited. By Phase Three, in 1986, AID recognized that for now the plantation owners were unlikely to become equal partners in spending on social welfare. The project's contribution towards housing rose to 80 percent, with the companies contributing to only twenty percent of costs. The social component now included the provision of latrines and deep tubewells on the labour 'lines'. In general, however, progress was slow. The social component was also beginning to look distinctly old-fashioned, with stress on service provision rather than new definitions of 'social development.' By the end of this phase, it was acknowledged by AID that substantial changes would be necessary if the project were to continue. Although funding was to come to an end in 1991, an extension of nine months was to be provided to allow for the preparation of a more sophisticated labour welfare component, to be fully incorporated into the project designs.

Meanings and Modes of Development in the PRP: 1977–1986

In her account of 'Women in Development' projects (1993), Caroline Moser outlines five main approaches, each associated with a distinct developmental philosophy. Although her focus is gender, I suggest that her typology can also be applied to projects which are not specifically aimed at women. It is thus a useful starting point for the disaggregation of developmental discourses. A 'welfare'-type project, for example, is linked to charitable notions of 'doing good' for women and children and involves the top-down provision of services and goods to beneficiaries, without demanding any return on their behalf. This approach was common in the 1960s and early 1970s, but with the growing influence of feminism into the 1970s, notions of 'equity' increasingly gained sway in some development circles. These aimed at boosting the rights and power of women within developing countries, again usually through top-down changes in governmental policy, state intervention, and so on.

Another approach which gained popularity during the 1970s and 1980s was 'Anti-Poverty', in which poverty was recognized as women's main problem. This was closely allied to the Basic Needs movement, which had gained momentum during the 1970s. Solutions included income-generation projects, skill-generation, and so on. These strategies were often identical to those advocated by an 'Efficiency Approach', though their underlying thinking was fundamentally different. Efficiency was central to much developmental philosophy during the 1980s, in line with the dominant political ideologies of the time. Women became the targets of development projects only because the centrality of their productive contribution was recognized. If projects aimed to improve recipients' well-being, their underlying philosophical justification, rather than being grounded in notions of welfare or universal human rights, was that this would in turn increase their efficiency in the productive process and thus add to capitalist growth.

In contrast, the fifth and last approach, 'empowerment', rejects the assumption that development is predicated upon economic growth and Western capitalism. Influenced more by indigenous movements within the South than the political ideologies of Northern governments, this argues that development (in this case the development of human potential rather than economic growth) can only come from within. Women can only empower themselves through self-reliance; aid-funded development projects are likely to foster dependency, unless they explicitly hand over decision-making power to participants.

Although Moser's typology takes us some way in under-standing the diversity of developmental thought, the problem remains that it presents each approach as discrete and bounded. Once we begin to unpick any given project or policy we see that things are not so simple. Instead, developmental approaches are better understood as ever-changing discourses, as knowledges and practices which are endlessly interlinked, negotiated and dynamic. The PRP has involved all five approaches in a variety of ways. While two of these, welfare and efficiency, were easily combined during Phases One and Two, it was with the introduction of anti-poverty, equity and empowerment approaches that the various meanings of development became explicitly conflictual and the delicate balance of negotiations between different parties began to fall apart.

It would be misleading to present these approaches as analytic-ally separate. As we shall see, different actors have taken a variety of positions throughout the project's history, sometimes even advocating apparently contradictory approaches at the same time. To understand the complexity and dynamism of developmental discourse, we also need to dig beneath official policies and objectives to reveal that these often have multiple meanings and are read in different ways by different people. Lastly, as any project ethnography will reveal, in the PRP there is an ongoing disjunction between practice and theory.

At the beginning of the PRP there were two project objectives: to improve the productivity of the estates (in Moser's typology, an 'efficiency' approach), and to improve labourers' welfare (efficiency plus welfare). At a more general level, these fitted into the 'modernization' paradigm of development (Long 1977). In this, 'development' is taken to mean industrialization, technological change and increased productivity; improved standards of living are assumed to be an automatic by-product of economic growth. Development is not a question of structural change; politics is only important at the level of government corruption, a much-cited 'obstacle' to development.

In its earliest stages, the PRP was a 'modernization' project par excellence. The main objective of the project was to increase the output of the plantations through technical advice and material support. To this end a number of expatriate consultants were appointed, many of whom had previously been colonial planters in pre-independence Africa and Asia. These consultants worked mainly with managers in participating plantations, advising and supporting them on ways to improve the quality of their output and the efficiency of their manufacturing processes. Over time, a substantial training programme was also developed. This was a reflection of AID's increasing concern throughout the 1980s with 'institution-building' (an expression reflecting a growing emphasis over this period upon increased efficiency and sustainability). The training was based around a diploma for assistant managers in the technicalities of crop-production and management. Although in theory it was to be carried out by their local counterparts, in practice the training was run by expatriate advisors.

In comparison with the training and technical activities, during the first phases of the PRP the social component of the project was relatively small and quite separate. Officially, the social component was presented almost entirely in welfare terms. It is worth noting that though not an explicit part of the component, it also easily combined notions of 'efficiency' held by the plantation owners. While aiming to improve standards of living on the estates (through the provision of 'model' housing, tube-wells and latrines), they also increased labourers' efficiency by improving their physical well-being. Understanding the component in these terms, the plantation-owners had no reason to object. Even if some might not have improved labourers' housing and sanitation themselves, the project's provision of these services was hardly threatening to their own objectives of increasing productivity and profit.

In general, the tone of the social component was heavily paternalistic and top-down. While it was hoped that the plantations would eventually run their own facilities, those who were supposed to directly benefit from them, the labourers, were treated as entirely passive recipients. This paternalism was wholly compatible with the prevalent culture of the plantations. Since European rule, labourers had been provided for by their estates, and those who were registered expected housing, a portion of land and medical services as their automatic right. This, plus their apparent subservience to those higher up on the hierarchy, gave them a reputation for having a 'dependence mentality'. This stereotype was mostly based upon hearsay, reports written by missionaries working in the area, and the views of managers and plantation owners, to which project officials were frequently exposed. At this stage of the project, knowledge of the labourers' own forms of organization and perspectives was not perceived to be relevant.

During the first decade of the PRP, the predominant understanding of development (as reflected in project objectives) was
therefore that it had to do with modernization and service
provision. Development was something 'done' by experts, most
of whom had gained their expertise through the colonial system.
Technical knowledge, in this case involving the growing and
processing of a plantation crop, was prioritized, for development
was perceived to be a technical problem for which there were
practical solutions. With the application of expert advice, material
support and various changes within the nation, it was hoped that
'development' (economic growth and industrialization) would
follow. Because of this, the expatriate consultants were expected
to have only technical and practical knowledge. Since many had
been in managerial positions in pre-independence plantations,
they had considerable understanding of technical, economic and
managerial issues, but their understanding of political and social
issues was generally limited. This was to become a substantial
problem during later stages of the project.

Just as the knowledge of the developers was derived from
colonialism, so were their practices. The life-styles of the consultants mirrored that of pre-independence plantation-owners. The
one area in which significant progress was made in the first years
of the project was in building what became known as 'the
compound' for the consultants and their families. This included
bungalows, a swimming pool, guest rooms and a club-house.
These were staffed by a full complement of servants, cooks,
gardeners and guards. Moreover, the compound was organized
along exactly the same lines as the plantations, with 'lines' of
housing: the consultants' bungalows were clustered at the top of
the hill, the counterparts' homes half-way down, and the
compound staff's at the bottom. The male consultants and their
wives (as was almost entirely the case until the last few years of
the project) needed do little for themselves. There were also
strict social conventions, laid down by the project's 'team leader',
which individuals contravened at their peril. Every Wednesday
evening, for example, they were expected to attend 'Club Night'
at the club house, eat the snacks and drink the drinks provided by
the resident cook, who like so many of the staff had been trained
within European-owned and managed estates, and socialize with
other members of the team. Dress codes were old fashioned and
again reflected colonial rule more than contemporary European

fashion – baggy beige 'empire' shorts, socks with garters and sturdy boots.

Shifting Meanings of Development: The Late 1980s Onwards

The tone of the PRP was not, however, static. By the end of the 1980s, various trends within developmental thought were becoming increasingly influential. The first of these was a movement away from old-style modernization projects within AID. Policy now stressed the ideals of sustainability and self-reliance. Projects were also expected to show clear returns; if they could not, then funding would be called into question. Anti-poverty and Equity approaches were increasingly dominant within some sections of the administration; there was a growing movement for projects to have a specific 'poverty-focus'. Income-generation, participation and 'the grassroots' were, by the late 1980s, key buzz words, both in AID and among Northern NGOs. Gender too was now very definitely on the agenda. Feminism had played an important role here, leading to calls for more gender awareness in policy-making. This involved not only project design, but also an attempt within the organization to rid its employees of sexism and to recruit more women.

These ideological shifts meant that as definitions of development and their attendant knowledges were increasingly debated within AID in the late 1980s, development involved a growing array of activities, for it now meant so many things. While for some it still involved helping the 'less developed countries' strive towards economic growth and modernity through the provision of technical and material aid, for others it was now increasingly a question of empowerment, of enabling people to change their own lives. This approach tended to weld notions of equity, poverty-alleviation and empowerment, with its advocates laying varying stress on different parts of the package. Associated activities included the provision of credit and income-generation opportunities, training, the setting up of committees, and so on. Within these discourses, 'development' meant enabling people to meet their individual potential; it was a human rather than an economic process. Emphasis was on bottom-up innovations, participation and indigenous knowledge of how to do things, rather than the provision of goods and services which might or might not be appropriate.

The intrinsically social, as opposed to technical, nature of change was also explicitly recognized. Within AID, all project proposals are evaluated by health, social, economic and environmental advisors, before being put to an official approvals committee. Advisors can therefore recommend that a particular project be funded or turned down. When project proposals were passed to social advisors, the first question they would usually ask was: 'Who will this help, and who might it disadvantage?' Innovations in health-care, housing or productivity could not occur in a vacuum, it was argued. Instead, what were rather loosely referred to as strategies for 'community development' (another increasingly fashionable phrase within international and national development circles) should take place alongside other changes. This would involve measures to strengthen the community or groups within it and to enable them to articulate their own needs and take ultimate responsibility for the changes promoted by the development project. Interestingly, this new approach shared much with the 'New Right' philosophies of Thatcher and Reagan in the 1980s, with their stress upon self-reliance, decentralization and the ideal of civilians' participation rather than governmental control.

Rather than the 'scientific' or 'hard' knowledge of the technocrats, within the new definition stress was therefore increasingly upon 'local' and 'appropriate' knowledge. The importance of policies and projects being sensitive to social and cultural conditions, combined with the need to understand the social implications of projects, became explicitly acknowledged. 'Local understanding' tended to be valued over hard technical knowledge. To this end, the insights of social anthropologists, the impossibility of accurately quantifying and measuring social change and the relevance of indigenous knowledge were all stressed. Since within this discourse 'development' is not simply a series of technical and material changes but more an increase in human potential and control among particular communities and groups, the role of the expatriate is problematized. While it is acknowledged that outside forces (the developers) might help facilitate processes of change, their long-term presence and involvement, it is believed, can engender dependency. This obviously has far-reaching consequences for those whose careers have centred around foreign postings.

These changing perspectives were not evenly spread throughout AID. Instead various internal factions (most notably the administration's social advisers) were increasingly promoting the new definitions of development. The 'social development faction' within AID represented a significantly different *modus operandi* from that of the majority of other administrators and advisors. From a mainly anthropological background, most had fieldwork experience, and all stressed the need for knowledge of local cultural and social conditions before embarking on a project. Although in the late 1980s their power within AID was still limited, they were able to influence the design of new projects and to lobby for changes in existing projects. They could also set the terms of reference for both short-term consultants and longer-term employees engaged as social development officers. It is hardly surprising that the presence of the 'social-development' faction, both within the administration and during visits to projects, evoked mixed feelings among other advisers and administrators. Although forced to operate within what were then the dominant discourses of development in AID (which stressed technical and welfare considerations), what they contested, in however subtle a way, was the very nature of development.

It would, however, be misleading to imply that these various approaches were wholly separate or that their proponents always belonged to opposing camps. It is important to recognize that individuals' definitions of development often vary internally according to what they are doing, when and where they are doing it, and to whom they are talking. Rather than developers holding one discrete definition of development, the majority hold several at once. Indeed, many have neither the time nor the disposition to analyse or label what they are doing. Ideological positions and the meanings given to development are therefore often mixed, and continually shifting. Likewise some strategies (for example, income-generation) may involve a variety of developmental approaches (efficiency, anti-poverty, equity and empowerment).

By the end of the 1980s there were, however (and still are today), several analytically separate meanings of development held within AID. Policy-making therefore was and is the result of complex negotiations between different parties, the outcomes of which invariably reflect power relations within the organization. At times these negotiations are non-conflictual. As we have seen, the various definitions are not necessarily contradictory; interests may even coincide. However, when conflict does occur, it often takes place over particular axes. Indeed, there are areas of inherent tension within much of development work. The first of these is that between policy and practice, a contradiction which is often embodied by differences between the 'office' or institutional centre and the 'field' or project site. Secondly, there is the tension between technical and social development. Both of these areas of conflict became important in the PRP.

Changing Meanings of Development in the PRP

With the end of Phase Three in sight by the late 1980s, it was hoped that the social component of the project could be redesigned to better express the new meanings of development held by the social advisers. Indeed, some individuals within AID expressed the wish that the PRP might even become a flagship for AID social development in the region, a model of the 'empowerment' type projects which, while many NGOs were now successfully running, did not as yet feature in AID's portfolio.

Co-incidental with this were a number of personnel changes among the consultants. First was the appointment of a health adviser. As part of a new generation of development workers, she recognized that little of the project was actually benefiting the labourers and internally lobbied both AID and the consultancy company which employed her to change policies. Secondly, while the consultant trainers and technical experts remained, a new post was created for a 'social development adviser', a meaningful shift from the former post of 'labour welfare adviser' whose remit had been simply to: 'Improve the living and working conditions of the workforce'. The new consultant's terms of reference as set by the AID's social advisers was to initiate a 'community development' programme. Although not explicitly defined, this phrase moved her work closer to the domain of 'empowerment', linking into a new definition and culture of development. While she was to support and extend the current programme of model housing, latrine-building and so on, she was also to test the viability of new initiatives in community and participatory development. This would eventually lead into a concrete project proposal at the end of Phase Three, which, if funded, would form the basis for Phase Four. Combined with this was an explicit recognition, at policy level, at least, of the integrated nature of the social development programme. This meant that the primary health component plus housing and sanitation improvements were supposed to be directly linked, rather than separate as they had been formerly.

Despite the changing AID definitions, within the project social development was still strongly associated with the provision of welfare for labourers, by individuals within AID, the consultants, local government and the plantation owners. The ideas embodied by the new social development adviser were not, however, completely new to the project, for Phase Three had involved some efforts to move towards the more contemporary model. Unfortunately these had led to a direct clash of interests. Recognizing the seasonal swings in demand for labour on the estates and the underemployment and poverty this caused, social consultants had recommended income generation schemes aimed particularly at the unregistered workers kept by the estates as surplus labour. Nothing could have been more threatening to the plantation owners, for the proposals directly interfered with the labour supply on which they depended. Not only might they lead to a labour deficit on the estates – a potential disaster, especially given the relatively skilled nature of some of the work – but in reducing the labourers' economic dependency on the estates, they might strengthen them politically. This was an extremely sensitive issue. Although often labelled 'passive' and 'dependent', labourers were also a source of considerable fear among owners and managers. Only recently a manager had been murdered by furious labourers when he could not pay them. The labourers' union is also famous for its militancy; the threat of union action hangs constantly over estates. Any policy which appears to strengthen and agitate labourers is thus immediately vetoed by the owners. As was generally the case over policy issues, the government supported the estate owners in their opposition. Plans for income generation had therefore been scrapped, but they lingered in the minds of many as synonymous with social development.

The first task of the new social development adviser was thus to reassure her colleagues on the project, the government and – most importantly, if any form of social development programme were to take place on the estates – the plantation owners of the notion that social development necessarily involved income generation. Instead, the new ideas were introduced more strategically. Discussions with managers and influential plantation owners were held on a regular basis, and social development was explained to them largely in terms of welfare and efficiency. Rather than phrasing them in terms of empowerment, equity and poverty alleviation, changes were packaged so as the meanings they had for social development advisers in AID (empowerment, equity and poverty alleviation) were obscured. Their presentation as non-threatening was, however, only partly accepted. Many individual plantation owners appeared to withhold judgement until the design of Phase Four was finalized; others simply claimed not to understand what 'social factors, 'integration' and 'the community' had to do with 'development'.

Confusion, possibly acting as a smokescreen for opposition, was not limited to local interest groups. Instead, most expatriate consultants on the project initially pleaded ignorance as to what the social development consultant's terms of reference could possibly involve. Age and gender were undoubtedly contributory factors: she and the health adviser, who was working closely with her, were referred to as 'the girls', and both had the strong impression that their work was not taken seriously by the rest of the 'team'. Despite attempts to explain what they were doing, informal conversations with several of the consultants at the end of the project revealed that some still understood social development in terms of labour welfare and the provision of services. Others, however, began to shift their definitions, especially when they realized that social development was to be key to Phase Four of the project.

Contested Knowledges: The PRP Redefined

In the day to day running of the PRP, it was quite possible for the consultants to hold their different definitions of development without coming into direct conflict, for the project was still very far from being 'integrated'. The female social development and primary health consultants were largely left alone by the male technicians and trainers, who rarely enquired into the nature of their work. They were also generally tolerated by local government and the plantation owners, so long as they pushed the 'welfare' and 'efficiency' lines. This uneasy stasis was not, however, to last. Ultimately the plans for the new Phase Four social component would have to be revealed. Before this, the social development consultant would also have to 'test' the viability of her ideas, which meant the gathering of specific forms of knowledge. With the help of AID's social adviser, terms of reference were drawn up for a short-term researcher, a job which went to me.

Unlike previous short-term consultancies, which had concentrated upon welfare conditions within the estates, the terms of reference focused directly upon the social structure of the labourers, their indigenous institutions, and hierarchies of class, gender and caste within the lines. For the first time, an anthropologist with specific local experience was hired to provide the requisite information. The terms of reference assumed that I would spend relatively long periods of time with labourers, and if possible live on the plantations. This, it became apparent, was viewed as the most suitable methodology for the type of knowledge my new colleagues wanted to gather. As I was to learn, this contrasted sharply with previous consultants, who, while having local experience, had not been anthropologists. For the first time, anthropological expertise was being recognized.

Combined with this, the job was designed for a local social scientist as well as an expatriate; both were to spend three months researching the issues outlined in the terms of reference. The long-term nature of anthropological methodologies was thus explicitly recognized and prioritized. Unfortunately both of these fine aims were eventually to be scrapped: a local researcher could not be found by the consultants in time, and due to internal project deadlines my own contribution was reduced to one month. Theoretically, however, the terms of reference represented an important shift in the prioritization of different forms of knowledge.

Though viewed by the social development and primary health consultants as central to their work, the findings of my month's fieldwork were not, at least at this stage, treated seriously by the other consultants. They did not, however, object to my presence, and at a practical level (the provision of rides in their jeeps to and from estates, for example) were supportive. To this extent anthropological knowledge was not seen as threatening, but (I sensed) was felt to have no relevance to their work. The plantation owners, however, had a quite different approach, for they objected strongly to my presence. This was particularly the case amongst those plantations still owned by Europeans. I was forbidden access to all of these; they would not even allow me to interview their managers. Clearly they were fearful of another 'expose' in the European media. More than this, however, there was a general sentiment among plantation owners that anthropological research (actually spending time with and talking to the labourers) might 'stir things up', that such knowledge could only mean trouble and was thus anti-developmental, for it threatened to interfere with productivity.

Though on the one hand being opposed to the 'dangerous' forms of knowledge my research might generate, objections were raised on the other to the impossibility of an outsider understanding the social organization of the labourers in so short a time. This was particularly expressed by officials within the government and local counterparts in the Project Management Unit. This type of cultural 'gatekeeping' is often experienced by anthropologists, when the most educated and powerful assure them that they will never be able to penetrate the complexities of local society. This view tends to interweave various perspectives. First, it involves a notion of unassailable cultural boundaries, in which 'outsiders' can never hope to understand the content of the 'inside'. Secondly, it tends to draw upon particular epistemologies, in which the status of any form of qualitative knowledge which cannot be measured or scientifically proven is denied. Thirdly, when made by the most privileged, it often involves undercurrents of cultural snobbery. What 'local' people do is the result of their own ignorance: researching local culture can therefore never lead to an appreciation of 'proper' culture. None of these gatekeepers were actually members of the cultural groups with whom I proposed to work. Lastly, it is a powerful statement of superiority, indicating scepticism about the understandings of expatriate 'experts'.

Despite the objections made by plantation owners and some members of the Project Management Unit, several of the estates with whom the project had particularly good relations offered me their hospitality and allowed me open access to the labourers. After a month's fieldwork I was therefore able to discuss my findings and their implications for a redesigned social development programme in Phase Four with the social development and primary health consultants.

When the concept of labourers' participation – for example, in making decisions about what services or activities were most desirable within the social component – was first introduced by the social development and primary health consultants, they were frequently told by plantation owners and governmental representatives that the labourers were too dependent and passive to be able to participate (for further discussion of the slippery nature of the concept of participation, see Adnan 1992: 27–33; Rahnema 1993). What I found in the three estates where I worked, however, was a huge potential for participation. Many of the features which the new style of social development sought to promote were already present in the lines. Women labourers, for example, often participated in savings and credit groups, which they ran themselves. Where tubewells and ringwells were broken, I found several instances of people on the 'lines' organizing themselves to mend them: the committee structure which community development generally worked through was already loosely in place. Combined with this, some women were already acting as informal leaders.

A strong case could therefore clearly be made for the long-term sustainability of community development in the plantations, for labourers already appeared to be well organized and, within obvious limits, self-reliant. To move away from the paternalism of top-down welfarism, then, it was proposed that the social component in Phase Four should be based upon a 'social fund', which would ultimately be controlled by committees of labourers. Through these committees, which would include representatives of unregistered as well as registered labourers and women as well as men, labourers could decide for themselves the services or material aid they wanted. They would also have to make a very small contribution from their earnings to the fund, to establish the principal of self-reliance and ensure that when funding eventually ended, the Social Fund would continue.

This model was very much the type of project which AID's social development advisers wished to promote. Indeed, it was becoming apparent that without such changes, funding for the PRP might well cease. Combined with this, different policy makers and administrators within AID appeared to agree that while technical improvements would still be a part of the project, the social component would now take centre stage. The model's message of self-reliance and empowerment was, however, a direct threat to existing power relations within both the plantations and the project. The proposed reorganization of decision-making powers, as well as the new emphasis on social as opposed to technical development, conflicted with pre-existing discourses of development within the project as well as those of the plantation owners and the government. The proposals therefore became a battleground for different interest groups in their struggles over how development was to be understood and what practices it was to involve.

The lack of interest on the part of many of the consultants in the social component of Phase Four soon ended when a delegation of AID advisers and administrators visited the project to have the new designs presented and explained to them. During a seminar held to discuss Phase Four, which was attended by AID representatives and the expatriate consultants, it became clear that due to political and ideological shifts within AID most of its representatives were strongly in favour of the proposed social development model, with its messages of empowerment and participation. Moreover, without their consent, Phase Four would not receive further funding. Reflecting the changing gender balance within the organization, it is worth noting that the AID team was wholly female.

Two things happened after the unveiling of the proposed social development component. The first is that the technical consultants realized very rapidly that the expertise on which they had based their careers was to have only a minimal role within the new definitions. It would be too simplistic to suggest that all were wholly opposed to the proposal. Instead, some offered advice based on their previous experience with plantation labour. Rather than directly questioning the new discourse, these actors took up the new jargon ('participation', 'social development', 'gender') without necessarily sharing its meanings with others around the seminar table. Interestingly, since their definition of development was seen as a primarily technical affair, it was technical advice based on their practical experience that they offered.

Other consultants were more explicitly hostile, arguing that the model would never be acceptable to the government or plantation owners. In these instances their long-term 'field' experience was often used to undermine the 'idealistic' plans of the policy makers and (substantially younger, and in their view less experienced) social development and primary health advisers. It should be stressed that these different positions were neither fixed nor absolute: many people had mixed feelings about the proposals. Actors were positioned differently according to context (whether sitting at the seminar table with the AID team, or privately with other consultants over a drink) and over time. Although to an extent the degree to which actors participated in or rejected the new discourse depended upon their individual leanings and personal beliefs, the constraints placed on them by their political positions should not be underestimated either. The allegiances of the team leader of the Project Management Unit were split between the donors, AID, and the 'client', the national government. For the consultancy company's contract to be renewed, he had to satisfy both of these groups. To say the least, his position was difficult.

The proposals were also presented and understood in a variety of ways according to context. The social development and primary health advisers, who were all too aware of the politically problematic nature of their proposals and who structurally had to answer to AID yet also gain the approval of the government and plantation owners, went to great effort to stress different dimensions to the various interest groups. For the plantation owners, the proposal was presented largely in terms of the provision of health-care, therefore substantially depoliticizing it. For the AID advisers, it was presented in terms of notions of empowerment and participation.

Compromise was not, however, possible. Although Phase Four was accepted by AID, when unveiled for the plantation owners and government they instantly vetoed it, even though efforts had been made to present it in more palatable terms. In the eyes of the plantation owners empowerment, the underlying ideal behind the proposed Social Fund and committee structures, could not be combined with improving the productivity of the estates, for if labourers were empowered they would be less malleable and thus less effective as labourers. Empowerment and efficiency thus ran contrary to each other. The proposed Phase Four has never been approved by the plantation owners or the government. Funding for the whole of the PRP thus ceased at the end of Phase Three.

Concluding Reflections

In this paper I have described how, in one particular project, various forms of action and types of knowledge are associated with particular paradigms of development. But rather than being fixed or bounded, these are constantly changing. While discourses are indeed produced by wider historical and political conditions, they are also the products of micro-political factors and the actions of particular actors. As the balance of power within the PRP changed at the end of Phase Four, social development became integrated into the language of the project.

Meanings of development are continually contested, negotiated and redefined by different actors. While analytically it may be helpful to disaggregate the paradigms of developmental thought which influence particular groups, the actions of individuals and institutions are guided by a range of other factors. A development worker may, for example, wholly subscribe to ideas of 'empower-ment' but still find herself hiring expatriate anthropologists (such as myself) and making efficiency-type arguments to the clients who pay her wages. Once we understand discourse as practice rather than as a systematized body of knowledge, we can see how it is produced through everyday conditions and activities and thus constantly subject to change and to the agency of individuals. Discourses of development within the PRP were substantially changed through the work of individuals both within the project and within AID. These in turn affected the understandings of others.

The various meanings of development touched upon here are not separate, but closely interrelated; in practice, there are no 'clean' breaks between paradigms. For example, although invoking notions of local knowledge and action, when used by bilateral agencies such as AID, 'empowerment' approaches still tend to rely heavily upon the 'expert' advice of outsiders (this is not, however, the case with NGOs, whose empowerment approaches are usually based on grassroots experience). For a variety of practical and political reasons, the use of national consultants remains rare, and the use of true 'insiders' (the tea labourers) is unheard of. Social development consultants are as much international experts as the engineers, economists and agronomists they differentiate themselves from. The insistence by some local officials that I would never understand social organization in the plantations was indeed an assertion of one type of knowledge (scientific) over another (non-scientific, unmeasurable). But it can also be given a different political interpretation and viewed as an ultimately unsuccessful attempt to undermine the authority of the foreign 'expert'.

The redefinition of meanings and the competing forms of

knowledge described here, while ostensibly to do with different notions of social and economic change, are also, at least in this account, to do with power between groups. Ideological differences (which, interestingly, coincided with those of gender) are only one part of this. At another level, power between donors and recipients is an issue, but it would be mistaken to assume that aid agencies are always the most powerful. In this case, local plantation owners and the government blocked the new plans by their refusal to accept Phase Four. The consultants, meanwhile, were caught between both parties. As Ferguson points out (1990: 20), development work involves multi-layered interests: intentional plans interact with unacknowledged structures and chance events to produce unintended consequences. In this case local political structures and the particular needs of AID to promote empowerment-type projects meant that the project lost its funding. In other circumstances and with different characters involved, the results may have been different.

References

Adnan, S. *et al.* (1992), *Peoples' Participation, NGOs and the Flood Action Plan: An Independent Review Report*, commissioned by Oxfam, Bangladesh, Dhaka.

Escobar, A. (1988), 'Power and Visibility: Development and the Intervention and Management of the Third World', *Cultural Anthropology*, 3: 4.

Escobar, A. (1991), 'Anthropology and the Development Encounter', *American Ethnologist*, 18/4: 658–82.

Escobar, A. (1995), *Encountering Development: The Making and Unmaking of the Third World*, Princeton: Princeton University Press.

Esteva, G. (1993), 'Development', in W. Sachs (ed.), *The Development Dictionary: A Guide to Knowledge as Power*, London: Zed Books.

Fairhead, J. (1993), 'Representing Knowledge: The "New Farmer" in Research Fashions', in J. Pottier (ed.), *Practising Development*, London: Routledge.

Ferguson, J. (1990), *The Anti-politics Machine: 'Development'*,

Depolitization, and Bureaucratic Power in Lesotho, Minneapolis: University of Minnesota Press.

Gardner, K. and D. Lewis (1996), *Anthropology, Development and the Post-modern Challenge*, London: Pluto Press.

Hobart, M. (ed.) (1993), *An Anthropological Critique of Development: The Growth of Ignorance*, London: Routledge.

Long, N. (1977), *An Introduction to the Sociology of Developing Societies*, London: Tavistock.

—— (1992), 'From Paradigm Lost to Paradigm Regained? The Case For an Actor-oriented Sociology of Development', in N. Long and A. Long (eds) (1992), *Battlefields of Knowledge: The Interlocking of Theory and Practice in Social Research and Development*, London: Routledge.

—— and A. Long (eds) (1992), *Battlefields of Knowledge: The Interlocking of Theory and Practice in Social Research and Development*, London: Routledge.

Moser, C. (1993), *Gender Planning and Development: Theory, Practice and Training*, London: Routledge.

Rahnema, M. (1993), 'Participation', in W. Sachs (ed.), *The Development Dictionary: A Guide to Knowledge as Power*, London: Zed Books.

Scoones, I. and J. Thompson (1993), *Challenging the Populist Perspective: Rural Peoples' Knowledge, Agricultural Research and Extension Practice*, University of Sussex: Institute of Development Studies (Institute of Development Studies Discussion Paper 332).

Chapter 7

Gender Politics, Development and Women's Agency in Rajasthan

Maya Unnithan and *Kavita Srivastava*

In India, especially in the 1980s, gender-oriented development programmes represented a convergence of two separate streams of research and related activities.[1] The two streams can be broadly identified as 'feminist' on the one hand and 'developmentalist' on the other. In the present paper, we examine the ways in which these two perspectives overlap in the context of the Women's Development Programme (WDP) in Rajasthan, north-western India, between 1984 and 1993. The WDP is regarded as a successful programme by governmental and non-governmental organizations alike and has recently been used as a model for women and development schemes implemented in four other states in India (Das 1992). Common to recent feminist and development agendas, and also manifest in the WDP, is the objective of 'empowering' women and poorer communities. Arising mainly in the context of work with poor women, the empowerment perspective is distinctive in its focus on the processual aspects of power (Kabeer 1994) and its critique of the assumption in earlier notions of women in development that women are fixed in positions of powerlessness.

One of the more pervasive images of women in developing countries has been informed by the idea that given the patriarchal contexts of their lives, women have universally been devoid of power and agency. Recent feminist ethnographic work (for example, Raheja and Gold 1994; Raheja 1996) in north-western India has shown that one should not assume that women in patriarchal systems necessarily internalize patriarchal values, and that, along with patriarchal structures, structures and institutions which empower women may co-exist. But to get at these structures, one has to use different mechanisms for observation and explanation. So, for example, Raheja and Gold show how an emphasis on narrative – on songs, prose and stories told by women – shows them to be active agents in their social relations, which is in contrast to the overriding picture of women as subordinate to oppressive patriarchal structures. A similar perspective informs the WDP, which has been most successful where it has worked within and strengthened existing forms of women's self-expression and identification. Linked to the importance of boosting women's self-confidence is the idea that this will encourage women's agency in the domains where it matters, i.e., where decisions are made, authority is exercised and prestige is manifest. The importance of such a perspective becomes clear once we understand that women's subordination is often a strategy for their long-term security in a system where men are given more social and cultural value. In other words, if women are not seen to act in their own interests and against their subordination, it is not because they are incapable of doing so but more because they may be unwilling to do so. As Sen (1990) and Agarwal (1994) argue, it is the negative perceptions of women's contributions, both by the women themselves and by others, which play a critical role in undervaluing their economic contributions. Agarwal further suggests that in the context of household negotiations, women adopt compliance rather than resistance as a long-term strategy to ensure their own security within both the household and the wider community of which it is a part. Even if women are seen to 'fit' their customary gender roles and seek to maximize collective interests, they may do so for reasons other than altruism precisely because individual and family interests are more linked for women than for men.

However, there is an extent to which giving priority to women's concerns in itself presents a challenge to existing social and cultural roles and relations in a community. It is precisely because these gendered relationships are so embedded and therefore difficult to challenge that the objective of 'empowerment' which concentrates only on women can never be fully realized. Therefore, as we argue in this chapter with reference to the WDP, while the development focus on poor women threatens men's appropriation of women's selves – the fruits of their labour and sexual reproduction and their standing in society – the main obstacle to the success of an empowerment approach ultimately stems from the different meanings of empowerment held by development personnel, that is, NGO-activists, government functionaries and members of academic bodies themselves. The differences between the women researchers, women co-ordinators and women workers in the WDP were differences based on their very different institutional locations and related ethics as well as their different life experiences and expectations. It is to the level of differences in what often emerged as conflicting approaches to empowerment processes that we turn our attention to in this chapter. Here, we look at both kinds of conflict, those addressed by the programme and those generated by it. We do not consider the presence of conflict to represent a failure of the programme. In fact, we believe that the WDP is the foremost initiative of its kind, especially in its attempt to be governed by the participants and to redress top-down approaches to development. We seek, however, to understand the kinds of differences that are generated by projects such as the WDP which aim to empower certain categories of people. We first describe the structure and processes of the programme in the social and cultural context of Rajasthan. We then move to look more closely at the nature of differences that arose as a result of the implementation of the Women's Development Programme.

The Women's Development Programme in Rajasthan

In September 1993, a local Hindi newspaper in Jaipur, the capital of Rajasthan, carried a report and accompanying picture of a group of village women in their *ghagra-odhani* (skirt and wrap) sitting in protest outside the offices of the state government officials. The women in the picture were a group of *sathin* (literally, female companions) or village-level workers of the Women's Development Programme (WDP) in Rajasthan. They were women who worked to 'empower' women in the villages they lived in. It is only in the past few years that there have been reports of village women protesting against the state. So far, the media reports of women who protested showed them as belonging to one of two categories: the 'feminist-type', college and university-educated women who wear *salwar kameez* (pants and tunic), jeans and sometimes the *saree*; and 'housewives', lower middle-class, *saree*-clad women protesting against a rise in the prices of household goods. The *sathin* protest marked a new and emerging phase in

the politics of gender and class in Rajasthan which at the same
time foregrounded the issue of 'development' in the state. On the
one hand, the September event could be seen as indicating the
overall success of the WDP programme in that village women had
been able to get together to articulate their own needs. On the
other hand, the demands made by the village women, which were
for increased pay and incorporation into the government structure,
contradicted certain fundamental values such as the need to move
away from government-type hierarchies, of those who had
formulated the programme in the first instance. It was the latter
issue which particularly raised several problems that the WDP
found difficult to address. Nevertheless, the dominant picture to
emerge from the occasion, especially for those familiar with the
lives of poorer, rural women in Rajasthan, was the collective
agency of village women in a public, political space previously
inhabited by urban, literate women and men. To understand the
significance of the visibility of rural women in Rajasthan, we briefly
describe some distinctive features of the state and the communities
within it.

Rajasthan is the second largest state in the country, with a
relatively low population density. Most of its approximately forty-
four million people reside in rural areas, making for a figure of
over thirty-three million people in the 33,000 villages in the state.
Environmental and historical factors especially set the state apart
from other states in the Indian union. Two-thirds of Rajasthan lies
in the arid and semi-arid region where drought is a recurrent
phenomenon. Most of the population is engaged largely in
subsistence agriculture, where the general productivity is low. In
economic terms, Rajasthan has all the indicators of being a
backward state (see Bhargava 1993). Historically, it was under the
domination of the Rajput noble lineages. The Rajput state was
officially dismantled only at the time of Indian independence in
1947. Rajput rule gave the communities in Rajasthan a social and
economic structure distinct from the other states in that they were
kin-based and stratified according to their genealogical or
occupational distance from the royal Rajput lineages. In the Rajput
state the power over land and peoples was intimately connected
with the interests of the brotherhood and 'in the shared male
substance which allowed it to rule over the land' (Ziegler 1978:
232). Rules of the Rajput code of ethics (*dharma*) stressed above all
the solidarity of the brotherhood. In this context, Rajput women

were seen as subordinate to and dependants of the brotherhood and the rulers, though at the same time they were venerated as status symbols of the brotherhood and were therefore objects of male protection. The violation of women more so than of other dependants (servants, for example) of a particular brotherhood was a cause of great concern to its members as it symbolized above all subordination of the brotherhood to the victimizing group, Rajput or non-Rajput. Here we find that women's bodies became symbols of honour and conquest in the battles between brotherhoods. As a result, the priorities of Rajput women became determined by the status concerns of their patrilineal brotherhoods. As depicted in Rajput folklore and oral history, in cases of military defeat at the hands of the conquering Rajput lineage, women committed *jauhar* (mass immolation) as a means of preserving the status of the defeated and shamed brotherhood.

The patriarchal and kin-based feudal ethic of the Rajputs still strongly influences the way life is organized in most Rajasthani villages. For most women, this entails a structural subordination to their husband and his kin, reflected in varying forms of seclusion and exclusion, for example, in the restrictions on mobility, prescription of attire, controlled access to food and weak participation in family and community decision-making. Women are largely defined in terms of their marital status and reproductive capacities. A survey undertaken by Srivastava into descriptions of village women by their communities showed that only one out of the eight categories used conveyed a positive image. The ideal role model for a good or 'normal' woman is to be married only once and to have borne sons. In contrast, the other categories describe 'abnormal' women, who are widows, women deserted or abandoned by their husbands, second wives, infertile women whose wombs only produce daughters, women who are much older than the husband or, conversely, women who are married to elderly men. Alongside these very real descriptions of women's low worth, we find images of great strength, both in physical terms and in the sense of having a presence, with which rural Rajasthani women in particular are associated. Village women are also perceived as forthright and outspoken by those living in the towns. These aspects of women are important markers of community identity and emphasize the difference in rural compared to urban upbringing. The differences that the references to women's behaviour convey may be perceived by outsiders in a positive as well as negative sense. Often the more marginalized a social group, the more 'deviant' (compared to orthodox caste rules) its women are depicted (see, for example, the images associated with 'tribal' women in Rajasthan; Unnithan 1994; Unnithan-Kumar 1997). It is, however, worth noting that these 'strong' women never pursue questions about their lack of control over resources, the devaluation of their labour contributions or the marginal positions they occupy in decision-making structures. It is more likely that women in villages in Rajasthan think of themselves as lacking in work skills and abilities and have generally a low self-esteem.

In India as elsewhere, issues of women's ideological devaluation were not addressed by the early efforts in development, which were instead driven by women's nutritional and reproductive roles (also see Kabeer 1994). The concept of women's development was initially influenced by the increasingly visible autonomous women's organizations in India. The mid 1970s particularly saw the growth of the autonomous women's movement in the country, in contrast to the much older, political-party affiliated women's organizations (such as the National Federation of Indian Women of the Communist Party of India, All India Democratic Women's Association of the Communist Party Marxist, the Mahila Dakhsata Samiti of the Janata Party and the All India Women's Conference of the Congress Party). The autonomous women's organizations were social-service oriented and had urban, middle-class women as its members (Calman 1992). These urban-based women's autonomous groups campaigned for women on issues such as rape, dowry and bride-burning, which received wide coverage in the media. The pressure on the government by the autonomous women's groups resulted in the research and publication of the first major official document which had women as its focus ('Towards Equality', ICSSR Standing Committee Report, prepared in 1974 by the Committee for the Status of Women in India). Certain women's groups also challenged the emphasis on the domestic role of women in government development schemes. Till then, women's development was popularly conceived as having to do with the provision of sewing machines and smokeless stoves, which, women activists pointed out, forced women to conform to their gender stereotypes rather than confront issues such as the rights to property, choice and decision-making, which involved challenging existing social and cultural arrangements. The early development plans for improving the position of Indian women did not acknowledge the triple burden of women (Moser 1989), i.e., that they often worked for husband, household and community without recognition or remuneration for their efforts. As a result of a greater awareness of women's positions, the shift in the objectives of women's development – from considering women's development as a provision of domestic aids to women, to their empowerment – took place in the 1980s.

Locating the WDP: Personnel and Perspectives

The WDP was launched by the state government of Rajasthan in 1984 in six of the twenty-six districts of the state. By the end of 1993, it had expanded to cover fourteen districts. A series of planning exercises preceded the implementation of the programme in 1984. These were primarily initiated by a member of the government Department of Development and Panchayati Raj along with women researchers and activists in Rajasthan in consultation with members of women's groups in India over a period of two years. Initially funded by UNICEF but solely state-government funded from 1990 onwards, the main aim of the programme was to 'encourage, create agencies, groups and individuals to articulate concerns towards indignities and discriminations . . . and to empower women through the communication of information, education and to enable them to recognize and improve their social and economic status' (Jain *et al.* 1986). Such forums were seen to enable women to identify their central concerns and think of ways of achieving them. The WDP had two key objectives. First, it sought to alter the self-image of village women (what they thought of themselves) as well as their social image (how they were regarded by their communities). Its second objective was to foster a common bond between village women in order to enable them to become active participants in the processes of decision-making in kin-related institutions such as the family, caste and village, as well as in relation to the state and markets. The focus on increasing women's decision-making powers was particularly challenging because married women lived in their husbands' villages, where they had few rights to property, little control over others' or their own labour and often no control over their sexuality and reproduction. The WDP work was all the more difficult because it had to counter the strong tendency amongst rural and urban people alike to believe that change in the rural hinterlands was neither possible nor valued. In this sense, the WDP was engaged in a much wider project which brought ideas that change was possible and could be critically reflected upon to a community which did not consider social change favourably.

The distinct features of the WDP were, first, that it involved a partnership of governmental, non-governmental and academic bodies in Rajasthan, and, secondly, that the planners, implementers and beneficiaries were all mainly women. As a whole, the WDP came under the Directorate of Women and Child Development (of the Social Welfare Department of the government), its director being the director of the WDP. There were three distinct structural levels of the programme – state, district and village (see Table 7.1). The planning and supra-coordinating body was at the state level and included an academic body, a non-governmental organization and a government department. The Institute of Development Studies (IDS) in Jaipur was chosen as the academic body to monitor and evaluate the progress of the programme. The voluntary agency (NGO) selected was the Rajasthan Adult Education Association, which housed the state and district Information, Development and Resource Agencies (IDARA). The NGO was to contribute by devising ways and methods of training for empowerment which would incorporate procedures for feedback and critical reflection. The NGO was seen not only as an equal partner in the imple-mentation of the programme but also as an important initiator in the course of development. The role of the government was envisaged in terms of the provisioning of funds and also as legitimating the programme in the eyes of both the administrative bodies of the state and the villagers. The government organization directly involved in the districts was the District Women's Development Agency (DWDA), headed by a project director and under the chairmanship of the district collector.

There was a distinct feminist research and activist component to the programme. This was particularly the case at the state and planning levels. Those who were significantly involved with the feminist aspect of the WDP were two women researchers at the Institute of Development Studies and their three colleagues from the NGO sector, who were freelance feminist activists mainly associated with the Social Work and Research Center in Tilonia and the state IDARA mentioned above. The main inputs of the

Table 7.1. Structure of Women's Development Programme (WDP)

	State level	District level	Block level	Village level
Government body	Directorate of Woman and Child Development	District Women's Development Agency (DWDA)	Woman Co-ordinator	Woman worker
	(Director, WDP)	(Project Director)	*(pracheta)*	*(sathin)*
Voluntary agency	State Information Development and Resource Agency (IDARA), Rajasthan Adult Education Association, Jaipur	District Information Development and Resource Agency (IDARA)		
Evaluation and monitoring body	Women's Unit, Institute of Development Studies (IDS), Jaipur			

latter were the guidelines arrived at in the initial training and fieldwork sessions and with the researchers, the evaluations of the programme which were published as reports of the IDS. One key area of feminist influence, for example, was in the explicit acknowledgement that there were no previous experiences to follow for the kind of empowerment-oriented development sought by the programme. Consequently, it was accepted by all the organizations and individuals involved that there would be few specified, defined trainer roles or training models to start with but that instead these were to be explored and developed with the participants. Apart from being involved with research and evaluation at the state level, women co-ordinated the programme mainly at the district and village levels, based on the idea shared by all three of the coordinating bodies that women would be most able to empathise with other women on the issue of subordination.

The most important level of the WDP to which all efforts and planning was geared was that of the *sathin* (women companions). The *sathin*, who were village women, were both the focus of change and also the key agents of development. A *sathin* was a resident of her village and was intended to be a voluntary worker of the WDP for an honorarium of Rs 200/- per month (raised to Rs 250/- by 1990; approximately US$ 8). There was one *sathin* to every cluster of villages (*gram panchayat*). *Sathin* were selected on the basis of their 'readiness to change and receive new ideas' and their 'enthusiasm for participation' (S. Jain, Srivastava and Mathur 1986: 6). Literacy was not an important criterion in *sathin* selection and often practical factors, such as her families' willingness to allow her to attend training programmes of up to a month outside the village, were important. As far as possible, *sathin* were to be chosen from families who were not politically powerful. The first batch of 22 *sathin* to be selected for the programme were aged between 16 to 55 years and came from different castes and from varying educational backgrounds. By 1993, there were approximately 800 *sathin* working for the WDP (state IDARA figures).

The WDP functionaries at the block levels were the *pracheta* (literally, 'women who impart awareness/consciousness'). A *pracheta* was responsible for ten *sathin* in the district. The *pracheta* were women belonging to the smaller towns in the district, selected by the government DWDA on the basis of their experience in government-related development work as *gram-sevikas* (village workers), *anganwadi* workers (training rural women for child health-care and nutrition) or as teachers in government schools. The *pracheta* in turn helped to select the *sathin*. The major role of the *pracheta* was twofold: first, to provide a link between village workers and the district and state bodies, and secondly, to provide guidance, support and advice to the *sathin* at the village level. By 1993, there were approximately 110 *pracheta* working for the WDP (state IDARA figures).

Processes of Empowerment

The official Hindi term by which the programme was known was *mahila vikas* (literally 'women, development/progress') which came to be understood and conceptualized in the local Rajasthani dialect as *mailo vikas* or 'the growth/development of that which was within' (from *mailo*, meaning internal). What is of interest in the use of the unofficial notion of development was that it translated women's development as having a much wider scope than the original term *mahila vikas*, thus capturing more effectively the aims and spirit of the WDP, which sought to bring about a qualitative shift in the attitudes of the people involved in the programme. According to the WDP planning body, development was regarded as providing the means to improve the quality of life through a control not only over economic resources but also over the ideologies that governed peoples' lives. In this sense, development was as much to do with the values, moralities, emotions and experiences of the communities involved and was a process which not only realized individual transformative capacities but also imparted a collective sense of agency.

'Training', one of the few English words to be used in the programme, was a complex term whose meaning varied according to the gathering of participants at any point of time. It could refer to the formal and informal meetings of the *sathin* with their block co-ordinators, the *pracheta*, or of the block co-ordinators with members of the government (DWDA), NGO (IDARA) or evaluators (IDS), or when the evaluators or NGOs met with the village women. The meaning of 'training' also shifted as the meetings progressed. In the initial stages of the programme, 'training' really meant an occasion when women got together, an opportunity for *sathin* and villagers to discuss what were otherwise regarded as mundane issues, their emotions and life experiences in the village. These were informal meetings which nevertheless provided insights into village life for the evaluators and co-ordinators (IDS, IDARA and *pracheta*) and conversely, for the *sathin* and other village women to learn about life in the city. The opportunity provided by a women-only gathering with an emphasis on the equality of members of the group was, however, often not enough to get village women to talk about themselves. Frequently, therefore, as a means of reaching their experiences, the discussions were about the daily activities in which women were involved: work, marriage, death, caste discrimination, the role of village elders and relationships between wives, mothers-in-law and daughters-in-law. One of the important aspects of the initial sessions was that the course of the meeting was unplanned, allowing the training to be guided by the immediate concerns of either the community or the individual. So, for example, if one of the members of the group became troubled previous to or in the course of the meeting, then it became imperative to centre the discussion around the source of this concern.

Only later did training sessions specifically address the potential for change in women's roles. It was a conscious decision by the planning body and evaluators (IDS, IDARA) to resist the incorporation of a rigid agenda and fixed targets for the early training sessions. It was believed that the setting of targets did not allow for sensitive responses to field situations. Furthermore, the pressure of meeting targets was considered detrimental both to building up the confidence of village women and to encouraging egalitarian relations between trainers and trainees. Participatory development techniques were seen as crucial in providing a non-hierarchical environment. As a result, there was no emphasis on lectures, but rather on interactive methods of learning together. Songs, drama, films and chart-making were important activities which brought the trainers, evaluators, trainees and even the onlookers together.

Songs were among the most effective tools for thinking about issues of power and subordination. In Rajasthan, songs are an important aspect of life for both women and men. There are historical songs and those sung at religious rituals, including marriages and funerals or for agricultural occasions such as at harvesting. The songs are often gender-specific in terms of who sings them and whom they are about. So, for example, at marriages, women will sing songs about the mother-in-law and how she must be kept in check. Songs can therefore be strong statements about the nature of relationships in the community. They can also be regarded as expressing the social and structural tensions that exist in a community, providing certain unprivileged categories (such as the daughter-in-law in the above example) with the means to cope with their social roles. Songs can also be a means of challenging the given order and bringing about change, precisely because they are so strongly embedded within the given culture. For Raheja (1996: 149, 150), for example, north Indian rural women's speech practices 'not only interrogate kinship ideologies' but also 'function as strategies in ongoing negotiations and contestations of kinship and gender identities'.

Apart from their rich repertoire of songs, villagers in Rajasthan also have a tradition of song improvization. It was the skill at improvization that was particularly useful for the WDP training, as, by changing a few words in a well-known tune, the song could be linked to central issues of the development programme. For example, a popular song about women's daily activities, such as grinding the grain, sweeping and cooking, became associated with her subordination and the fact that fame never came her way, even though she worked from dawn till dark.

> Awake since four o'clock, I sat to grind
> The grinding stone
> Grinding and grinding my knees gave way
> Whom to tell, not a soul to be found
> (Women have to move ahead [later addition])
> Getting up from the grinding stone, I
> Started sweeping
> Sweeping and sweeping my back became
> Bent
> Whom to tell, not a soul around
> Having made the vegetable, I
> Started cooking *roti* (unleavened bread),
> Cooking and cooking I remained hungry
> Twelve, twelve children have I borne but still no one to tell

For women, the act of creating songs together around an issue was not only a means of focusing on the nature of the issue at hand but also an effective way of bonding for the women of a single village. This in itself was an important achievement, as most married women in rural Rajasthan came from different natal villages. Introducing songs composed by *sathin* in one district on, say, the effects of drinking, would immediately open up the discussion in another district and perhaps lead to an addition, modification or completely new song. Songs were thus important elements of 'training' which linked village women across the district. At the same time, the creation and improvization of songs cut across the trainer/trainee divide in that the *sathin* and other village women assumed the role of teachers to the urban, educated women of the programme. Informal theatre was another highly successful forum in which empowerment could be experienced and experiences communicated. In the skits, women would take on different roles and question the status of individuals, the hierarchy and the values and moralities of the community.

While songs and theatre enabled women to think critically about their own lives and relationships, films and meetings with specialists such as lawyers, academics and government officials were organized by the *sathin* and *pracheta* directly to provide village women with information on a specific subject. Most of the issues discussed in these sessions were those which affected not only the women but the villagers as a whole. Some examples were the functioning of the village handpumps, the distribution and nature of famine work, the provision of minimum wages, government rationing, grazing problems, health facilities and the government's birth-control campaigns. The two important components of the programme built around the felt need to increase women's access to knowledge and information were the *jajam* and *shivir* meetings. The *jajam* was a monthly meeting of *sathin* which brought them together to discuss and exchange information on their common experiences and problems as *sathin*. In some cases, the *jajam* became a *gram sabha* or village gathering. Often these discussions led to the formulation of new ways of action as seen in the example of a *jajam* in Jodhpur district in 1985– 86. The following account appeared in the IDS report in English (Jain *et al.* 1986: 18) and was extracted from *pracheta* reports written in Hindi:

> Sathin Rambha came up with the issue of the polluted river water in Salawas village. She pointed out that the wastage from the neigh-bouring factories is dumped into the river. Apart from discolouring the water, the pollution had lead to alarming health hazards. It was observed by some women that even when the animals drank that water they had serious problems. The villagers felt that being a Sathin, it was Rambha's duty to find a solution to this problem. During the discussion in the Jajam it was clear that Rambha could not do anything by herself. Everyone suggested that she should try to involve the community, have discussions with them and make them realize that without a group effort this would never be solved. As a result of taking up this issue at the Jajam level, Rambha understood what to do about this problem. She had a series of meetings at the village level with

women, men and the Sarpanch. Soon the community realized that they all would have to pool in their efforts to tackle this issue. In these meetings they decided to erect a wall outside the factory so that the water would not flow out of the factory, in case the management failed to find some solution. The Sathin discussed it with the *pracheta* and the DWDA and Idara. This led to the intervention of the Collector. He promised that purifier plants would soon be installed in the factories.

The report gives an idea of the processes which are involved in participatory development for which the *jajam* was a catalyst. The *jajam* and *shivir* meetings were organized by the *sathin* and depended on their initiatives. The *shivir* was a 'camp' (the English word was used in the IDS reports) held to discuss an issue which was considered common to all participants in the district and not just restricted to members of one village, as in a *jajam*. The camps required careful planning by the *sathin*, as they involved bringing together members of the coordinating and evaluating bodies (DWDA, IDARA, IDS) and, with their assistance, experts on an issue considered important by all *sathin* in the district. For example, a *shivir* was held in Jaipur district around the role of the village leader (*sarpanch*) and the system of village governance (*panchayat*). As a result of the *shivir*, the *sathin* and villagers received information on, among other areas, the political, administrative and revenue bodies of the government, the function of elections and the meaning of representation. The *shivir* resulted in detailed discussions among the villagers, especially the women, on the extent to which their village leader (*sarpanch*) was representative of the needs of the villagers. Thus in the process of training, *sathin* and village women moved from being completely excluded from the realms of power to being able to participate through their enhanced understanding in the political processes of their community and state. In another instance a *shivir* was held on the issue of health and family planning. As a result, the *sathin* became aware of and able to state figures for the adverse sex ratio in Rajasthan (913 females for every 1000 males). This in turn earned them the respect of the community leaders as well as the health and development officials. Such knowledge was a particularly effective tool in countering the pressure on women to undergo sterilization operations carried on under the banner of family-planning focused development programmes.

The meaning of training to emerge from the above examples contradicts the assumption that there are fixed categories of teachers and trainees bound in a relationship of transferring identifiable skills from one to the other. The *sathin* emerged both as trainers and as trainees in different situations, imbibing information and skills and equally imparting them. They used methods they had learned and others which they had developed and created for other *sathin* and trainers to use. The *sathin* methods were particularly effective, as they stemmed from their experience and understanding of the cultural and social fabric of the communities targeted for development. As a result of their increasing skills and consequently indispensable position within their communities, the *sathin* began to take on most of the burden of the WDP at the village level. The next section considers the impact of this increased responsibility on the *sathin*, their communities and other levels of the programme. It also examines the shifting direction of the programme as a consequence of the different conceptions of empowerment and development which emerged at the various levels of the WDP.

Different Experiences, Different Agendas

The WDP brought together not only different organizations in its project of empowerment but also women of very different social, economic and cultural backgrounds. There were thus many areas of difference, organizational as well as individual, caste, class and gender related. In this section we focus on the dissent which arose as a result of the differing ideologies, expectations and experiences that surfaced as the work of the programme proceeded. At the outset, the programme was bound to be taken to task at the village level by the council elders, husbands, fathers and brothers of the women involved in the WDP. The WDP was initially regarded by the village elders and councillors, in the light of previous government programmes for development, as a project to facilitate health and nutrition amongst women. But as the training and meetings went on, women formed wider groups and networks and began to take issue with the restrictions imposed on them by their husbands, families and village leaders. The honorarium of Rs 200/- per month paid to each *sathin* was a major factor, at least for the husbands and extended families, in permitting their wives, sisters and daughters to work for the WDP. However, as the *sathin* devoted increasingly more time to the WDP activities, their role changed from being part-time workers to becoming fully involved in the programme and 'trainers' in their own right. The increasing commitment and leadership they assumed led to confrontations with the authority structures in their community on the one hand and with the state institutions on the other. There were few mechanisms within the programme to deal with these differences.

An example of the conflicts generated by the programme can be seen in training in the Ajmer District in 1987–88, which focused on health and on women's bodies and sexuality. Among the issues of concern which were raised at the meeting was the population programme of the government; in particular its emphasis on female sterilization was questioned. The criticism gained further force when the participants in the training learnt that the employment of poorer women on government relief works had the former's sterilization as a precondition. The negative sentiments of the *sathin, pracheta* and other members expressed at the meeting were conveyed to other officials of the programme and in the district. In response, the district collector and village leaders criticized the WDP for instigating anti-government feelings. The village elders used the occasion to demonstrate how the WDP encouraged their women to discuss 'shameful things'. Their observation that women had learnt to keep a record of their menstrual cycles in order to have greater control over their fertile periods had particularly upset male sentiment in the village. The health trainers were mostly feminist activists working in the NGO sector and were unwilling to be deterred by what they saw as an essentially male-biased criticism of their programme. The response of the health activists and the feminist members of the IDS and IDARA to the criticisms of the training was to insist that the WDP as a whole take a stance against the government. However, the project director of the WDP, who was a government employee, and the state programme director, felt that the approach of the health project would have to be revised for fear of the government preventing such training from taking place in the future. The debate on the approach to be taken in the health training sessions was related to a wider controversy between the voluntary and activist sections of the programme and those employed by the government over who had final control over the issues to be prioritized and the methods of training used. We shall return to this disagreement shortly.

Another, more recent example of the nature of opposition the WDP, and more directly the *sathin*, met in the course of their work were the events in 1992 involving a *sathin* named Bhanwari. Bhanwari tried to prevent the child marriage of the one-year-old daughter of an influential and powerful man in her village. Giving sufficient notice to the family concerned, she informed the state authorities of the preparation for the marriage. As a punishment for reporting them to the police and state officials, she was raped in September 1992 by four members of the girl's family (upper-caste Gujjars) and another upper-caste (Brahman) man. Bhanwari reported her rape to the police authorities of the district but found little sympathy and no immediate action. The local police, in fact, supported the Gujjar claims that the whole incident had been fabricated by Bhanwari, who, they claimed, was herself a prostitute. It was only when the other *sathin, pracheta,* IDARA and IDS members rallied to her support and pushed the government for justice and compensation for Bhanwari in a rally in October 1992 that her situation was considered at all. With the support of other women's groups and networks, the WDP members were able to pressurize the government of Rajasthan to transfer Bhanwari's case to the Central Bureau of Investigation at Delhi, which they believed would conduct a fairer investigation of the case than the state officials. As a result of the CBI deliberations, the five accused Gujjars were arrested in January 1994, sixteen months after the incident. The state high court had simultaneously rejected the bail applications of two of the five men accused. At the time of writing this article, the WDP and several women's groups in Jaipur and Delhi are fighting for the accused to be tried and sentenced and for compensation to be granted to Bhanwari by the supreme court. As a measure of interim relief, Bhanwari received Rs. 10,000 from the Prime Minister's Relief Fund, and IDARA gave her son a job as messenger at their Jaipur office. The judgement and conviction in the Bhanwari case was a considerable achievement for the WDP, not least because it was unusual for upper-caste men to be convicted for raping lower-caste women in Rajasthan (by and large, cases of rape went unreported). Bhanwari's case also further reinforced the demands made by the women's groups that the state provide legislative guidelines against the sexual harassment of women in the workplace.

Bhanwari's rape was above all a stark reminder to the other *sathin* of their difficult working conditions, and it reinforced their general feeling of dissatisfaction with the programme. Here we see how community feelings against the programme became related to conflicts between its functionaries. Questions were again raised by the *sathin* about the physical and financial security guaranteed them by the WDP (the issue of payment had first arisen at the *sathin mela* or jamboree in 1990). The honorarium of Rs. 250/ - was regarded by the *sathin* as totally inadequate considering the circumstances of their work. It was in this context that protests for higher wages and the security of permanent government employment were made in Jaipur in September 1993. For the *sathin*, the government was the main facilitator of the WDP, providing funds and employing all the workers, trainers and evaluators. Thus an association with the government was to be desired. This in itself was a shift from previous attitudes. Before their participation in the WDP, most village women found it difficult to have a proper conversation with government officials, let alone conceive of being one of them. Even the local elected representatives such as the headman (*sarpanch*) and village revenue collector (*patwari*) were considered *mai-baap* (like parents), whose orders were to be obeyed and not questioned. Now the *sathin* demanded to be part of that status structure and to perform defined roles, earn fixed government salaries and be accorded the prestige accompanying such posts. Towards this end, we find that by September 1993 the *sathin* had formed close links among themselves rather than between them and the other village women, as had been envisaged by the programme. The state authorities, particularly the Department of Social Welfare, were, however, unwilling to undertake what they saw as an increased financial liability in raising the *sathin* honorarium. They saw the *sathin* as providing them with cheap labour to promote government programmes against child marriage, in favour of female sterilization etc.

Both the IDS research team and the IDARA (NGO) supported the *sathins'* claims for increased remuneration but were not in favour of more fixed terms of employment. One of the factors favouring higher wages for the *sathin* was that members of the coordinating levels of the programme had been similarly rewarded – for example, the IDS members associated with the programme received promotions and higher salaries, and some, including Kavita Srivastava, felt guilt about their rewards, which should

have gone equally to the *sathin*. They also felt that the amount of
remuneration for the *sathin* was unjustifiably low given increasing
inflation and the full-time nature of the *sathin's* work. The IDS and
IDARA were, however, ideologically opposed to the issue of
permanent government employment for the *sathin*. In this, they
differed from the *sathin*. One of the main points to emerge from
the self-assessment exercises undertaken during training and
referred to in the review of the programme carried out by the
IDS in 1990 was the value the *sathin* placed on links with the
government and their desire to become government employees
(Srivastava *et al.* 1990). The review exercise especially highlighted
the fact that villagers, men and women, including the *sathin*, saw
the government from a different perspective from that of the
voluntary organizations and feminist researchers. For the NGO
and feminists of the programme (IDS and state IDARA), the
disjunction in their and the *sathins'* perceptions of the government
was seen as a failing on their part as trainers to make the
programme and its institutions itself a focus for discussion and
reflection. The fact that the *sathin* had formed support groups
with other *sathin* rather than with other village women further
highlighted the NGO-feminist concern that the beneficiaries of the
programme would be the functionaries, not the poorest village
women. As a result, in 1992 and 1993 there was a change in the
WDP organization with regard to the *sathin*. The WDP planning
and coordinating body moved to form direct links with women's
groups in the villages rather than communicate with them through
the *sathin*. In this scheme, the honorarium would be given to the
group as a whole rather than to one person.

There were further ideological differences between programme
workers at the level above that of the *sathin*, i.e. between the
pracheta and the activist members of the IDS and the IDARA. The
pracheta were initially found to treat the *sathin* as unequal
participants rather than co-workers. As the programme unfolded,
the IDS report (1990) claimed in retrospect that a greater emphasis
on *pracheta*-training should have been made in the programme,
so that the *pracheta* as much as the *sathin* could 'imbibe the spirit
of the programme' and rethink their own values and morals of
hierarchy and inequality in order to make the programme effective.
Towards this end, it was evident that the *pracheta* needed to be
empowered themselves, to bond with women of their own
backgrounds and to be able to externalize the frustrations of their

own work and lives. The *pracheta* also needed to have fora, otherwise provided for the *sathin* and village women, to explore creative means of expression. From the point of view of the *pracheta*, they faced practical problems which were not taken into account in the programme design. For example, their work in the villages took them away from their home in the city, and as a consequence married mothers in particular had little contact with their children. In general, the *pracheta* felt that the WDP was insensitive to their household responsibilities, this being a major cause of conflict between the *pracheta* and their husbands. The *pracheta*, like the *sathin*, also felt that monetary compensation and job security were lacking. Without any specific goals or aims for their own growth being addressed in the programme and no clear channels for upward mobility in their jobs, a high level of dissatisfaction was registered at this level of the programme.

Dissent was also registered by members of the coordinating body at higher levels (above that of the *pracheta*) in the programme, and here we return to the controversy mentioned earlier between the voluntary and activist members and the government functionaries. The support given by the state IDARA and IDS to the *sathin* protest against the government at the same time conveyed the increasing distance felt by the IDS and state IDARA from the district government functionaries. Their position reflected earlier doubts which, for example, had arisen over the health awareness training, as to whether a government organization could be an effective partner in encouraging a form of development which would question the government itself, and whether the aspect of the WDP which envisaged such a partnership was itself misconceived. There was a growing rift between the voluntary and government organizations of the WDP, which contributed to the growing dissatisfaction of the *sathin* and *pracheta*. The NGO (IDARA) and the DWDA (government department) each saw the other either as trying to take over their functions or as not doing enough for the programme. The IDARA perceived themselves as the guardians of the values of the WDP and considered the DWDA as uninterested in the processes and minutiae of the programme and geared only towards the production of results. The DWDA, on the other hand, felt that their role as administrators was undervalued and began to seek support from government bodies outside the WDP, for which they were further criticized by the IDARA. The tension between the project director of the DWDA and members of the IDARA was the cause of further dissatisfaction among the *sathin* and *pracheta*, who had to work with both organizations and often became pawns in the politics of the higher levels of the programme.

What became increasingly clear as the WDP entered its ninth year was the fact that the structural relationship between the coordinating bodies set up at the beginning of the programme could not continue. Over the past two years of the programme, some changes have been consciously implemented, such as the emphasis on village women's groups rather than on single *sathin*. Other changes have resulted from the movement of WDP personnel. The IDS feminist input has decreased significantly, as has the effectiveness of the district IDARAs. The remaining NGO component (state IDARA) has tended to follow the government in its organization and orientation, thus further reinforcing the WDP as a government programme. The declining feminist-NGO component has been particularly detrimental to the environment of critical self-awareness in which the programme was conducted.

Some Conclusions

Most of the problems associated with the WDP could be seen to occur at two levels. First, there were differences which were manifest at the level of those targeted by the programme, i.e. the *sathin* and members of their village community. Secondly, differences were seen to arise at the level of those who organized and co-ordinated the programme. Within this level, a further dichotomy of opinions and positions was discernible between the IDS, IDARA feminist researchers and activists on the one hand and the district and middle-level government officials and functionaries, including the *pracheta*, on the other. To a certain extent, these levels of differences could both be seen as related to the strong ideological agenda underlying the programme, which was driving social change.

The agenda for empowerment had been set by feminist-led development concerns. The feminist position was an important component of the WDP, which significantly enabled the pro-gramme to achieve not only first-time goals for women, but also to develop creative participatory methods which connected the aims of development more centrally to the lives and concerns of the communities and individuals involved. The participatory nature of the WDP brought to bear a focus on social relations in the programme which successfully connected the goals of development with local-level social structures and processes. While the concepts, aims and methods of the feminist developmentalists were crucial to the success of the WDP, at the same time – and contrary to their expectations – these very aspects imparted a hierarchical and alienating element to the programme. The different ideological perspectives among those involved in the programme were reflected in the structural differences of language, education and culture at its different levels. Those who were part of the IDS and NGO came from well-educated, largely English-medium, urban backgrounds. The government functionaries prominent at the district level, including the *pracheta*, were educated in Hindi-medium schools and lived lower-middle-class lives in smaller towns and cities. The *sathin*, who spoke the Rajasthani dialect and lived in the villages, had comparatively little education. Although the WDP was successful in removing the conceptual barriers between the categories of trainers and trainees, it had been unable to provide the opportunities for vertical mobility, especially for lower-level functionaries such as the *sathin* and *pracheta*.

A number of the feminist developmentalist concerns of the WDP are also shared by anthropologists today. This is particularly the case as regards their common interest in understanding categories, institutions and processes in terms of people's own conceptions and the need to draw upon individual and community experiences. Methodologically, they increasingly share an emphasis on participatory forms of research and on a plurality of views and voices in the collection of information (also see Moore 1988). But perhaps, as is evident from the WDP experiences, feminists, unlike anthropologists, are less able to deal with ideological positions different from their own (a result of the very different construction of the 'other', as Strathern 1987 and Caplan 1988 suggest), precisely because of the committed nature of their work. The gap in developmental perspectives between the feminist minority and the rest of the programme workers (mainly lower government functionaries) perhaps indicates why the feminist component of the WDP has become weaker in more recent times. It also points to the fact that until the language and idioms of empowerment are shared across communities and the concept of empowerment is continuously re-addressed in the local context and at the level of the state – outside the context defined by development – development programmes themselves will remain only partially effective.

Note

1. We would like to thank Ralph Grillo for his helpful comments. For us, writing this paper together was a result of the realization that we shared more than our memories of school and undergraduate years in Jaipur. We both went on to work in rural Rajasthan, but from the different perspectives of social anthropology and development. Kavita became involved with several districts and villages in the course of her work in the Institute of Development Studies and particularly with the Women's Development Programme. Maya spent a year in a village doing fieldwork for her doctoral research in social anthropology. Although we have come to address different audiences (village women, government and NGO workers in one case and university students and colleagues in the other) and have been engaged in the different concerns of our disciplines, we nevertheless share similar orientations. This paper provided us with an opportunity to put together our experiences in Rajasthan in a manner which prioritized local-level interpretations, ideologies and needs, strengthened our interest in feminism as an epistemology and at the same time allowed us to move beyond the boundaries of our disciplines.

References

Agarwal, B. (1994), *A Field of One's Own: Gender and Land Rights in South Asia*, Cambridge: Cambridge University Press.

Bhargava, P. (1993), *Rajasthan*, Jaipur: Institute of Development Studies.

Calman, L.J. (1992), *Toward Empowerment: Women and Movement Politics in India*, Boulder: Westview Press.

Caplan, P. (1988), 'Engendering Knowledge: The Politics of Ethnography', *Anthropology Today*, 14(5): 8–12, 14(6): 14–17.

Das, M. (1992), *The Women's Development Programme in Rajasthan: A Case Study in Group Formation for Women's Development*, Washington D.C.: World Bank (policy research working paper on women in development, series WPS 913).

Jain, S., K. Srivastava, K. Mathur *et al.* (1986), *Exploring Possibilities: A Review of the Women's Development Programme, Rajasthan*, Jaipur: Institute of Development Studies.

Kabeer, N. (1994), *Reversed Realities: Gender Hierarchies in Development Thought*, London: Verso.

Moore, H. (1988), *Feminism and Anthropology*, London: Routledge.

Raheja, G. and A.G. Gold (1994), *Listen to the Heron's Words: Reimagining Gender and Kinship in North India*, Berkeley: University of California Press.

Raheja, G. (1996), 'Limits of Patriliny: Kinship, Gender and Women's Speech Practices in Rural North India', in J. Maynes, B. Solnad, U. Strasser *et al.* (eds), *Gender, Kinship and Power*, London: Routledge.

Sen, A. (1990), 'Gender and Cooperative Conflicts', in I. Tinker (ed.), *Persistent Inequalities: Women and World Development*, Oxford: Oxford University Press.

Srivastava, K., S. Rajan, D. Bhog *et al.* (1990), *WDP: Emerging Challenges*, Jaipur: Institute of Development Studies.

Strathern, M. (1987), 'An Awkward Relationship: The Case of Feminism and Anthropology', *Signs*, 12/2: 276–92.

Unnithan, M. (1994), 'Girasias and the Politics of Difference: 'Caste', Kinship and Gender in a Marginalised Society', in M. Searle-Chatterjee and U. Sharma (eds), *Contextualising Caste: Post-Dumontian Perspectives*, Oxford: Blackwell Publishers.

Unnithan-Kumar, M. (1997), *Identity, Gender and Poverty: New Perspectives on Caste and Tribe in Rajasthan*, Oxford: Berghahn.

Ziegler, P. (1978), 'Some Notes on Rajput Loyalties during the Mughal Period', in J.F. Richards (ed.), *Kingship and Authority in South Asia*, Madison: University of Wisconsin Press.

Chapter 8

Three Critical Issues in Community Health Development Projects in Kenya

David O. Nyamwaya

Introduction

After political independence was obtained in Kenya, many Kenyans held the view that the government should shoulder full responsibility for providing health and related services to Kenyans as promised by the politicians just before independence. Non-governmental organizations, especially religious ones, were regarded in like manner. However, because of a rapidly increasing population and the escalating capital and recurrent costs of health-development projects, both the government and some non-governmental organizations soon realized that it was not feasible for health services to be provided to Kenyan communities without the participation of those communities.

The shift of opinion noted above was strengthened by the Alma Ata Declaration (1978), which called for the incorporation of local resources in health development. Another push came in 1983, when Kenya initiated the 'District Focus of Rural Development' strategy for development. It was stated that the objective of this new strategy was to broaden the base of rural development and encourage local initiatives in order to improve problem identification, resource mobilization and project design and implementation (Government of Kenya 1987: 8).

The District focus strategy was hailed as an important step towards enhancing local participation in the development process. Even non-governmental development personnel quickly embraced the concept and began working through the government machinery established to facilitate operationalization of the strategy. However, a decade after the strategy was initiated, there exist divergent views between communities and development agencies and personnel regarding the origination of development projects, the units on which development should focus and the constitution of the missing link in development activities. Health development is still planned, managed and assessed almost exclusively by 'experts', with communities playing only insignificant, non-decision-making roles.

The author has carefully studied community-based health projects in several districts of Kenya during the 1980s and early 1990s. Examples used to illustrate the discussion are selected at random and presented in such a way as to hide the identity of specific individuals and/or projects.

The main argument is that while in theory communities are supposed to play a leading role in the health-development process, that process is still largely controlled by government and NGO development 'experts' who do not allow communities to play major roles. Examples are taken from the Kenyan community health development scene, including those based on both governmental initiatives and projects. The lumping together of governmental and non-governmental approaches may be questioned, but I think it is justified. While there are some differences between governmental and non-governmental spon-sored projects, critical scrutiny of what actually happens on the ground (at project sites) indicates that conceptual differences between the two sides as far as development is concerned dissipate on the ground because non-governmental organizations depend almost entirely on official (government) structures, mechanisms and personnel to implement development strategies. Furthermore, government rules and regulations about community development have to be adhered to by whoever is involved in development. The period covered is post-Alma Ata to the present, and specific-ally 1980 to 1993.

Origination and Implementation of Projects

Successive development plans developed by the government of Kenya and health-development agencies stipulated that com-munities should be involved in the planning and implementation of project activities. For example, in Kenya's District Focus for

Rural Development, it is stated that:

> Divisional, locational and sub-locational development committees should encourage inputs from community members on development opportunities and problems in their local areas, the types of projects that are needed in their communities, and ways to maintain the utilization of completed development infrastructure (Government of Kenya 1987: 8).

In practice, project beneficiaries are rarely involved in deciding which health or any other problem should be addressed. For example, in a project in a semi-arid area, a development agency, in conjunction with the local Ministry of Health, decided to initiate a maternal and child health (MCH) project whose objective was to reduce the number of child deaths and enhance safe motherhood. Ministry of Health staff at district and lower levels were contacted together with the local administration officials. Community leaders volunteered to mobilize the people.

A number of meetings were organized by the development agency to explain project objectives and activities to the people. The focus was to be 'education for child survival and development' and the beneficiaries were to be adult women. Initially, the women showed much enthusiasm and attended scheduled meetings regularly. When the planting season came some women began to skip meetings, and by the time the planting season had come hardly anybody attended the much publicized 'development' meetings.

It took detailed investigations to discover what the problem was. In the semi-arid region, women's lives revolve around the ownership and exploitation of goats and goat products. Since the 'health' project being proposed did not make any reference to goats, the project could not sustain the initial euphoria. Furthermore, the project did not have a water component, in spite of the fact that the women spent fifty percent of their working lives looking for water.

Fortunately, the development agency, having learned of the centrality of goats and water to the community, reset project objectives, shifting the focus towards improving goat production and reducing time spent on fetching water through the purchase of donkey carts. A revolving fund for goat production was set up and the vaccination of goats supported. The women today have more income and more time, both of which are largely devoted to improving the health of the children. It must be pointed out that such a re-adjustment in project objectives is the exception rather than the rule.

In many of the projects observed, it was established that in most cases project strategies were decided on without consulting the community concerned. In one project, the aim was to increase the number of latrines in a community. The 'demonstration unit' strategy was adopted to promote the construction and use of latrines. Different models of latrines were constructed in schools, the chief's office and the homes of opinion leaders (for which read powerful people). The models were extremely well constructed, with expensive finishes. The idea was to make the models attractive enough for community members to replicate. By the time the four-year project was completed, hardly any community member had 'copied' any of the models displayed. A joke developed within the community to the effect that you only needed any of the models if you became a chief or leader or occupied some elevated position in the community. In any case, most of the models cost far more to build than an ordinary house.

In other projects, equally inappropriate strategies have been adopted. For example, village health workers (VHWs) were trained to improve the nutritional status of women and children. The VHWs were trained on the different food groups and on food preparation. Nothing in the project referred to improving food production or storage. Today, many of the mothers reached by the VHWs know that fish contains proteins and that vegetables are a good source of vitamins, but there are no fish ponds or kitchen gardens on the project sites, nor has the status of nutrition improved.

In an attempt to stick to project work plans and budgets, development personnel ignore people's own work plans and commitments. In many cases, project schedules are developed so as to suit the project's needs, rarely those of the beneficiaries. A few years ago, an international agency in collaboration with the Ministry of Health decided to increase immunization coverage in one of Kenya's coastal districts. There was much pressure from the agency headquarters to show results 'quickly' so as to justify continued funding for project activities in the district. A crash programme was developed to promote people's understanding of the importance of immunization and to vaccinate all children

under five who had not been vaccinated. Four weeks of promotional activities were planned and strenuous efforts made to
create awareness about immunization. The promotional activities
were planned to culminate in a day-long vaccination campaign.
In spite of the immense investment in creating awareness and in
logistical arrangements, the campaign planners had not taken
cognizance of the religious festivals going on during the month.
Since most people were fasting, the turn-out on the final day was
extremely low.

What happened in the vaccination campaign is not unique.
In many 'community-based health projects', individuals and
communities are driven by the sponsoring agency's time plans.
The argument usually given for such sponsor-driven time plans
is that the project has a specific life-span which must be taken into
consideration. The not-so-obvious assumption here is that beneficiaries have all the time to spare, so they have to 'accept' what
others have decided. Furthermore, there is an implicit assumption
that since beneficiaries are receiving assistance, they have no right
to choose the timing of project activities.

The Construction of Social Units as the Focus for
Development Activities

The health projects studied in preparation for this paper indicate
an insidious interest by agencies and the government to create
objects of development from social categories. References to
'development', 'youth group', 'women's group', etc., are common.
This tendency to objectify and categorize people for purposes of
development seems to stem from the need to construct social
categories merely for development purposes. Once a group is
identified, development is seen to constitute a visible transformation of all or at least some members of that specific group,
without due consideration for the other members of a community.

Our observations indicate that the project 'groups' that are
constructed are largely artificial. Take, for example, a health project
which seeks to train 'village health workers' for community A.
When an agency initiates a project in A, certain assumptions are
made. First, it is assumed that the group being constructed is a
bounded group with shared characteristics and aspirations.
Secondly, it is assumed that the health needs delineated as the

focus for intervention are perceived as such by all members of the group. Thirdly, in order to facilitate the use of specific strategies to effect changes, it is assumed that all members of the group are at the same socio-economic level. Fourthly, it is taken for granted that members of the group wish to work together. In real life, even small communities are extremely heterogeneous, requiring diverse strategies for health improvement.

In some communities, different agencies form different groups, to implement health activities. Some members of the community belong to several such groups, all set in the same locality. Little if any attention is paid to existing organizational structures which might undertake project activities. Situations exist where, for example, project committees formed in the same community bear the names of the sponsoring agencies. Such agencies dictate when 'their' committees can meet, what they can talk about and who chairs the meetings. Records of meetings are seen to belong to the sponsoring agency and not the community. Some agencies insist that no committee meeting should take place in the absence of a representative from the agency. The agency determines whether committee members are enumerated or not and whether committee members are given some allowance during the duration of the 'project'. Most such committees fall apart when the agency enumeration is removed. However, in most cases, committee members work as 'volunteers'.

In real life, communities in rural Kenya are not homogeneous. Some members of, say, a village have more economic capacity than others. In these cases, interventions such as introducing indiscriminate sale of subsidized mosquito bednets within the group may not be appropriate. Equally inappropriate is the distribution of supplementary food to all members of a group, including those who do not need it. Such distribution is justified in the name of equity: all members of the group must be given equal access to project handouts. We have witnessed many cases where the most economically able members of a group are the only ones who can meet the 'community contribution' requirement for project handouts. In one project, an offer was made to all members of the group to receive certain materials for constructing VIP latrines, with the requirement that before receiving the materials a recipient had to dig a pit. Poorer members of the community could not meet the requirement and were therefore unable to benefit from the project. Many more examples could be given to show the overemphasis on the homogeneity of social groups in health projects; suffice to say that a focus on such groups is quite common. In fact, there is hardly any project which does not identify a specific social group as the target for development intervention while excluding other members of the community. In many cases, such groups have to be mobilized or even constituted before project implementation can start. Anthropological and community development studies indicate that there is need to pay more attention to community heterogeneity. Such studies provide evidence for the merits of an approach which sees the community as composed of many parts and separate ideologies (Chambers and Young 1979: 65).

In my view, much effort is spent on mobilizing or constituting social groups because projects are planned without due regard to the heterogeneity of communities and their felt needs. Such efforts are expended because development agencies and the government wish to have visible objects in development interventions. The quest for visibility leads to the construction of social groups which may exist only in the project personnel's imagination and reports. Visible social groups can be controlled, and this seems to be the hidden agenda of development agencies. The construction, ownership and control of such groups make good reading in project progress reports. Neither government nor development agency staff wish to see 'uncontrolled' developments in a project situation.

It is usually a requirement for development assistance that expected outcomes are clearly listed in the project proposal in order that funding may be forthcoming. Outcomes in health projects are seen to include visible groups of people, not single individuals. A focus on reaching individuals of households may prove risky because the numbers may be too small to justify the investment involved. In my view, if development in health is to be meaningful for the perspective of the beneficiary, it must focus on the individual or households, besides being set in a specific community.

Missing Links

What are the missing links to be addressed through community health development interventions?

If community health development in Kenya (as elsewhere in Africa) were to be viewed as a chain, both development personnel and community members could agree that there are missing links in it. The links must be missing because there are many preventable health problems which abound in the country. However, there does not seem to be any agreement as to what the missing links are. There is even broader disagreement as to who should put the links in place for health development to be realized.

At and soon after independence, the government saw itself as the 'supplier', literally, of all 'missing links' in development. In the case of health, the missing link was seen to include the provision of curative services. Communities were regarded as receptacles and were expected to make use of the services provided as a way of improving their health conditions. It soon became clear, however, that health development required more than just the provision of curative services. Attention turned more and more to public health interventions and improvements in nutrition, water and housing. By the time the Alma Ata declaration was signed in 1979, in principle the government and development agencies had accepted the need to promote public health and other interventions required to improve people's health. Despite the conceptual shift from curative to preventive health services which occurred, there is still no agreement as to what the critical interventions in this area should be.

Ministry of Health personnel at almost all levels claim that the missing link in community health development is 'lack of proper knowledge'. This claim is used to explain the existence of problems such as malnutrition, low immunization rates and epidemics of cholera, typhoid and meningitis. On the other hand, community members blame health personnel for not intervening in time to prevent the occurrence of these problems. An observer may see that both sides are right, in the sense that the elimination of health problems requires both the health specialist and the lay person, but there is something more. The problems listed above are due largely to socio-economic conditions rather than just ignorance on the part of community members or the negligence of health providers.

Development personnel, especially those working with non-governmental organizations at grassroots level, argue that the main obstacle to community health improvement is lack of adequate financial resources. While this thinking may not be articulated verbally or in project documents, it is discernible in the form of health-development assistance. Money and materials constitute the largest component of assistance given to communities in pursuance of health development. It is only recently that, due to financial constraints, attention is being turned to human-resources development, an issue we examine later on in this section.

Both governmental and non-governmental organizations, for example, attempt to encourage better environmental health through support for latrine and dish-rack construction and small water sources protection (e.g. springs) by providing funds. Usually, the amount of money involved is quite small. In some cases, only a slab or ventilation pipe may be provided to individuals who wish to construct latrines. It is usually argued that the community cannot 'afford' the investment. True, there are households which are so poor that they cannot afford a pit latrine. However, if careful analysis of household expenditure is made, it is sometimes clear that where latrines have not been constructed the problem is not just one of lack of funds. In one case, a fairly well-to-do member of a community put up an impressive pit latrine, complete with a permanent superstructure, then asked for the reimbursement for expenses from project personnel!

In another instance, a community asked to have piped water instead of the hand-pumps which were being promoted by a project. Members of this community argued through their representatives that they could afford running water and a water-borne sewage system. However, project personnel turned down the request because it was not in line with project policy and objectives. In another case, powdered milk was made available for all households of a community. The only requirement was that the household should have one or more children under five. The community perceived the offer as a good gesture from the government and each household requested the milk. Some members of the community did not really need the milk for their children, so they used it for making tea.

Some development personnel think that in order for community health development to occur, all indigenous health-seeking behaviour must be abandoned. To such people, abandonment of such practices is an important part of the missing links. Sometimes even useful or at most harmless practices are the focus of health education. An example may be taken from indigenous forms of growth-monitoring. In many parts of rural Kenya, mothers and others in the community seek to monitor the growth of babies by tying a cloth or leather band around the wrist, waist or neck. The point is that if the baby is growing normally, the band should be extended from time to time. However, the author witnessed several cases where health personnel providing MCH or family-planning services cut the bands to pieces and lectured the mothers on the dangers of witchcraft which the bands were seen to signify!

For the recipient of assistance for community health develop-ment, the missing link may be seen to relate to physical conditions, health facilities and services, and requirements such as water, food or housing, depending on the specific local conditions. Thus in some places, people may say that their most critical health problem is water, while in another, it may be stated to be a lack of adequate services. It is therefore difficult for communities to fathom why health projects should focus on issues such as immunization or the control of a specific disease, diarrhoea, say – without addressing more pressing health needs. To most communities, therefore, the concern is not the attainment of some global health goals, but rather the problem which the community faces and whose solution is seen to depend on both internal and external resources. In the communities observed, there is a determination to address problems pertaining to health using local resources. Assistance is called for when local resources are not adequate. As demonstration for this argument, it is enough to observe how households pay for quality private services even where free government services are available. As much as possible, house-hold and individuals are prepared to spend money to improve their health in a manner that ensures quality, convenience and confidentiality and does not compromise individual or family dignity.

From the foregoing, it is arguable that though there is much rhetorical support for 'development from below', our experience indicates that the rhetoric has yet to be put into practice. Develop-ment is still effected in a top-down manner, and there is always the implicit assumption that communities can only develop once they have assimilated specialized technical and material inputs from the outside. Few attempts have been made to utilize indigenous resources to provide the missing block in health development. This issue is discussed further later.

When the locus of control of initiatives, construction of social units and determination of the missing links in community health projects are considered carefully, a number of patterns pertaining to community health development emerge. Here main patterns are presented and attempts made at explaining them.

Patterns of Intervention

A clear pattern observable in most community health projects relates to the attempts of the government and development agencies and personnel to modernize communities. Perhaps more than in any other sector, modernization strategies in health have been extended to include not only pharmaceutical drugs but also management, financing and communication aspects. The perceived superiority of biomedical drugs over indigenous pharmacopoeia is now seen to be extendable to virtually all aspects of health development. It is unquestioningly assumed that Western medical drugs, service delivery financing and even communication systems are universally applicable. In fact health planners and workers in general take it for granted that such Western systems should be promoted actively as the basic prerequisite for health improvement. Modernization is seen as the employment of external resources to effect changes in and around communities. This view accounts for the almost total neglect of indigenous approaches to health-care delivery, financing and even communication systems, which are known to be not only more effective but also affordable and acceptable to many Kenyan communities. I go along with these scholars, who point out the necessity for development planners (and others) to take into account the accumulated knowledge and traditional skills and technology of the people among whom they work.

Health-care providers in particular see little room for indigenous resources in health development. Such resources, including practitioners, materia medica and delivery systems, are regarded as 'backward' and therefore not suitable for promotion (Nyamwaya 1982). Even in the few cases where such 'non-modern' resources are utilized, attempts are made to 'modernize' them, although such modernization – actually Westernization – is not necessary. For example, traditional birth attendants are dressed in uniform or given badges to make them look like their hospital-based counterparts, who themselves strive to look as untraditional as possible in speech and general deportment. New social units have to be created to facilitate health development, since indigenous ones are perceived by development agencies and personnel to be incapable of handling 'modern' health services. Even when pre-existing units (such as women's groups) are used to promote health, the groups, or at least their leaders, have to be trained in modern ways of leadership and management. Modern here is seen to imply non-indigenous! Even the holistic approach to health delivery employed by many Kenyan communities is hardly seen as critical to community health development initiatives. This is the case even when there is increasing evidence that the holistic approach to the management of health problems leads to a greater success of initiatives.

Because of the overemphasis on 'modern' resources and approaches in community development, the 'missing link' in many community health projects is, as pointed out earlier, seen by project implementors to be something coming from outside the community. This accounts for the fact that there is little emphasis on empowering communities to address health problems the way they think is best. As has been emphasized, even the determination of what constitutes the missing link is done for the community because of its assumed backwardness.

The second pattern observable in community health projects is the tendency toward providing universal, standardized package solutions to problems. There is an unwritten rule used by both governmental and non-governmental agencies and personnel running community health projects. The rule revolves around the need for the application of 'package' solutions to similar problems occurring in different socio-economic contexts. All the packages so applied are intended to help reduce or eliminate completely some specific health problems. Packages for dealing with diarrhoeal disease (CDD), immunization (EPI), drug supply (EDP) and others such as community-based health-care (CBHC) have now acquired universal acclaim. Each package has its basic strategies, including IEC systems, evaluation and even essential staffing. The package approach dictates not only project budgets but also activities and beneficiaries (usually referred to as the target population). Little is done to adapt project designs to specific circumstances. Even project management structures and systems are applied universally. The package applied is seen to constitute the only missing link in the process of community development. The more pressing missing links perceived by community members are not even acknowledged.

In my view, the package approach to community development is flawed in many different respects. In the first place, it is assumed that a set of strategies is suitable for application in many different settings. In a way, there are some problems which may present themselves in more or less similar ways. However, when it comes to providing or applying solutions, there is a need to look for home-grown solutions which address local situations more effectively than universal standard ones. There is also the question of sustainability. If solutions are developed locally, or at least with a local flavour, the solutions are more likely to be sustainable in the long run.

Secondly, the use of universal package solutions in communities assumes a degree of homogeneity between and within the communities which does not exist. Different communities have unique socio-economic capacities and are affected diversely by the same health problems. So-called target populations are rarely completely similar.

Thirdly, universal packages of the nature discussed here reduce the significance of local resources in health development. The systematic application of such packages leads to states of dependence. Communities are made to depend almost entirely on external resources for solving problems which do not necessarily require external inputs. Thus the culture of dependence in health (as in other) development has reached alarming proportions, even after the Alma Ata Declaration, which emphasized self-reliance.

A third pattern which is closely related to the two already discussed concerns the lack of solid databases for community health planning. Certainly baseline, feasibility or pre-investment studies are undertaken before some health projects are implemented. However, such studies hardly yield a meaningful sociocultural database for development planning. There are strong epidemiological and sociological influences on such studies when they do occur. They do not, therefore, produce evidence for intra-community variation such as is required for participatory development planning. Interactive data-collection methods such as are used in applied anthropology and rural appraisal approaches (Chambers 1992) are required to correct the situation. For example, participant observation, focus-group discussions, informal interviews and related techniques need to be brought into play to unearth realities about communities so as to facilitate participation.

A fourth pattern observable in community health projects relates to participation. Most such projects usually include community participation as a strategy in project implementation. I suggest that the phrase 'community participation' is a misnomer. Although it is now commonly employed in health and other development, its use implies that the community is only an objective, a receptacle, for ideas, techniques and materials. There is an implicit assumption that people other than community members hold the primary responsibility in developing the communities. While this view may not be stated overtly, it is implied not only in the use of the phrase but also in the control of the development process itself as indicated elsewhere in this paper. Use of the phrase indicates an unequal power relationship between development agencies and personnel as opposed to the community. It is taken for granted that communities should 'accept' the views, approaches and materials controlled and disbursed by agencies or government. This is what Paulo Freire (1972) has called the 'banking' concept of development. In my view, the question of community participation should not arise, since communities should decide who or what they require to enhance their own development. It is health workers and others from outside the community who should be invited to participate in community development. If this view is accepted, it would imply that communities would be supported and encouraged to hold the responsibility for making decisions about their own destiny. Development agencies and personnel should, in this scheme, play a supportive rather than a directing and controlling role in development.

Medical Anthropology in Community Health Development

The existence of the three major issues relating to community health development in Kenya points to the need for social scientists to be involved in the process. A case for such involvement has been made ably by Eisenberg and Kleinman (eds) (1981). In this section the role of medical anthropology in community health development is examined.

Anthropological involvement in public health development on a large scale started in the 1950s. At that time, the major role of anthropologists in health programmes was seen to lie in isolating cultural barriers to the acceptance of new public-health interventions. The aim was to use anthropologists to help governments and health personnel to overcome resistance to change grounded in traditional values, institutions and practices (Hoben 1982). During the 1960s, the number of anthropologists involved in health programmes declined, largely due to the shift away from community development and towards technology transfer. In the health field, the emphasis shifted to hospital-based services and other areas requiring the application of advanced medical technology (Coreil 1990: 6). Anthropologists were not regarded as important in the process. From the mid-1970s to date, anthropologists have become more and more involved in health-development activities. This has been facilitated by two major developments: the increased interest in traditional medicine and the Alma Ata Declaration which called for more community participation in development. Recently, anthropologists have made important contributions to health development because of their interest in the role of women, community participation and child-survival intervention in community health.

Although anthropologists involved in health development use quantitative and epidemiological methods, the strength of the discipline is still seen to lie in the qualitative, in-depth methods it employs. It should be noted that the qualitative label has also led to anthropology being viewed as a weak or soft discipline which has yet to make any significant impact on health policy and planning (Pelto, Bentley and Pelto 1990).

While it is now widely acknowledged that social sciences have an important role to play in community health development, it is my view that applied anthropology possesses a number of comparative advantages in dealing with community health issues. The fulcrum of anthropology is its people-centered approach to community life. This approach, together with the discipline's interest in epic perspectives, can facilitate effective community involvement in health programmes. As indicated earlier, current perspectives on community participation are based on the external control of health-development processes. By stressing the power and organizational structures in communities and local potential for programme implementation, anthropology can facilitate a type of people-centered health development which is based on community decision-taking and control over health matters. It is also possible to envisage the development of health services which are more responsive to community needs through the sensitization of health-care providers using anthropological knowledge on the basis of health-seeking behaviour.

Because of its interest in the study of pluralistic health systems, anthropology has helped to explode the myth of 'hierarchy of resort' in community health-seeking. The discipline has opened the door to the study of various therapeutic alternatives, both indigenous and cosmopolitan. There is an ever-increasing need for anthropologists to help transform the rhetorical support for indigenous health services into action. Attempts have been made in Kenya to use herbalists and traditional birth attendants to deliver basic PHC services, including family-planning. At experimental level, this initiative has worked quite well but has yet to be fully institutionalized in official health services. Anthropological methodology is well suited to the explication of the human, material and conceptual bases of indigenous health services. Anthropological studies of indigenous health resources is gathering momentum and could be sharpened and expanded to include explorations into planning and policy matters.

Anthropology as a tool in health development has an overwhelming advantage over other social sciences in terms of its holistic approach to human thought and action. Anthropology seeks to explain human thought, organization and behaviour within the broader context of socio-economic conditions. This holistic approach enables the discipline to focus on the context of community health development and the diverse and wide range of possible interventions. Other social sciences tend to focus on the search for simple 'human-factor' solutions which do not entail changes in the socio-economic status quo nor even the reorganization of health-care (Coreil 1990: 17).

Anthropology can help planners, health-care providers and development personnel guard against the concept of the magic bullet syndrome which is rapidly gaining currency in developing countries. Anthropology seeks to address the totality of structures, concepts and materials which require modification in order for improvements in health conditions to occur. Such an approach moves away from the 'technologic intervention' view so common in the 1970s. 'Development with a human face', as espoused by Charnel, Chambers and others, resonates with the anthropologist's concern for the emic perspective of people's community lives.

While anthropology may have the advantages and methodology to handle a number of community health matters, the discipline faces a number of constraints which stem largely from its very nature. I will discuss three of these obstacles.

In the first place, anthropology is still regarded as the 'don't disturb the people' discipline. In the minds of most planners, health and other development personnel, the discipline belongs in the same class as classical music and fine art, implying that it possesses little practical value. Because of this misconception, hardly any resources are set aside for anthropological inputs into community health projects. Health providers in particular often dismiss anthropology as non-technical and only turn to it when cultural barriers to community health development need to be explained. Anthropology needs, therefore, to provide itself with a better track record of effective inputs into health programmes.

Secondly, anthropology is still seen as a 'soft' discipline because of its qualitative approach. Many development experts believe that quantitative information is of more value than qualitative. Although the discipline has incorporated quantitative and epidemiological techniques, it is still lumped with literature in terms of its intellectual contribution to development. Two comments about this view are relevant here. First, social knowledge, whether quantitative or qualitative, is critical to the success of health (or other) development. There is a need for anthropologists to 'sell' the value of the social knowledge they 'discover' so that it is accepted as a relevant contribution to development.

Thirdly, anthropology is viewed by many people as a discipline which takes a long time before the results of studies are seen, and also as a largely theoretical rather than an applied discipline. To a large extent this is true. However, during the last two decades, anthropologists have exhibited much interest in the application of anthropological knowledge and skills to the solution of human health (and other) problems. There is room for more work in this area. The evolution of applied forms of anthropology such as the Rapid Assessment (anthropological) Procedure (RAP) is a step in the right direction. RAP, a condensed form of anthropology, is now widely used in HIV/AIDS work, nutrition and in a number of primary health-care programmes. Mainstream anthropologists still regard RAP as an upstart, but it seems to be making major inroads into the community health development arena.

In conclusion, there is a need to state that anthropology as a discipline – or in the case of health, medical anthropology – can occupy an important niche in community health development, as has been argued above. Medical anthropology has developed primarily as an applied branch of the main discipline, but as yet it lacks a clear theoretical basis. However, with the publication of numerous books and papers in the subdiscipline and the strengthening of journals, as with the Medical Anthropology section of *Social Science and Medicine*, the development of the appropriate conceptual framework is only a matter of time. It is also important to mention here that for those of us who hail from developing countries, applied anthropology and especially medical anthropology is a more attractive alternative than conventional anthropology. This is so because the people and issues studied happen to be within our living environment and do not pertain to 'other cultures'.

References

Chambers, E.J. and P.D. Young (1979), 'Mesoamerican Community Studies: The Past Decade', *Annual Review of Anthropology*, 8: 45–70.

Chambers, R. (1992), *Rural Appraisal: Rapid, Relaxed and Participatory*, University of Sussex: Institute of Development Studies (IDS Discussion Papers 311).

Coreil, J. (1990), 'The Evolution of Anthropology in International Health', in J. Coreil and D.J. Mull (eds), *Anthropology and Primary Health Care*, Boulder: Westview Press.

Eisenberg, L. and A. Kleinman (eds) (1981), *The Relevance of Social Science for Medicine*, Dordrecht, Boston and London: D. Reidel Publishing Company.

Freire, P. (1972), *The Pedagogy of the Oppressed*, Harmondsworth: Penguin.

Government of Kenya (1987), *District Focus for Rural Development*, Nairobi: Government Printers.

Hoben, A. (1982), 'Anthropologists and Development', *Annual Review of Anthropology*, 11: 349–75.

Nyamwaya, D.O. (1982), *African Indigenous Medicine: An Anthropological Perspective on PHC Managers*, Nairobi: AMREF.

Pelto, J.P., E.M. Bentley and H.G. Pelto (1990), 'Applied Anthropology Research Methods: Diarrhoea Studies as an Example', in J. Coreil and D.J. Mull (eds), *Anthropology and Primary Health Care*, Boulder: Westview Press.

Chapter 9

Towards an Ethnography of Participatory Appraisal and Research

Johan Pottier

Drawing on recent experience with directing a series of participatory workshops[1] on food security in Africa, in this chapter[2] I argue that the level of participation in such workshops depends by and large on a country's politico-intellectual climate. This climate may favour or thwart critical questioning by 'ordinary' citizens. More generally, occasions for participatory appraisal and research are shown to be structured encounters marked by hidden agendas and strategic manoeuvres, no matter how informal and relaxed the set-up may appear to outsiders. Against this backdrop, I argue that anthropologists must continue to be detached observers. A commitment to participatory appraisal and research must not tempt anthropologists away from every conventional task and role. Especially, they must continue to contextualize research activities and events, reflect on how knowledge is produced and write it all down as reflexive ethnography.

Challenging Research Orthodoxy

Anthropologists in development know that collaborative research has become imperative on at least two levels. The first is that of research itself, where, on the basis of identified problems of development, social and natural scientists have begun to work in tandem. This is common now in research on agricultural development (de Boef, Amanor and Wellard eds 1993; Moock and Rhoades 1992). The second level, and here the debate is more recent, regards the actual field site where academic 'researchers', 'policy makers', 'informants' and 'ordinary people' have begun to work together in the search for solutions (Chambers 1992a, 1992b). It is the latter level with which this chapter is concerned.

Regarding the practice of field-level research, and indeed most types of research, the core challenge is that the extractive orientation must be reversed. The standard practice is for outsiders to come in and do *their* research *on* people, after which they take away *their* data for analysis *elsewhere*. Ethically and methodologically, this practice is suspect. That such extractive orientation can no longer be justified is already understood in (some) development circles, especially by professionals concerned with food security. The challenge now is to work towards decentralized planning and to re-focus research priorities and practice. Food security planning, Maxwell argues (1992: 11–12), must 'begin with the diversity and complexity of food insecurity as experienced by the food insecure themselves. The primary focus needs to be on individuals and households who lack, or fear they may lack, secure access to enough food at all times for an active, healthy life'. In methodological terms, the forecast is that '[more] modest approaches to food security planning, as a process and often with a strong local government component, are likely to be more successful than over-centralized, top-down models. Food security planning should *foster data collection, planning and action with the communities on which people depend*' (ibid.: 12; emphasis added).

Participatory research is particularly desirable in relation to food security, a policy area where urban and rural poor still have little or no say. As McMillan highlights in her introduction to *Anthropology and Food Policy* (1991), poor people may even lack the information to understand which policies affect them.

> One important aspect of studying food and hunger at the grassroots is that one quickly discovers that most people have no understanding of the nature of the policies – or even the existence of the policies – which by and large determine how and what they eat . . . .. Local people have virtually no idea what determines the prices they receive for their products or the types of food they find in the market place. Also impressive is the fact that these same local people have virtually no participation in the policy-making process that determines market prices and products . . . .. It seems to the authors in this volume that for people to take a more active role in determining what food policies they want, a more adequate foundation of information and analysis is necessary (1991: 2–3).

McMillan calls upon fellow anthropologists to step in as mediators. Anthropologists are ideally placed:

> Starting from a base of extensive anthropological fieldwork . . . an anthropologist can talk about food preferences and how mal-nourishment occurs within a family or community context and can raise questions from this base about the nature of national and international food policies which, unknown to local consumers, directly affect their well-being and, indeed, their social and political lives (ibid.: 2).

This local lack of understanding and control has provided the ideological and practical underpinnings on which the Food Systems Under Stress (FSUS) collaborative research programme was launched in 1993 (Pottier 1993, 1994b). The programme began with an exploratory workshop involving social and natural scientists interested in local-level research on food (in)security, then led to a series of participatory workshops on local-level perceptions of food stress, which resulted in a further conference (Pottier 1995). The immediate and longer-term challenges which the FSUS group has taken on were agreed from the onset: food-insecure people must participate in research, as partners working with (elite) academic researchers and (elite) policy-makers, with a view to co-authoring the policies that affect their lives. As with project evaluations, the group acknowledged the need to build up 'local knowledge repositories to support sustainable development' (Honadle and Cooper 1990: 188). All too often, what is learned from project evaluations, mostly carried out by outsiders to the project, is not appreciated by those running the project and therefore not incorporated into implementation actions or policy thrusts (ibid.: 186). The proposed solution is to design ways in which project beneficiaries can take a full part in evaluation not just by offering opinion and insight, but by becoming engaged in the research process and through learning from analysis.

The full Food Systems Under Stress (FSUS) programme aims to contribute to the development of social awareness in food-security planning by providing an avenue for collaboration between African researchers, policy-makers and food-insecure rural producers. On a modest scale, the programme encourages research into the food crisis as it is lived and perceived by food-insecure groups and individuals. It focuses on how their views can be used to help realize the transition from top-down to more decentralized approaches to food security planning.

In 1993, FSUS participatory workshops were organized in five African countries, Uganda, Tanzania, Zambia, Zimbabwe and Botswana. They aimed to collect baseline data on local perceptions of food stress at the community and the household level; to start involving local people in policy matters by inviting them to formulate proposals for future action research on food (in)security.

Established Views on Participatory Appraisal and Research

An important argument against continuing the practice of extractive field research is 'the growing recognition by professionals of the obvious fact that rural people [are] themselves knowledgeable on many subjects that [touch] their lives' (Chambers 1992a: 4). Most strongly developed by RRA/PRA practitioners, the participatory approach aims

> to enable rural people to do their own investigations, to share their knowledge and teach us [the 'outsiders'] to do the analysis and presentations, to plan and to own the outcome. In a PRA, knowledge is articulated and generated in more participatory ways; in which interviewing, investigations, transects, mapping and diagramming, presentation and analysis are carried out more by the rural people themselves; *in which they 'own' more of the information; in which they identify the priorities* (ibid.: 5; emphasis added).

The new thinking on appraisal and research correctly portrays the 'outside' researcher as a socially determined being, an actor who, no matter how sympathetic to the cause of development and the plight of the poor, also has prejudices, aspirations and privileges to defend. The formerly presumed value-free researcher thus joins the developers, bureaucrats and policy elite and becomes a potential class obstacle to development (see e.g. Keesing 1990: 69).

Today, fieldworkers are only too aware that they are part of the research scene, not detached from it. They are social actors endowed with an array of attributes and biases that influence the nature and outcome of their social inquiries (Long and Long eds 1992; Wilson 1993: 181). Barnes already argued the point thirty years ago:

[The] division between those under the microscope and those looking scientifically down the eyepiece has broken down. There may still be an exotic focus of study but the group or institution being studied is now seen to be embedded in a network of social relations of which the observer is an integral if reluctant part (1967: 197).

In line with the current development emphasis on *Putting People First* (Cernea 1990: 10) or *Putting The Last First* (Chambers 1983), the role of anthropology has been recast in terms of the researcher's greater responsibility towards the research community. If research is to be ethical, it no longer suffices merely to want to 'protect' the informants and the host community. The researcher now has a duty to reciprocate, and responsibilities continue until well after the fieldwork itself. One way in which reciprocal relations can be met is through enabling local groups to regain control over and responsibility for their own resources (Bennett 1990: 193). Anthropologists should 'do their best to bring local expertise into contact with the planners' (ibid.: 185). The challenge is fraught with notions of hierarchy and paternalism (postmodern stumbling blocks in recent discussions on ethics and anthropological fieldwork; cf. Fluehr-Lobban 1991, 1996), yet research 'with people' cannot continue if the need for reciprocity is not addressed.

The new research ethics distinguishes between the 'products' of research (data, analysis) and the 'process' of research, with the former 'objects of research' now receiving more credit for their routinely unrecognized contributions as researchers. Field research really is an ethical minefield requiring a good deal of reflexivity. It is erroneous, for example, to assume that a single, 'true' version of reality might be possible. Fieldworkers can only hope to produce their own best 'true' version, along with a full exposure of their own biases and shortcomings. Researchers also know they must take greater care not to reify the particular version(s) of reality formulated by particular informants. Instead, 'many voices' need to be listened to and articulated, even when, or especially when, these voices are in conflict. It has finally dawned that 'there is no single, authentic, indigenous voice or reality that the researcher can discover and present to the world' (Wilson 1993: 181). Increasingly forced to drop the 'authoritative', 'lone-ranger' approach to fieldwork and text (for a milestone discussion, see Owusu 1978), anthropologists have begun to acknowledge that one of their primary tasks is to enable the consumers of ethnography 'to hear the voices and appreciate the actions of as many of the different people involved as possible' (Wilson ibid.).

But some want to go further still. Once it is recognized that the 'many voices' are capable of doing their own analysis, it becomes ethically incorrect to deny these 'voices' their rightful status as 'analysts'. Helping build that capacity for analysis is one new challenge for the fieldworker of today. The challenge involves opening up communication lines with the powers that be: policy-makers, bureaucrats, politicians, sometimes even academics.

Participatory Workshops

In the remainder of this chapter, I first provide a window on the analytic capabilities of the former 'objects of research', capabilities which anthropologists have begun to appreciate. Then follows a critical sketch of certain FSUS workshop activities and discourses (Case Studies 1 and 2), in which I build up an ethnographic account of what I believe happened 'in reality'. In so doing I show, first, that the people who attend participatory workshops (the villagers, the community workers, the policy-makers, the facilitators) are a highly diversified group, and secondly, that there is more at stake for participating anthropologists than a simple recording of the plurality of voices.

Specifically, I argue that facilitators too work with assumptions, have opinions, have agendas. Taking 'the facilitator' to be an actor, I ask reflexive questions and invite those who facilitate in participatory workshops to look at their own identities and roles. Can facilitators live with that self-questioning, uneasy conscience so familiar to anthropologists working in development? The crux of the matter is how to reconcile the desire to intervene (often justified as an attempt to ease the burden of rapid change) with the desire to protect the integrity and self-determination of human groups (Bennett 1990: 185). In lifting the veil on the politics of participatory workshops, I suggest that participatory research practices must move in the direction taken by interpretative anthropology (see e.g. Holy 1984). Facilitators must strive critically to appreciate the overall context in which participatory develop-ment, including PRA workshops, is situated.

The workshop ethnographies presented here derive from the 1993 Food Systems Under Stress workshops (for a full account, see Pottier ed. 1995). In the Uganda FSUS workshop, participants witnessed an interesting incident during which research *product* and research *process* intersected. It began with a discussion on why millet grows well near swamps, when one Mr Obi, a much respected 'big farmer', volunteered a lesson in how to grow millet successfully. He offered the group data and analysis (*product*), along with his recipe for success. He was challenged, however, in a way which brought home the importance of the search for data, the re-search *process*.

Mr Obi shared his thoughts on millet, saying that after he had lost his bulls during raids by Karimojong, he picked up the hoe and started digging. This he did mostly with the help of his wife and children, but *timing* was of the essence.

> My wisdom is that I start preparing my land in December, so that by the end of January I am already sowing millet. The seeds are left in the soil until the rains come. I also make the garden very clean before sowing. And, as soon as the rains come, I plant groundnuts in a different field when others are just starting their millet cultivation. Then, as soon as possible, I prepare a third garden for potatoes. This is the order in which I grow my crops. When you delay broadcasting millet until the rains have started, the germination will be poor.

Mr Obi gave two reasons for poor germination: a) the soil is cold; b) continuous rain chokes the seeds and prevents germination. With early planting, in contrast, germination is fast and cannot be destroyed by the impact of the rain. When asked, 'what is your advice for those who cannot copy you?', Mr Obi replied: 'It depends on one's decision; we are responsible for our own affairs.'

Hearing this, a woman farmer challenged him. Speaking for other women too, she said: 'The problem with early planting is that a lot of weeds sprout up, which is not the case when you delay until the rains start.' She implied that Mr Obi's method might be the best, but that farmers need access to sufficient labour power if they are to weed thoroughly. And most farmers in the workshop area simply do not command a sufficiently large labour pool. What was impressive was this farmer's awareness of how food insecurity is best understood as a problem rooted in social inequalities that restrict access to labour.

Although short, the intervention added a full social chapter to

Mr Obi's wisdom, the kind of analysis that fieldworkers might end up appropriating as their own. In other workshops too, skilful facilitation regularly resulted in good analysis, for example, when women in Zambia argued that analysts must look simultaneously at food markets and labour markets (Pottier 1994b). Skilful facilitation, it will now be shown, is also a prerequisite for building or restoring people's confidence in agricultural extension. Facilitation can foster open dialogue, as in Case Study 1, or may reinforce the status quo, as in Case Study 2.

The Political Culture of Information-sharing and Dialogue.
Case Study 1: Talking about Cassava (Wera-Angole, Uganda)

Besides the loss of their cattle and rice crop, the people of Wera-Angole (Soroti District) were having to cope with cassava mosaic. Extension workers were now advising that any diseased cassava must be uprooted, but farmers were still reluctant to do this. What to do about cassava became a focus of the Uganda workshop.

Early in the workshop, participants had told the Assistant District Agricultural Officer (ADAO) about stiga (*amoto*), a weed new to the area. They wondered about its emergence and spread. The ADAO explained that the weed was typical of overcultivated, unfallowed land, especially when sorghum or millet are grown. The connection between the spread of stiga and changes in cultivation became very apparent during a transect walk. Farmers were impressed that the ADAO visited the fields and that *his* theory and *their* reality linked up. The walk also resulted in a discussion of the new mosaic-resistant cassava variety introduced two years earlier. Farmers were glad to have a chance to discuss this variety, which, they complained, was not totally resistant in second-generation crops. The ADAO agreed that the new variety was not perfect, pointing out that the one which was fully resistant had a high cyanide content. 'This is dangerous, because people like eating cassava raw.'

During the transect walk we spotted the whitish amphids that transmit the mosaic virus. The ADAO's explanation of the behaviour of amphids helped farmers appreciate the need for uprooting all the infected plants. Farmers, in turn, explained how they thought the infection came via the soil, but now (they said) they understood it was different. Asked whether spraying would get rid of the amphids, the ADAO replied that this would just drive them temporarily into the grass. To this farmers responded that, from now on, they would uproot more willingly. The ADAO also learned there were two reasons why farmers remained reluctant to uproot. First, the disease is not visible in the early stages. Secondly, even when attacked by mosaic, cassava still yields something. The ADAO indicated he now understood farmer reluctance better.

Whether uprooting will become the norm is not the main issue here. Farmers are unlikely to change their behaviour until the new mosaic-resistant varieties become less toxic. The point, however, is that a dialogue was achieved in which both parties listened to each other without imposing their own views. Because the ADAO seemed genuinely interested in farmers' views, his visit *may* have laid the foundation for a more open-ended, participatory collaboration in future. While some other local government workers came in for heavy criticism during this workshop, the ADAO's aptitude for *learning with farmers* was appreciated by everyone who attended. He had clearly come to the workshop to learn and advise, not to *teach them*.

Although certain themes were not explored (see Pottier and Orone 1995), the participatory set-up in Wera-Angole encouraged open discussion. Why? Several reasons can be suggested. For a start, the frankness may have had something to do with the long years of war. With so many men killed and cattle raided, the people of Wera-Angole have nothing to lose from non-violent confrontation. At some point, the PRA team was reminded of its promise that there would be no victimization: 'We are happy that this should indeed be the case,' people said. Soroti had been a 'rebel district' until 1991. A second factor could be that the village had had a secondary school in pre-war days. This had given many villagers a good command of English. Being articulate in at least two languages including English (the language of government), people were confident that their voices would be heard. This confidence was boosted by the presence on the PRA team of a Deputy Minister who is also a researcher. Thirdly, workshop exchanges benefited from the current climate of honesty which the Ugandan government encourages. Its leadership style puts a premium on constructive dialogue and accountability, as exemplified in the ADAO's approach to learning.

**The Political Culture of Information-sharing and Dialogue.
Case Study 2: Talking about Maize (Magindu, Tanzania)**

Magindu's history (and reason for its selection as a site for collaborative research) is a succession of well-remembered droughts and famines. Participants recalled the famine of 1975–76 when many people moved to Bagamoyo, the 1977–79 drought when people migrated again, the 1984–85 drought when many moved to Chalinze and Dar es Salaam, and the 1990–91 drought and hunger which were exceptionally severe. In Magindu, land is a limiting factor. Some land is fertile, but most is dry and suitable only for grazing.

The day before the Tanzania FSUS team set off for Magindu, I recalled the frankness of the Wera-Angole workshop. I particularly recalled how inefficient local-government workers had been criticized, even summoned before the workshop. The Tanzania team leader responded that such frankness would not be possible in his country, since the act of taking local-government workers to task would lead to post-workshop reprisals. He explained that anything so sensitive as evaluating the performance of, say, the agricultural extension staff would need to be done anonymously.

That it would be difficult to create transparent conditions became clear the moment the team met the *selected* participants. So many minor officials had turned up that the workshop's non-Tanzanian facilitators immediately wondered how 'ordinary voices' would be articulated. Participants included the District Agricultural Officer (DAO), the District Community Development Officer (DCDO), the Deputy Ward Chairman, the Ward Secretary, the Ward Education Co-ordinator (who is also the Ward Executive), the Ward Agricultural Officer, the Ward Health Officer, one Ward Councillor, one woman health-worker, a woman representing women's groups, one elder, one shopkeeper, two Maasai livestock keepers (men) and four men representing their village settlements. When the PRA team commented on the absence of women, two more women joined, followed by another two the following day. Also conspicuous by their absence were young people, who were represented by an elder.

Following a short discussion among the FSUS/PRA team, smaller groups were formed in such a way that each had a range of representatives. The groups dealt with (and were referred to as): Natural Resources; Farming Systems; Socio-Economic Issues. Their composition was fixed throughout the workshop, and they worked separately. There was no reporting back between the groups at the end of the day. Only in the final plenary session did all participants reconvene. By contrast, the FSUS/PRA team exchanged findings and impressions at the end of each day. What follows are selected highlights from the discussions, the 'research journey' (de Vries 1992). These aim to demonstrate not only how exchanges between PRA facilitators need to be situated in their proper context, but also how such exchanges can result in genuine learning experiences.

At the end of the first day, the rapporteur for the 'Farming Systems' group summarized what was learned during the transect walk. As the group included both the DAO and the Ward Agricultural Officer (referred to as *Bwana Shamba*), its attention had soon turned to the question of maize:

> We were interested in what types of crops are grown in the area, which we deduced from the remains of crops we saw in the fields, such as maize, sorghum, simsim, pigeon peas . . .. These were either intercropped or grown pure stand. Regarding our observation that there were many empty spaces between plots, farmers explained they practise shifting cultivation, as plots are depleted after about three years. We inquired about crop rotations (e.g. maize this year, simsim next year and sorghum in year three), but the answer was negative.

As the discussion unfolded, it became clear that the 'Farming Systems' group's main concern had been to find out whether Magindu farmers followed extension workers' advice on crop selection for semi-arid areas. The team had set the terms for the discussion rather than allowing farmers to do so:

> We asked them a question. 'We know that two years ago there was a serious famine in this area. What were the possible causes for this?' They said it was due to rainfall shortages, which is something that repeats itself every three years. But the agriculturalists were smart enough to say there were other causes . . .. They said they had very poor tools for farming, and referred especially to the hand hoe, with which you can do little. Someone else suggested another cause: the depleted soils, because of which people need to shift. This contributes to famine conditions.

At this point, *Bwana Shamba* remarked that Tanzania is divided into agro-ecological zones and that each zone has been allocated specific crops that are suited to it. Since the workshop area has insufficient rainfall, the Ministry of Agriculture recommends that drought-resistant crops be grown, especially sorghum and cassava. 'Unfortunately,' the *Bwana Shamba* added, 'in this area [Magindu] people do not want to grow sorghum or cassava. Sorghum has no taste, so they much prefer maize – which fails from one year to the next!' The rapporteur agreed:

> With the most recent failure of the crops, the area here was badly hit, because [people] did not grow the recommended crops; they grew something else, maize. In contrast, a neighbouring village, Lukenge, never experienced any famine at all. Lukenge villagers grew cassava and sorghum, as recommended by government.

As there was still some confusion within the PRA group about where all these crops were grown, one team member (TM1) and principal facilitator offered some background information:

> We learned that during the cultivation season people move to where their farms are, taking their property and children. The distance is long. People leave in March and return in July after the first harvests, when repairs begin or new structures are erected. [The distant fields are still within the village boundary.]

The DAO then recalled that the main crops (simsim, maize and some sorghum and cassava) are grown in those distant fields away from the village centre.

The *Bwana Shamba*'s words were taken at face value, the team arrived at a shared understanding on maize. Without visiting the more distant fields, the team agreed at the end of Day One that maize dominated the local production system at the expense of sorghum and cassava, and that the villagers' obsession with maize had been the main human cause of the 1990–1991 famine.

The participatory activities on Day Two, however, revealed a different picture when a facilitator from Zambia (TM2) worked with villagers to construct a 'Seasonal Availability of Food' calendar. This gave the following results (Table 9.1):

Table 9.1.

Season	Availability
time of cultivation (January–March)	sorghum declining little maize
time of planting (March–April) time of weeding (April–May) time of moving to the temporary residences (May–June)	sorghum depleted
time of harvesting (July–August)	cassava much eaten sorghum in plenty maize available rice available
time of land clearing (September–December)	sweet potato-snacking sorghum in plenty maize available rice available

Villagers commented that sorghum and maize were eaten on a daily basis except during the hungry season, but that *maize was grown only on a small scale.* Cassava, not much liked, was eaten only when nothing else was available, while rice was only eaten on festival days.

A discussion of local intercropping regimes confirmed that maize was not grown extensively. Villagers mentioned that the following were common: sorghum with cassava (preferred by the government); pigeon peas with sorghum; green gram with maize; ochra with sorghum or maize; simsim with sorghum. The rationale for these combinations was also discussed: cassava with sorghum reduced the risk of crop failure; the other combinations were labour-saving strategies.

That maize was grown only on a small scale, *a conclusion which contradicted what the team 'knew' at the end of Day 1,* also emerged from the discussion on crop-soil associations, and was reinforced further through information obtained from a 'Crop Preference Matrix'. The latter showed beyond doubt that maize, a hugely popular food, was grown in only small quantities when compared with sorghum. Farmers restricted maize as a field crop because of post-harvest storage losses, the crop's poor resistance to drought, diseases and pests, and the demands on labour, especially during weeding. The maize they consumed was predominantly maize they bought.

At the end of Day Two, the PRA team should have concluded that the people of Magindu like eating maize but that it was not extensively grown. Despite the new information, however, the team leader (and team) stuck to the theory/assumption that Magindu had suffered severe hunger in 1990–91 because farmers had ignored the government policy on suitable crops.

The simplicity of a disaster narrative grounded in farmer ignorance and stubbornness remained attractive to the team, despite clear evidence to the contrary. With the benefit of hindsight, it is clear now that the team failed to spot the important contrast between, on the one hand, what it had learned/imagined during the walk on Day 1, which was that the villagers grew 'maize and some sorghum' (the official view) and, on the other, the information which local farmers provided on Day 2, which suggested that villagers grew 'sorghum and some maize'. This failure to respond to new evidence may be striking, yet it is not alien to the practice of PRA (cf. Mosse 1994) and is indeed common in the practice of environmental policy-making in Africa (see e.g. Hoben 1995; Leach and Mearns 1996; Moore and Vaughan 1994; Pottier 1996). The power and persistence of simple explanatory narratives were much in evidence at the end of Day Two. After failing to pay due attention to what 'ordinary people' had said about maize (as against sorghum), the team leader persisted with the theory/assumption arrived at on Day One.

Here is a fragment of the in-team discussion:

TM1:	In my group it was agreed that water was the major problem in the area. Transport came second, followed by food, medicine, low awareness of health issues, lack of drugs (for people and animals), crop destruction by Maasai animals, poorly equipped dispensary, poor houses, no milling machine, no latrines. We then discussed two of these in detail. First food. What causes shortages? I asked: what solutions (other than migration) could people think of?
Team Leader, interjecting:	Was anything said about the poor selection of crops? . . . I mention this because people here are trying their very best to hide the fact that the country is divided up in various agro-ecological zones and that there is

> sound government advice about what
> should be grown in terms of specific crops.
> This area has to grow drought-resistant
> crops. And that is what they do not do. And
> they did not want to mention that!

The interjection revealed much about the spirit in which the workshop was held. The team leader toed the official line, paying no attention to what people said about actual farming practices.

The poor quality of the analysis had implications for the so-called participatory search for solutions: local participants suggested only those solutions the PRA team wanted to hear. In doing so, they declared themselves guilty of ignorance or in need of education and other forms of assistance. The team showed little interest in discovering whether the local participants knew of any solutions that might replace those proposed by government. The following reflections bring this out:

> TM1: We asked if the causes of food shortage could be solved. People
> said bush fires were something they could control better. 'What
> we need is bylaws.' People also thought that more trees should
> be planted, but for this they needed saplings and water. This
> solution came from the teachers and the government workers,
> who said that planting trees would enhance rainfall. People
> also said there should be stricter control of illegal charcoal
> burning. On the misuse of food, the proposed solution is that
> whoever is in charge of educating people regarding good
> practices to do with food should instruct. Equally, to reduce
> alcohol abuse, more health education is needed. To reduce the
> destruction of crops by insects . . . insecticides are needed.
> People also said they would need to take more care to plant on
> time, within the appropriate seasons.

The ingrained message, that the masses are ignorant and the enlightened must teach them, also ran through the Team Leader's concluding thoughts on the supposed opposition to cassava:

> We asked about cassava. They said it is extremely unpalatable, which
> is why they do not like it. We asked what the solution could be.
> Someone said, 'Government should use force to make us grow it'.
> We asked, 'Are you really serious?' They said: 'we can swear, after
> years of famine, we are prepared to face force, we will adopt the
> recommendation for growing.'

By the time the FSUS team met for post-workshop reflections, it was clear that two opinions had formed within the team, that a rift had emerged. Some of the group still stood by the team leader's analysis (assumption), while others (TM2) were overcome by a sense of failure, a sense that the team had failed to distinguish between what the extension workers believed to be 'good practice' and the views of the villagers themselves. The difference of opinion came into the open when a team member challenged his colleagues.

> TM2: Whenever we asked for solutions, the people stressed government interventions. I am suspicious about this. Perhaps we should look at these 'solutions' more critically, perhaps the people associated us with Government policy.

This team member then asked: 'Could it be that there is a particular political culture at the root of all this self-blame?' TM1 agreed:

> People are used to being ordered about and they have forgotten about community development by their own efforts. This has created a passive attitude towards development, which is thought of as being 'brought' to the people by a donor.

That workshop participants should blame themselves for everything was an issue that slowly began to trouble the *entire* team. Members started thinking more deeply about the possibility that they themselves might have caused this self-blame, since they went along with the political culture that prohibits the articulation of 'disparate voices'. The team's long evening discussions were now paying off: the 'research journey' had begun. Researchers were showing greater awareness of how they influence the information they collect.

> TM2: We seem to have aided people in heaping up this blame upon themselves. *We* have agreed that *they* are not responsible, they don't build toilets, they get pregnant frequently and ignore the rules about growing drought-resistant crops . . . .. I really wonder what the cause of all this is. We must address this.

The Team Leader agreed: 'We should go further even and make sure that the issue of self-blame is included in our plans for long-term research.'

On reflection, the contrast between the two research experiences described here seems to be linked to the fact that the Tanzania team was more interested in collecting data (research *products*) than in bringing local people into the research *process*. In Wera-Angole, Uganda, both aspects of research were equally valued. The divergence may have roots in the fact that the two countries differ in terms of the leadership styles they foster, with open dialogue being an intrinsic part of the Uganda approach, while Tanzanian officials (extensionists, political leaders, researchers) prefer a top-down approach.

Participatory Workshops: Narrowing or Recreating Social Distance?

The case studies illustrate how discourse can be used to knock down or re-create social distance. On the basis of these illustrations, I wish to argue that anthropologists must not let go of their familiar roles, which are to provide context and ask epistemological questions. With reference to *all* the actors involved in participatory appraisal and research, facilitators included, the central anthropological question surely must be, why and how do people with different access to knowledge and power interact in the way they do? Despite the analytical insights that local actors contribute, it still takes an informed outsider, someone who can apply an anthropological perspective, to contextualize the research process and its outcome.

The problem with the Tanzania workshop was that its facilitators did not question their own preconceptions until after they left Magindu. During the workshop they had a mission to fulfil, had to do something about (for) those villagers they deemed ignorant and in need of education. It was an approach the villagers went along with. They agreed that government should 'punish if we digress', that they had specific medical or nutritional problems (the ones suggested by the team), that failure, including hunger, was clearly 'our fault; we blame ourselves!' The outsiders' diagnosis was their own, even though (or perhaps because) PRA team members were 'speaking patronizingly for others' (Torres 1992: 88). The outsiders did so because as academics they are part of a political universe from which they cannot easily establish a distance. They were not only part of the actual research scene, but also part of a specific political culture of development research.

The Magindu case study revealed further that PRA facilitators can create or reinforce 'boundaries between "us" and "them" in the ways they express themselves' (Seur 1992: 118; Fairhead 1993). The particular discourse of the facilitators at Magindu reinforced social distance and attempted to bring 'disparate voices' in line with their own dominant discourse as if all participants spoke with 'one voice'. Language was used to construct and legitimize particular sets of codes, rules and roles (Apthorpe 1986: 377). Hyped perhaps by the challenge of multiparty democracy and less autocratic approaches to rural development, certain facilitators set out to rationalize and reinforce the hegemony of their own way (the government way) of thinking.

Such an imposition may carry implicit threats. As Andrew Long puts it, 'Certain types of discourse may appear more persistent or forceful than others. They may, that is, have the backing of authoritative voices (e.g. the chief or central government) who can – though never absolutely – set the terms of the debate and apply certain sanctions on those in opposition' (1992: 168). Even a cursory look at the discourse of participatory workshops is an invitation to question the claim that workshops involving PRA become relaxed informal gatherings in which people speak freely (Chambers 1992b: 21–2). Anthropologists must conceptualize participatory workshops as structured events, as politico-intellectual exchanges on a continuum going from highly structured and backed by authoritative voices, to more interactive occasions in which multiple voices are encouraged.

That dominant discourses are difficult to quell, and that even the most 'open' workshops remain to some extent *formal and political in character*, was clearly conveyed in the 1993 FSUS workshop in Zimbabwe, during which local participants were invited to draw up a research agenda for the future. Local participants acknowledged a hierarchy of voices.

Facilitator: I was saying to you that if people should come from Harare and they wanted to research in the area, what would *you* want them to research on?

Woman: We have told you all our problems. Now we ask you to look into the issues that you would like to research on. [In plain language, she was urging that the facilitator and the team should make up their mind.]

Man: We do not know how we can help ourselves and we want you [researchers] to help us solve our problems. We want *you* to say, 'try this, try that'. And you must be prepared to meet resistance, because not all of us will agree with whatever is said here in this meeting. Let me say it again. We want money and can those in research find out why our children are not going to school?

Facilitator: Are there any other suggestions?

Man: We want to give you all our seeds so that you can go back and test them for us to find whether they are suitable for this area. Perhaps we are using the wrong seeds after all. We want you to test our soils, so we want you to look at our soils.

Facilitator: Any other questions? What about the women?

Woman: We cannot go into that area [of research], it is too big for us.

Reacting quickly and correctly, a Second Facilitator reassured her:

Women must remember that sometimes men speak about things they want as men. We saw it on the map [i.e. during resource mapping], when men demonstrated different things from women, so we want you women to show us which areas we should look into.

Man: We might be talking endlessly. Why cannot you tell us from your world of experience? You should be giving us examples about what you did in other areas rather than go on asking us. If you continue asking we shall become like sheep that have seen a dog!

The villagers' use of idiomatic language did the trick, and the team abandoned its attempt to discuss research as a more abstract category. It seemed they had reached deadlock, because the whole notion of 'having local people set the research agenda' remained alien to the locals. It was a situation very similar to the one Torres describes in rural Mexico, between himself (the researcher) and the local cane-cutters, during which certain shared understandings emerged along with messages that were at cross purposes and failed to bring about a response (1992: 109).

Whatever the PRA pundits say about 'relaxed settings', participatory workshops remain structured encounters marked by hidden agendas and strategic manoeuvres. Part of the problem is that facilitators do not have access to information on interactions before and after the workshop. In a participatory workshop there may well be an open discussion, for instance, between extension staff and certain participants, from which facilitators may then draw certain positive conclusions. But what happens once the facilitators leave? What was interesting in Zimbabwe (and this I know thanks to the excellent observations made by certain team members, and because I recalled an incident involving a smartly dressed visitor on the first day) was that a certain type of information – namely that district officials were already in possession of a proposal for more boreholes and might approve it – was deliberately kept from the FSUS/PRA team. The issue here could have been that there is 'public' knowledge and 'private' knowledge (Pottier 1994a), and that PRA facilitators must not imagine that the settings they create are always conducive to stimulating debate on issues deemed to be private.

Researchers involved in long-term fieldwork are aware that informants often withhold information, sometimes unconsciously. As Seur puts it: 'Actors do not always feel the need to detail the knowledge or resources they share or are supposed to share with others. Instead they tend to formulate partial statements, situationally relevant statements or give only the answers asked for' (1992: 141; cf. Holy and Stuchlik 1981: 22–3). This is understandable, because 'knowledge [is never] fully unified or integrated in terms of an underlying cultural logic or systems of classification. Rather, it is fragmentary, partial and provisional in nature, and people work with a multiplicity of understandings, beliefs and commitments' (Arce and Long 1992: 211–12; also Fairhead 1993). To understand this wider context in which knowledge is continually shaped and reshaped, long-term fieldwork is imperative.

Against the backdrop of the debate on participatory research, the anthropologists' challenge is twofold. First, they need to work harder to provide an active forum for the articulation of multiple voices, especially weaker ones. Anthropologists should not be content just to write about the voices of the weak. Secondly, when anthropologists take this challenge seriously, they will find that 'informants' often turn into good analysts, who must be given credit for their analytic contributions. However, as the second case study shows, the role of the anthropologist does not end here. The further challenge – and here the anthropologist steps back in as someone with a distinct identity – is to set all voices, including those of the facilitator-researchers, in their full social and political context. Researchers too, whether fieldworkers or workshop facilitators, must be contextualized because they too are social actors with ideologies, beliefs, values and agendas. As an interest group, they may side with others and (unconsciously?) attempt to validate their own viewpoints and positions.

To change the jargon, to turn 'researchers' into 'facilitators' and 'the researched' into 'fellow researchers', is a step in the right direction, but the task of finding out 'who's who?' in terms of access to knowledge and power does not evaporate as a result. Rather, the contrary holds: the harder PRA practitioners try to reduce social distances between 'them' and 'us', the more important it is not to assume that social distances would not exist locally. Outsiders may be uncomfortable about the 'them' and 'us' dichotomy, and with good reason, but to abolish the distinction does not mean that the highly diversified 'them' ceases to have meaning. Actors and opinions still need situating.

The challenge of participatory appraisal and research requires both a new ethical stance and a cool head. For a start, anthropologists must let go of certain pretences, privileges and claims to authoritative authorship. No longer can they claim always to be the sole creators of their data and analyses. The challenge involves moving away from an obsession with the exclusive value of 'the product' of research to paying more attention to finding ways in which more voices can be drawn into 'the process' of research. But here lies the paradox. When committed to participatory appraisal and research, anthropologists will become aware that someone must also reflect on the total context of the research process. I am not implying that only anthropologists can do this (see Garber and Jenden 1993), although, for the time being, they are comparatively well placed to take on the job of providing context to collaborative, participatory research activities. The paradox, then, is that in the act of giving up authoritative authorship, the anthropologist rediscovers the importance of holism and reflexivity, the familiar roles that give the anthropologist a distinct voice.

Notes

1. The term 'workshop' refers to a series of focus group meetings and plenary sessions for conducting preliminary research. Meetings were spread over three days. Stress factors in the food system of each area were identified through the use of participatory appraisal methods.
2. I wish to thank the International Development Research Centre (IDRC, Canada), the Ford Foundation and the School of Oriental and African Studies, University of London, for supporting the Food Systems Under Stress (FSUS) collaborative research project. I also sincerely thank the many colleagues involved in FSUS. The opinions in this chapter are, however, mine alone.

References

Apthorpe, R. (1986), 'Development Policy Discourse', *Public Administration and Development*, 6: 377–89.

Arce, A. and N. Long (1992), 'The Dynamics of Knowledge: Interfaces Between Bureaucrats and Peasants', in N. Long and A. Long (eds), *Battlefields of Knowledge: The Interlocking of Theory and Practice in Social Research and Development*, London: Routledge.

Barnes, J.A. (1967), 'Some Ethical Problems in Modern Field Work', in D.G. Jongmans and P.C.W. Gutkind (eds), *Anthropologists in the Field*, Assen: Van Gorcum.

Bennett, J.W. (1990), 'Anthropology and Development: The Ambiguous Engagement', in H.M. Mathur (ed.), *The Human Dimension of Development: Perspectives from Anthropology*, New Delhi: Ashok Kumar Mittal Concept Publishing Company.

Cernea, M. (1990), 'Putting People First: Social Science Knowledge for Development Interventions', in H.M. Mathur (ed.), *The Human Dimension of Development: Perspectives from Anthropology*, New Delhi: Ashok Kumar Mittal Concept Publishing Company.

Chambers, R. (1983), *Rural Development: Putting the Last First*, London: Longman.

—— (1992a), 'Participatory Rural Appraisal: Past, Present and Future', *Forests, Trees and People Newsletter*, 15/16: 1–9.

—— (1992b), *Rural Appraisal: Rapid, Relaxed and Participatory*, University of Sussex, Institute of Development Studies (IDS Discussion Papers 311).

de Boef, W., K. Amanor and K. Wellard (eds) (1993), *Cultivating Knowledge: Genetic Diversity, Farmer Diversification and Crop Research*, London: Intermediate Technology.

de Vries, P. (1992), 'A Research Journey', in N. Long and A. Long (eds), *Battlefields of Knowledge: The Interlocking of Theory and Practice in Social Research and Development*, London: Routledge.

Fairhead, J. (1993), 'Representing Knowledge: The "New Farmer" in Research Fashions', in J. Pottier (ed.), *Practising Development*, London: Routledge.

Fluehr-Lobban, C. (1991), 'Ethics and Professionalism: A Review of Issues and Principles in Anthropology', in C. Fluehr-Lobban (ed.), *Ethics and the Profession of Anthropology: Dialogue for a New Era*, Philadelphia: University of Pennsylvania Press.

—— (1996), 'Developing the new AAA Code of Ethics', *AAA Newsletter*, 37/4: 17.

Garber, B. and P. Jenden (1993), 'Anthropologists or Anthropology? The Band Aid Perspective on Development Projects', in J. Pottier (ed.), *Practising Development*, London: Routledge.

Hoben, A. (1995), 'Paradigms and Politics: The Cultural Construction of Environmental Policy in Ethiopia', *World Development*, 23/6: 1007–22.

Holy, L. (1984), 'Theory, Methodology and the Research Process', in R. Ellen (ed.), *Ethnographic Research: A Guide to General Conduct*, London: Academic Press.

—— and M. Stuchlik (eds) (1981), *The Structure of Folk Models*, London: Academic Press.

Honadle, G. and L. Cooper (1990), 'Closing the Loops: Workshop Approaches to Evaluating Development Projects', in K. Finsterbush, J. Ingersoll and L. Llewellyn (eds), *Methods for Social Analysis in Developing Countries*, Boulder: Westview Press (Social Impact Assessment Series, No. 17).

Keesing, R.M. (1990), 'Development Planning: An Anthropological Perspective', in M. H. Mathur (ed.), *The Human Dimension of Development: Perspectives from Anthropology*, New Delhi: Ashok Kumar Mittal Concept Publishing Company.

Leach, M. and R. Mearns (1996), 'Challenging Received Wisdom in African Environmental Change and Policy', in M. Leach and R. Mearns (eds), *The Lie of the Land*, London: James Currey.

Long, A. (1992), 'Goods, Knowledge and Beer: The Methodological Significance of Situational Analysis and Discourse', in N. Long and A. Long (eds), *Battlefields of Knowledge: The Interlocking of Theory and Practice in Social Research and Development*, London: Routledge.

Long, N. and A. Long (eds) (1992), *Battlefields of Knowledge: The Interlocking of Theory and Practice in Social Research and Development*, London: Routledge.

McMillan, D.E. (1991), 'Introduction', in D.E McMillan (ed.), *Anthropology and Food Policy: Human Dimensions of Food Policy in Africa and Latin America*, Athens and London: The University of Georgia Press for the Southern Anthropological Society.

Maxwell, S. (1992), 'Food Security in Africa: Priorities for Reducing Hunger', *Africa Recovery Briefing Paper*, 6: 1–12.

Moock, J.L. and R. Rhoades (eds) (1992), *Diversity, Farmer Knowledge and Sustainability*, Ithaca and London: Cornell University Press.

Moore, H. and M. Vaughan (1994), *Cutting Down Trees: Gender, Nutrition, and Agricultural Change in the Northern Province of Zambia, 1890–1990*, London: James Currey.

Mosse, D. (1994), 'Authority, Gender and Knowledge: Theoretical Reflections on the Practice of Participatory Rural Appraisal', *Development and Change*, 25/3: 497–525.

Owusu, M. (1978), 'Ethnography of Africa: The Usefulness of the Useless', *American Anthropologist*, 80: 310–34.

Pottier, J. (ed.) (1993), *African Food Systems under Stress: Issues, Perspectives and Methodologies*, Brighton: Desktop Display.

—— (1994a), 'Agricultural Discourses: Farmer Experimentation and Agricultural Extension in Urban Rwanda', in I. Scoones and J. Thompson (eds), *Beyond Farmer First*, London: IT Publications.

—— (1994b), 'Understanding Food Stress at Local Levels', in R. Vernooy and K.M. Kealey (eds), *Food Systems under Stress in Africa*, Ottawa: International Development Research Centre (IDRC).

—— (ed.) (1995), *African Food Systems under Stress (FSUS): Proceedings of the Second International Conference*, Brighton: Desktop Display.

—— and P. Orone (1995), 'Consensus or Cover-up? The Limitations of Group Meetings', *PLA Notes*, 24: 38–42.

—— (1996), 'Agricultural Rehabilitation and Food Insecurity in Post-war Rwanda: Assessing Needs, Designing Solutions', *IDS Bulletin*, 27/3: 56–76.

Seur, H. (1992), 'The Engagement of Researcher and Local Actors in the Construction of Case Studies and Research Themes: Exploring Methods of Restudy', in N. Long and A. Long (eds), *Battlefields of Knowledge: The Interlocking of Theory and Practice in Social Research and Development*, London: Routledge.

Torres (1992), 'Plunging into the Garlic: Methodological Issues and Challenges', in N. Long and A. Long (eds), *Battlefields of Knowledge: The Interlocking of Theory and Practice in Social Research and Development*, London: Routledge.

Wilson, K. (1993), 'Thinking about the Ethics of Fieldwork', in S. Devereux and J. Hoddinott (eds), *Fieldwork in Developing Countries*, Hemel Hempstead: Harvester Wheatsheaf.

Chapter 10

Alternative Vocabularies of Development? 'Community' and 'Participation' in Development Discourse in Sri Lanka

Michael D. Woost

Mainstream development in Sri Lanka has long been spearheaded by discourses about community, with the latter often being positioned as the motor of progress.[1] During the late 1980s and into the 1990s, the discourse about community has been complemented by an increasingly ubiquitous discourse about 'people's participation' and 'empowerment'. While community has by no means completely disappeared from public and private discourses on development, everyone, from village farmers to international donors, has begun to speak the language of 'participation' and 'empowerment'. Yet in many ways the discourses of participation and community are not all that dissimilar. Both make certain suppositions about how development and change are to occur, namely, through more democratic means. In one case development is supposed to occur through the movement of the community as a whole. In Sri Lanka, as in most other places, this community was generally equated with the village. Villages were assumed to act as a unit bringing about development. The advent of participatory discourses about empowering the people seems to take this apparent drive for democracy in development practice a step further, leaving open the possibility of many different forms of group and individual effort. Community participation is still an option, presumably, but there are supposed to be allowances and spaces created for people to create their own insertions into the development process. This is also supposed to give them a greater voice in the drive toward 'progress' and, yes, even in the debate over what 'progress' is supposed to mean.

The emergence of a participatory element in the authoritative discourses of development in Sri Lanka and elsewhere should undoubtedly be hailed as a good thing. However, one must keep in mind that participatory discourse, like the notions of community that preceded it, clearly has many different connotations, only some of which hold the possibility for a more 'bottom-up' debate about the social, economic and cultural arrangement of the present and the future (cf. Rahnema 1992). My contention, outlined below, is that the mainstream use of participatory rhetoric in Sri Lanka offers little in the way of alternative development. Rather, the notion of participation has been laundered and reshaped in official discourse to fit the mould of an increasingly ruthless drive to implement market-led development strategies intended quickly to turn Sri Lanka into a NIC (Newly Industrialized Country). What is more, the drive for NIC status has also significantly changed the way the rural community is envisaged in development discourse.

In what follows, I will describe these shifts in development discourse in Sri Lanka and how they are related to the implement-ation and acceleration of market-led/open economic strategies of development. In many ways, the shifts in discourse illustrated by the redefinition of community and participation represent attempts to smooth over some of the glaring contradictions that have emerged with the drive for NIC status. I will conclude by indicating how the official ideological and economic push has limited the activities of Sri Lanka's many NGOs (non-governmental organizations). Overall, my goal is to document how the insertion of an alternative vocabulary of development into mainstream discourse in Sri Lanka has actually done little to redefine the boundaries of 'community' and 'people's partici-pation' in ways that would positively undercut common people's sense of powerlessness on the terrain of development, or for that matter in their struggle for survival. In fact, it can be argued that the manner in which alternative vocabularies of development are incorporated has tended to reinforce mainstream notions about how progress can be achieved.

Community and the Discourse of Participation

While the vocabulary of alternative development may arguably have come late to Sri Lanka,[2] it has undergone a more long-term incorporation into mainstream discourse of the global development hierarchy. This incorporation began gradually in the late 1960s and by the early and mid 1970s was clearly evident in mainstream development, as can be seen in Robert McNamara's farewell speech as President of the World Bank 1973 (McNamara 1987). Now, in the 1990s, the vocabulary of alternative development, particularly that of 'people's participation', has been adopted at nearly all levels of the global development hierarchy. As one Sri Lankan development specialist noted recently, it is the 'citizen' or the people who hold centre stage 'in the development drama in the present historical period' (IRED 1991: ii).

The mainstream adoption of participatory discourse entails some important repositioning of both the subjects and the objects of development. In this regard, 'the people' seem to be replacing the idea of community as the motor behind development. Nevertheless, contrary to what one might expect, 'the people' appear more as an ideological apparition than a real presence in the process of development. What is more, the power 'they' are supposed to wield in development is anything but liberating. I will illustrate these points after a few words about the notion of 'community' in development discourse in Sri Lanka.

During the 1980s, the development terrain was populated by a host of public rituals that celebrated village community as the engine of development.[3] Much of this rhetoric reflected Sinhala Buddhist nationalist concerns to create a new future by 'reviving' the supposed social order of Sri Lanka's precolonial past. I say supposed, because nationalist constructions of the past are political representations that often have little resemblance to historical realities (Spencer ed.1993). In any case, the village community of the Sinhala Buddhist nationalist past is usually argued to have worked as a unit to provide food and shelter for all its members, without regard to status. While there were royal castes, the king functioned more as a facilitator of this village economy by following Buddhist doctrine and supporting the monks who maintained it. The king also supported public works that provided paddy farmers with water and other resources. The emphasis, then, was supposedly on the small paddy farmer, living with his family and surrounded by the essentials of village life: the irrigation tank, the temple and the paddy field.

Contemporary nationalists have contended that this ideal village community was undermined through colonial contact (Ariyaratne 1982). This is why there is so much poverty in the land. In short, the contention is that in order to have real development, one must 're-awaken' the ideal village community of the past which is believed to be lying dormant in the rural areas. For instance, farmers are often said to have an inborn capacity to engage in paddy farming, an ability apparently passed on to them by their precolonial ancestors. Some development officials I interviewed in the mid-1980s went so far as to claim that paddy cultivation flowed in the blood of Sinhala people. By this reasoning, present-day farmers only need to be provided with land and water and they will know what to do.

The goal, then, of development, from the mammoth Mahaweli irrigation system (Tennekoon 1988) to single village projects, was to provide needed resources by restoring the basic building blocks of village community: the irrigation tank, the temple and the paddy field. Once these resources were in the hands of farmers, a cultural reawakening of village communities across the island would inevitably follow. As one NGO official told me in 1985: 'Once a village is re-awakened, the people can do the work of giants.' In this way, 'participation' in development is defined as a community affair in which villagers rediscover their cultural roots and band together to usher in a national economic revolution. Without this revitalization of community, development is impossible.

This general scenario was in widespread use during the 1980s (Brow 1988, 1990; Woost 1990, 1993) and still pervades development discourse in Sri Lanka. Nevertheless, the official drive for NIC status has necessitated a repositioning of community as well as the subject of development in ways that smooth over the many contradictions entailed in this drive. Additionally, the emergent voices of protest against this development strategy[4] and the outright failure of some massive development projects[5] have affected the way in which people's participation in development is officially envisioned. Further impacting on the reconstruction of development discourse is the fact that international donor institutions from the World Bank down have jumped on the participatory bandwagon. With donors linking their funds to some demonstration of increased people's participation, it is also no surprise that participatory rhetoric has become integral to the ideological legitimations of official development strategies. In short, these historical trends have together engendered a reformulation of development that more fully incorporates a concept of participation, but one that does not detract from the effort to establish a market-led form of development. So, before further discussion of the ideological shifts alluded to thus far, I will provide some details about the drive for NIC status.

The Open Economy and NIC Status

The drive for NIC status in Sri Lanka is geared toward rapid industrialization and the expansion of agribusiness ventures. Successive Sri Lankan governments have contended that it is possible for the country to convert its sagging agricultural economy into an industrial/export economy on a par with Singapore and Hong Kong in the very near future.[6] Toward that end, the UNP (United National Party) government has initiated various strategies encouraging private investment from home and abroad. These include leasing out lands under the large irrigation schemes constructed over the last decade and a half to corporations interested in agribusiness (this includes the Mahaweli projects as well as land in the sparsely populated southeastern hinterland). Many of these agriventures produce export commodities like sugar and pineapple. This investment strategy has been coupled with the privatization of state industries and services, including transport and tea. This effort has officially been referred to as 'peoplization', a term which is supposed to mark the fact that these industries and services are being 'returned' to the people, albeit in the form of stock (USAID recently contributed funds and technical assistance in setting up a stock exchange in Sri Lanka). Turning over these industries to investors is also said to be a more democratic endeavour.[7]

The most recent, and probably most important, of all NIC strategies is one in which the entire island was declared to be an Enterprise Promotion Zone or EPZ.[8] This measure is aimed at encouraging new investment in industry throughout the island and is an expansion of efforts by an earlier UNP regime under former President J.R. Jayawardana, a regime that came to power in 1977. The UNP under Jayawardana ended the country's reliance on import substitution strategies and opened the way to a 'liberalized' economy. This shift was given a jump start with the creation of the first EPZ near the international airport outside Colombo. It was there that some of the first garment factories were set up with special provisions, including tax holidays and the curtailment of union activity (Rupesinghe 1983; Shanmugaratnam 1985).

Under the new all-island EPZ plan, investors can take advantage of cheap labour and other incentives, similar to those initially offered in 1977, anywhere on the island. This has encouraged many foreign and local investors to start ventures in textiles, other light industries and agribusiness. This is the basic character of Sri Lanka's current development thrust. Corporate and individual investors provide the fuel for the economy to expand (i.e. capital), while the people of Sri Lanka provide the labour to build these industries from the ground up.

The adoption of these strategies marks Sri Lanka's fully fledged entry to the world market. Yet to survive in this game requires attention to certain characteristics of the global system. As David Harvey contends, the contemporary world economy is one characterized by 'flexible accumulation'. This marks a shift from mass production in a single, large and rigidly organized factory to a more 'flexible system [of] production with . . . [an] . . . emphasis upon problem-solving, rapid and often highly specialized responses, and adaptability of skills to special purposes' (1989: 155). It is also characterized by 'an increasing capacity to manufacture a variety of goods cheaply in small batches' (ibid.). This represents a shift from economies of scale to what Harvey calls 'economies of scope', in which production takes place through an intricate web or network of sub-contracting and out-sourcing (ibid.: 155–6). 'Flexible accumulation' also entails a 'time-space compression' due to improvements and declining costs in communications and transport that make it possible to shorten decision-making and production processes and to spread them across the globe. Consequently, employers enjoy greater control over labour, part-time and underemployment being the hallmarks of this new era (ibid.: 147, 155).

Under these conditions, markets for certain goods come and go very quickly, and production arrangements can change quite rapidly as well, with corporations moving their operations in the face of increased competition and risk. As a result a different sort of approach is required, one in which governments, corporations, businesses and individuals must all be ready to respond to rapid changes in the market. As Harvey argues, survival entails the development of 'flexible specificity' such that one is always prepared to make the specific changes in production that enable survival in the market.

For Sri Lanka to meet the demands of this kind of economy, it is necessary that at least some of the labour force become accustomed to its production requirements. In short, the country as a whole can no longer depend on the forms of production that previously dominated rural life, i.e. growing tea and cultivating rice. Moreover, to make the transition to production based on flexible specificity, it is necessary that people change the way they live their relation to production. As Antonio Gramsci noted with regard to Fordism in the 1930s, new types of workers, communities, ways of life, sexuality and identity are needed to implement a given form of production (1971: 279–318). Thus, the people of Sri Lanka must not only incorporate new kinds of commodities and work into their lives, they must also re-orient their identities and how they perceive their participation in development. Yet this is not an ideological re-orientation that the people are doing all on their own, even though the often heard term 'peoplization' might imply that. It is a process that receives ideological guidance from official sources. What is more, though the ideologies that are aimed at renovating popular notions about development and the people's role in it are couched in a rhetoric of participation, the kinds of participation sanctioned under the market-led form of development remain fairly limited. What options there are, can be easily discerned by examining the rhetoric supporting the recent 200 Garment Factories programme, just one of the many development ventures now being touted as the way to progress.

'Production by the Masses'

Attempting to discern how participation is constructed in mainstream development discourse in Sri Lanka is not too difficult. Exposure to development discourse is a fact of everyday life.

Merely walking through the cities, towns, villages and junctions, one is subjected to a cacophony of signs and symbols related to development, from development lottery booths to sign boards, from public spectacles celebrating development (seminars, official openings, speeches and so on) to news headlines and stories extolling the virtues of a government bringing about development for the people (Tennekoon 1988; Woost 1993). An important addition to this cultural terrain in 1992 was a complex of rituals and routines surrounding the '200 Garment Factory Programme'. The goal of this programme was to open 200 more garment factories in one year. During 1992 about 120 factories were officially opened. The stated purpose of this programme was to promote investment in the rural areas, thereby improving the employment situation in these depressed areas.[9]

In addition to its stated goal of easing unemployment in the rural areas, the 200-factories programme can also be seen as an attempt to construct a greater, more broadly based, legitimacy for this style of development. In this vein the programme provided ongoing opportunities for officials to promote export-led strategies, since each factory was ceremoniously opened much in the way that had become customary with regard to irrigation schemes and other agricultural projects (Tennekoon 1988; Woost 1993). While the late President was himself at the podium at a large proportion of these events,[10] he often enlisted the aid of celebrities, from investors and government officials to foreign dignitaries, including the US ambassador. The openings were widely attended events (if newspaper and television accounts are to be believed) and were broadcast daily on television and advertised in newspapers. The attendant press releases extrapolated further on related issues, while providing 'news' about the economic advances being made as a result of these policies.

In short, a large, complex set of rituals emerged in which every garment factory was opened with great fanfare. Every day on television one could see the late President on stage in the grounds of some garment factory, or working at a sewing machine while marvelling at the results of the export-led economy. His own testimonial was invariably supported by those of happy workers from the factories, usually young women, telling how the garment factory had saved them from a life of poverty. There were also all-night *pirit* ceremonies, often performed by notable monks, to invoke the Buddha's blessing on these enterprises.

The rhetoric emanating from this ceremonial complex proclaims an awakening of a village society bearing only a faint resemblance to the notions of community mentioned earlier. In contrast, the great socio-cultural revolution said to be taking place currently is supposedly marked by the emergence of 'textile villages'.[11] The latter are ideologically constructed as the new hub of economic activity in the areas where they are located. Aside from the influx of currency into the rural areas, textile villages are supposed to spur economic development in surrounding villages, since farmers will be able to sell their produce to factory workers. Local men can also provide periodic labour for factory construction and renovation as needed. It is also said that the proximity of the factories to the village will encourage villagers to explore avenues for the production of other export-oriented commodities. The location of the factory in the village is also supposed to keep 'the girls' close to their natal homes, free from the alienating environment of the city. In this way they will stay out of trouble, whether related to sexual or union activity. This strategy is also supposed to stem the tide of urban migration, with all its attendant problems. In other words, the 'textile village' is supposed to provide an economic and social boom for everyone in its vicinity, with the factory itself expanding into 'a centre for the economic development of the village'.[12] Gone are the references to the triad of paddy field, temple and irrigation tank. No longer is the re-emergence of the village community positioned as the motor of development. That prerogative is squarely in the hands of the investor.

In this scenario, the investment capitalist is usually constructed as a kind of guardian deity or patron of the village, who provides employment and some gratuities to villagers, thus replacing previous forms of village patronage.[13] The investor is also said to be motivated by Buddhist principles, not by the lust for profit. For instance, at one garment factory opening 'President [Premadasa] said that the investors in the garment industry were following the golden principle in using wealth advocated by the Buddha'.[14] Moreover, he continued:

> If he [the investor] was interested only in making profits, he could have made that investment in a more profitable venture. He could have made a fortune if he lent money for interest. [He] wanted to provide a lifeline to . . . poor families . . .. He was motivated by love

and compassion for the less fortunate. He realized the worth of the poor. He wanted to fulfil their need . . .. This is a trend that is gathering momentum in the country today. I can foresee an administration where the rule of love will prevail, in the near future.[15]

In this way, Premadasa argued that the programme was one way the government was 'humanizing' the use of wealth and giving the economy a conscience.[16] It was a programme that 'not only generated jobs for rural youth and opened up a source of foreign exchange', but was also 'converted *danapatiyas* (capitalists) into *danapathiyas* (philanthropists)'.[17]

In an attempt to link this construction of investment to a national past, Premadasa and other politicians often claimed that wealth held by the elite was a resource they ostensibly held

in trust, for the benefit of the entire society . . . Even in the society in the time of our ancient kings, economic activity was guided by social conscience and collective effort . . . *kaiya* (collective work) and *panguawa* (sharing of the harvest) were the main characteristics of the economic activity of that society. Even the king took part in the *kaiya* and he too claimed only his share.[18]

Thus there was continuity between the national past and the present in that investors used their wealth to work with the villagers to produce something collectively, while claiming only their fair share of the bounty.

Accordingly, investment-led development is said to create a brotherhood between the 'poor' and the 'rich' by forging a link between the 'big investor and the small producer'.[19] Time and again Premadasa and other politicians emphasized that villagers must not be seen as simply labourers or factory workers but as producers working collectively with investors to make a product. This was not to be mass production, it was 'production by the masses'[20] in league with the investor. Therefore, it is argued that a more 'humanized economy' will emerge in which 'everyone will get the opportunity to realize his human potential and each will recognize the other's need and worth. The resulting mutual respect and goodwill will banish class hatred'.[21]

This construction of development sets definite limits on people's participation. It does not give them the power to define development for themselves. Rather, development is a process in which the 'poor' benefit from the patronage of the 'rich'. Wealthy people can help 'to strengthen the weak' and make them more self-reliant.[22] Therefore, the 'poor' do not lift themselves up through a resurgence of community but find their worth, strength and power through the philanthropy of the wealthy, who retain the right to define the viable forms of production. Consequently, the 'poor' are only empowered to the extent that they become participants in an economic process fostered by wealthy investors, who come from outside their own rank, status and village.

The 'poor', in short, are not really empowered at all but are ushered into a new form of dependency. So even though this strategy for development is ideologically rendered as one that will eliminate the need for welfare (exemplified in slogans like 'trade not aid'), poor people are still being enlisted as participants in a programme that positions them as recipients of the goodwill of a wealthy patron. In some respects, this is probably an easy way to sell a programme of development, since the majority of the rural population has for decades been living development as a process initiated by powerful outsiders, whether they be government officials, wealthy traders or investors.[23] On that account, this strategy hardly seems revolutionary.

But there are still other ways in which the dominant discourse of development limits the popular interpretation of participation. For example, while the late President contended that 'every family in the country is in a position to share the benefits to the extent of its participation in the production process',[24] just how they share these benefits is not allowed to be questioned. This is made apparent in the way that lower-class Sri Lankans who provide the labour for these economic ventures are lumped into categories like the 'poor', 'the masses', 'the silent masses', 'labour', or even as 'little people'. These categories lump lower-class peoples into an undifferentiated pool of individuals who are on the one hand consumers, and on the other hand resources to be tapped by export-led industries. The people confined to these generic categories, who are often described as 'enterprising and skilled',[25] are supposedly waiting to be given an opportunity to express their 'talents'.[26] This usually means contributing labour to some enterprise initiated by a local or foreign investor. Bluntly stated, the people addressed by these terms are simply resources *for* development, not its progenitors.

The interpretation of participation as a resource for development in the Sri Lankan context resonates with Rahnema's recent comments about the concept of participation. He notes:

> participation has come to be 'disembedded' from the socio-cultural
> roots which had always kept it alive. It is now simply perceived as
> one of the many 'resources' needed to keep the *economy* alive. To
> participate is thus reduced to the act of partaking in the objectives of
> the economy, and the societal arrangements related to it . . .. For the
> modern construct of participation, a person should be part of a
> predefined . . . economic project, in order to qualify as a participant
> (1992: 120, emphasis in original).

This passage describes the interpretation of participation in the
Sri Lankan drive for an export-led economy in a nutshell. The
'masses' have no voice in the definition of this economy. In any
case the 'masses' are usually by nature 'silent', a designation that
also ignores the voices of protest that do exist. But in this scenario
the 'masses' need not be vocal, for, as the late President claimed,
the government understands their needs in spite of their silence.
The government, it is said, has adopted the path most beneficial
to the 'masses' and thus there is no need to discuss alternatives.
This is indeed a very tight-lipped form of participation.

These forms of discourse produce several 'ideological effects'
(Hall 1977). The first effect is to 'mask' the contradictions inherent
in the conflict between labourer and investor. As noted above, this
relationship is characterized not as one of struggle, but as one
involving love and mutual respect. Investment is not rooted
in the profit motive or greed, but in a compassionate use of
wealth that is sometimes presented as an outgrowth of Buddhist
religiosity.

The second effect is to fragment the body of labourers into
individuals. For instance, the late President was fond of saying at
public rallies that the people employed in the garment factories
were not 'factory workers' but 'producers', people who had a
resource that investors needed. Thus the people of Sri Lanka were
not to confront the investor/owner as a class or some other larger
social group, but as individual producers. In fact, everyone who
is not an investor has, according to this discourse, the potential to
become a producer. Everyone can make a contribution by making
themselves and their individual resources available to the investor.
The decision to make a contribution or not, to participate or not,
is not a social or collective decision but an individual one.

The third effect is to reunite the fragmented body of individuals into benign categories like 'the poor' or the 'masses'. By so doing, the individuals are re-identified, not as a group that is exploited, but as a group that has needs and desires that can readily be filled by market-led development strategies focused on investment. And while they may be disadvantaged as a group, they represent a latent pool of talent that can be made to bloom through the goodwill of the capitalist.

Taken together, these 'effects' set limits to the kinds of activities that can be construed as 'participation'. They organize ideas and assumptions about how development works in ways that support the drive for market-led development. In sum, they yield an ideological environment in which the 'people's' only real option in the struggle for development is to fulfil their roles as producers. They are not to decide what to produce or under what conditions they will do it, but simply to provide the resources needed to make the items that investors deem marketable in the world economy. The people thus remain silent; their only real opportunity to speak comes at the ceremonial factory openings, when representatives from their 'mass' are selected to tell the rest of Sri Lanka how much improved their lives are and how happy they are to be working for the factory owners. But even in that instance, they must wait until they are called upon.[27]

NGOs and 'Participation' in the market economy

It is important to emphasize that these 'effects' are not just part of language but have 'practical' ramifications that can be discerned in a multiplicity of social contexts. These practical effects, however, can readily be illustrated by looking at some of the ways in which the dominant discourses of development actually limit the activities and goals of NGOs working to develop the rural 'masses'.

Non-governmental organizations have often been singled out by both local and international development workers as having the ability to play an important intermediary role in the effort to empower the people and gain their participation in development. This is evident both in the literature on NGO activity in Sri Lanka (cf. IRED 1991: v) and from interviews I conducted with leaders and staff of many international and Sri Lankan NGOs in 1992. Nevertheless, while many NGO workers in Sri Lanka do describe their work in rural communities using a grassroots discourse (Sarvodaya, for example), one must concede that NGOs are still part of the development hierarchy with links to international donors and development institutions. Most are not autonomous people's organizations that actually grew up from the grassroots (cf. IRED 1991: iv–vii). Even so, development NGOs are usually said to provide a vehicle for helping the poor to participate more fully in their own development.

This is in many ways a very precarious position for NGOs and the people who run them. As I have already noted, participation is a concept that has a wide range of meanings, a range that the government seems very interested to limit. Thus the potential for conflict is great. While some NGOs have adopted the government position on participation, others continue to work on the basis of very different definitions, definitions that often conflict with the official rendition of how development works. While in Sri Lanka in 1992, I was able to interact with the personnel of NGOs at both ends of this spectrum and to document some of the ways the dominant interpretation of 'participation' practically effected their activities.

NGOs that situate their activities squarely within the limits of participation set out in official discourse often provide some service, educational or otherwise, which they believe will empower people to the extent that they will be allowed to operate more effectively within the market system. The majority of the organizations of this type that I visited were involved with 'income generation'. These strategies generally entail some kind of credit scheme in which attempts are made to set up local-level credit systems so that villagers can initiate productive activities aimed at the national and global markets. The hope is that this will allow entrepreneurs to blossom at the grassroots. This in turn is supposed to convince larger lending institutions to extend credit to the poor by providing examples of how trustworthy and industrious the poor can be if given a chance. Community development is rarely mentioned in these kinds of schemes. Rather, the focus is on individuals working on their own initiative to better their lot in life.

There are also efforts by a number of NGOs to teach budding entrepreneurs how to 'read' the rapidly changing market. These efforts are also portrayed as endeavours to increase 'people's participation'. These projects relate directly to the notion of 'flexible accumulation' discussed earlier. As one NGO leader explained to me, what nascent village capitalists need to learn is that just because there is a market niche for a particular commodity today, it does not mean there will be a demand for it tomorrow. They must learn to read the market and to adjust their operations rapidly to fit the way it is changing. As an example, I was told a story about a woman in one of their programmes who came up out of poverty by starting a pig farm on her land using a small loan provided by the NGO. As her neighbours saw her example and started raising pigs too, she got out of that business and sunk her modest capital into a new venture that she felt would have greater demand in the future.

According to many of the NGO leaders with whom I spoke, programmes such as these have become very popular in recent years with the government and with international donors. Some representatives of international donor organizations and government officials I spoke with also remarked that such programmes were the 'cutting edge' of development. Such strategies were said to fit well with the global emphasis on market-led development and with the Sri Lankan government's stated focus on 'investment not aid' or 'trade not aid'. Thus, while NGOs involved in this type of activity may not yet be in the majority, they are increasingly the ones that catch the donor's eye. For instance, one foreign donor agency gave me the names of several NGOs being funded.[28] Nearly all fit the general description above. But even more interesting is the fact that when I visited these organizations, the credit schemes they sponsored were represented to me by staff members in terms of 'empowerment' and 'people's participation'. Such programmes were said to be empowering because they taught individuals how to operate systems of credit successfully and to start their own businesses. This would in turn create jobs so that others who work for these new entrepreneurs could also take control of their lives. The programmes were said to be participatory because they obtained people's participation in the market-led development strategies.

I should make it clear that I am not berating the efforts of organizations trying to help people in whatever way they can. What I am taking issue with is the use of alternative vocabularies of development to describe activities that are clearly part of the mainstream. This is a concern voiced by many NGO workers themselves. One NGO staff member confided to me that while he worked to implement strategies like this, he did not feel they were truly emancipatory in the way implied by the rhetoric of partici- pation. He said that in the final analysis such programmes are funded because they resonate with the discourse of privatization that is currently in vogue. He also maintained that the limited success of some of these programmes was due to the fact that the poor already have a lot of experience working for the better-off members of their communities. In that sense, the majority of poor people's lives are not substantially changed: they simply take up work with emerging village entrepreneurs. The new entrepreneurs are meanwhile paraded around in the press as the harbingers of the new economic revolution that would be sweeping the countryside. The frustration for him was that he and other NGO workers were increasingly being forced to take up such strategies while adopting participatory rhetoric in order to obtain funding.

Thus while the intentions of most of these organizations are good, the overall effect of their activities has been to bolster the dominant strategies of development, strategies that set stringent limits on opportunities for participation. As just noted, this is even the view of many people who worked in these organizations. These activities also help create and spread new myths about self- improvement. The success stories displayed in the media often have the feel of old Horatio Alger stories. They recount how people who once had nothing have been able to make it to the top of the village hierarchy through ingenuity and initiative. The head of one NGO told me a story about a woman who had started a small business with a loan of only a thousand rupees. She now had ten or more people working for her in her village and was thinking of expanding. This woman, I was told, was a person who had all the skills necessary to become a successful entrepreneur, but who simply lacked the capital.

Another effect of these activities is that they tend to produce structural positions at the local level that are linked to the drive for a market-led economy. By creating more enthusiastic entre- preneurs at the local level, more people at the village level are exposed to the ideologies and activities that have become essential ingredients in the kinds of productive processes being pushed by the state. In this way, such ideologies and activities become naturalized. With members of one's own village engaging in these kinds of activities and speaking this particular language of development, the dominant strategies of development and definitions of participation begin to fit much better into local knowledge about development.

The 'Village Logic' of Development

While it is easy to trace out the possible functions of these 'participatory' practices of development in relation to the larger economic picture that is unfolding in Sri Lanka, it is often difficult to recognize how these strategies impact on the daily lives of people and their common-sense understanding of how the world works. In the remainder of this chapter, therefore, I would like to make some preliminary observations regarding the manner in which these new ideologies and practices of 'participatory' development might impact upon on the way villagers live and interpret their relationship with the processes of change that are referred to as development.

While I cannot claim to know how all villagers respond to the mainstream discourses of development, I have spent a fair amount of time since the mid-1980s (1985–87 and 1992) looking into the way in which the members of a settlement in southeastern Sri Lanka have lived and experienced development. This settlement, called Suduwatura Ara Gama, is home to 300 or so people, most of whom came to the region in search of a better life. They did this for various reasons, but scarcity of land was the prime factor for most of the inhabitants. The majority of the householders were very poor, working as wage labourers in addition to farming slash-and-burn plots and mining for gems in the nearby forest. Only two or three families out of fifty could rely entirely on their harvests for sustenance throughout the year. Additionally, there were few facilities, such as reliable transport and marketing facilities. Adequate health-care is also largely absent from the area. In general, then, the people lived below the poverty line and the majority of households experience hard times more often than good.

Even so, they also clearly understood that they were living in a period when great changes were supposed to be sweeping the country. As I have discussed elsewhere (Woost 1993), development is a major part of public discourse in Sri Lanka. Villagers are inundated with development in the form of lotteries, development projects large and small, seminars, rituals celebrating development, television and radio dramas, advertisements and political speeches, all touting development in some form or another. Through these media they hear constantly of the 'economic revolution' the government claims to be introducing. They have also learned to talk the talk of participation, even using the English words 'participation' and 'peoplization'. It is no surprise in this climate that the villagers sometimes remarked that they were living in the 'development era' (*sangwardana ugaye*). What is more, they were clearly aware of the ideological importance of development in the politics of both nation and village. I witnessed, for instance, the ways in which villagers capably adopted and manipulated the dominant discourses of community and participatory development in their interactions with development officials in their efforts to gain for their families and friends the resources they so desperately needed to make a better life for themselves (Woost 1990, 1993).

However, my observations of 'development' in Suduwatura Ara Gama revealed something else very interesting about villagers' ideas of development. Put succinctly, in spite of the various references to community and participation, the villagers generally saw development as a class-oriented project. While they never stated that overtly, when I asked them about what development meant and what it meant to be developed, nearly everyone responded by noting characteristics usually associated with upward class mobility. For instance, when I asked people (women, men and children) to give me an example of what it meant to be developed, they invariably defined it as a process of acquiring more material goods. They listed such things as having a car or motorbike, a two-storey house with servants, kitchen appliances, televisions and stereos, all good indicators of developed status. In short, to be developed was to be wealthy, having a lot of money. When I asked them to give me an example of a person who had become developed (*diyunu unna*), they would usually refer to a local individual who had recently become wealthy through gem mining. Alternatively, they might point to me as an example, since they believed generally that I was infinitely wealthy. While I would bring up the issue of improving irrigation tanks, roads and so forth, they usually saw such infrastructural improvements as things that would allow individuals to better their class position. In sum, there was rarely any talk of community development more generally. Their vision of the future was one in which individual families were able to raise their class position and thus participate more fully in at least a modest form of conspicuous consumption.

This was a view of development that directly affected my identity in the village, for Americans like myself were thought to be infinitely wealthy and thus, by definition, developed. Villagers were keen to situate me as a benefactor of development in the village on that account. I was a resource to be tapped in both individual and factional quests for a piece of the economic pie. This created all sorts of difficulties for me in that I really had few resources to share with them to make their lives better. However, the way they viewed my relation to development and the role I was supposed to play was indicative of how they understood development to work more generally.

By and large, development was understood to be a process in which outsiders brought wealth and improvement to a settlement or to individual families from outside the village boundaries. In general development was something that someone powerful and wealthy brought to you or gave you access to. It was not usually thought to be a process over which poor villagers themselves felt they had any control. Villagers did not often express this view outright, but in nearly all of their actions they reproduced this approach to the development process. Thus whatever development had occurred in the village was attributed to the goodwill of some outsider. The only real role for the villager was to work hard to incur or maintain the favour of powerful and wealthy outsiders so that they might look upon the village or some of its members sympathetically and grant them some resources. They never expressed to me a feeling that, through their own effort, they could develop the village or their families. The only way development was going to happen was if someone decided to give them a development project. As one man put it: 'Sir, we are but lowly and poor children in need of help. How could we develop this village ourselves or improve our family's position all on our own?'

To put it succinctly, they interpreted development as a status that was attained through the cultivation of good patron-client relationships. Their sense of powerlessness in relation to development was immediate in this sense. They never situated themselves as the source of development. Their participation was only as the recipients of whatever trickled down from a wealthy and powerful patron. A prime example of this occurred in 1992, the year the village was selected to be an Awakened Village in former President Premadasa's Gam Udawa ('village awakening') programme. Under this programme villages received loans and other assistance to build new homes and improve the village infrastructure. The people of Suduwatura Ara Gama pointed out that this would never have happened had not a former government official, who had set himself up as a benefactor of the village, taken it upon himself to petition the former President to 'awaken' Suduwatura Ara Gama. As a result of his intervention, one man in the village explained to me, 'the village is now receiving the assistance it needs to become developed. Had he not intervened on our behalf, we would have just gone on as before, struggling to make ends meet.'

The latter statement, and others like it that were made to me on many occasions, make it clear that the villagers of Suduwatura Ara Gama saw development as a fortuitous and unpredictable process. It was like the Development Lottery they were urged to play whenever they went to junction towns and or listened to the radio. Today just might be the day you'll win. In most cases, development just came out of the blue. As a result, they generally lived with very low expectations of the future, and these were often expressed in very anguished statements about what the future held for their children. One man told me many times he was sure his son would probably grow up and be killed as a member of some rebel political group protesting at the lack of jobs and means of subsistence. Yet he and others held the hope that some sympathetic and powerful outsider would come along and bring them the resources they needed to make yet another leap up the development ladder. In this respect, their expectations for development in some ways mirrored the logic of a cargo cult. Through the cultivation of various patron-client links with powerful outsiders, they were working to set the stage for another day when development would touch down in their village and leave some resources that would better their lives. In the meantime, they would go on doing what they do, struggling for survival on the land.

The manner in which notions of participation are being incorporated into mainstream development strategies like those I described above is unlikely to foster a sense among these or other poor Sri Lankans that they have more control over their future. Mainstream participatory development in Sri Lanka still cultivates a patron-client, cargo cult-like mentality: one participates in whatever development activity the well-placed patron decides to bring into your community or household.

Conclusion

What I have attempted to do in this chapter is to present some of the ways in which development discourse is changing in Sri Lanka. In particular, I was interested to show how the notion of 'participation' has been incorporated into a market-led strategy for development. I have briefly outlined some of the ways in which these limiting definitions have constrained the range of development activities that can be included under the guise of participation. In my view, these facets of the development terrain in Sri Lanka can lead to only one conclusion. Though the concept of 'participation' has been incorporated into the dominant discourses of development, this concept has been stripped of its alternative potential, whatever that may have been. What we have instead is a rhetoric with faint glimmers of Marx's statement about people making history – the people *can* participate. What is glossed over, though, are the stringent conditions under which people are allowed to participate.

Following the official rhetoric, the conditions under which the people are allowed to 'develop', to make their history, are not readily subject to re-organization or even to question. The conditions remain outside of the field of participatory development and in the hands of the market, the state or investors (i.e. in the hands of a patron). The poor can participate in development, but only in so far as they do not attempt to change the rules of the game. In short, we are still riding in a top-down vehicle of development whose wheels are greased with a vocabulary of bottom-up discourse. In fact, I would go so far as to argue that within the dominant rhetoric of development in Sri Lanka, the vocabulary of participation has become one of subordination rather than of constructing an alternative development. For under its terms, to participate is to bend one's purpose, goals and strategies to fit the official mould. Attempts to reshape that mould leaves one open to sanction. Whether or not it will be possible to rescue this vocabulary from the dominant framework of development in Sri Lanka or elsewhere remains an important and practical challenge in the struggle for a post-development world.

Notes

1. The research upon which this paper is based was conducted in Sri Lanka over a ten-month period in 1992. The research was funded by the South Asia Program of the Social Science Research Council.

2. As Majid Rahnema has recently pointed out in a recent discussion of participation (1992), the idea of people's participation has been around since almost the beginning of the development era (the late 1940s). However, he notes that many of the ideas commonly associated with this notion in an alternative sense were spawned and expanded upon during the 1970s. So while some movements for people's participation did emerge in Sri Lanka early on in the development era (for example, the emergence of the Sarvodaya Shramadana Movement in the 1950s), participatory rhetoric has only taken the ideological foreground in Sri Lanka in the last few years.

3. I have discussed this nationalist version of community elsewhere (Woost 1990, 1993). See also Brow 1988, 1990; Spencer 1990. For an example of nationalist writing in this vein, see Ariyaratne 1970, 1980, 1982.

4. For example, there were protests in 1992 against the construction of a huge hotel complex near a Buddhist holy site at Kandalama and against the lease of large areas of land in the south-east to multi-national agribusinesses.

5. For instance, the massive irrigation system at Lunugamvehara in the south, which ran completely dry in 1992, while up in the highlands the Samanalawewa dam sprang very serious leaks.

6. *Daily News*, 8 August 1992, p. 8: 'Foreign Investors Flock to Sri Lanka.'

7. *Daily News*, 30 June 1992, p. 1: 'Peoplisation: Towards a Share-owning Democracy.'

8. *Daily News*, 17 November 1992, p. 8: 'The Whole of Lanka Now Converted into an EPZ.'

9. *Daily News*, 6 August 1992, p. 6: 'Two Leading Manufacturers say: Garment Factories Can Provide Solution to Rural Job Program'; *Daily News*, 2 January 1992, p. 1: 'Scientist Lauds President's Initiative.'

10. President Premadasa was killed by an assassin's bomb on May Day, 1993.

11. *Daily News*, 25 November 1992, p. 6: 'Socio-economic Revolution in Villages through Garment Factories'; *Sunday Observer*, 15 November 1992, pp. 37–40: 'Building New Centres of Economic Growth'; *The Island*, 17 October 1992, pp. i–iv: 'Boom-time for Garments Industry.'

12. *Sunday Observer*, 15 November 1992, pp. 37–40: 'Building New Centres of Economic Growth.'

13. *Sunday Observer*, 15 November 1992, pp. 37–40: 'Building New Centres of Economic Growth.'

14. *Daily News*, 29 October 1992, p. 15: 'President Vows to Usher in New Order Bound by 'Spirit of Caring and Sharing.'

15. Ibid.

16. *Daily News*, 29 October 1992, p. 1: 'President Urges Humanising the Use of Wealth.'

17. *Daily News*, 1 December 1992, p. 1: 'Govt carrying out its people's plan, says President.'

18. *Daily News*, 31 October 1992, p. 17: 'New Value to People's Latent Skills and Creative Talents – President.'

19. *Daily News*, 3 July 1992, pp. 11–12: 'Investor-Producer Link Paves the Way to Freedom.'

20. *Daily News*, 21 May 1992, p. 6: 'Manpower Our Most Abundant Resource.'

21. *Daily News*, 29 October 1992, p. 15: 'President Vows to Usher in New Order Bound by "Spirit of Caring and Sharing".'

22. Ibid.

23. See, for example, Woost 1993.

24. *Daily News*, 17 November 1992, p. 21, Advertisement: 'Today Dialtex Interweaves into Kuliyapitiya.'

25. *Daily News*, 25 September 1992, p. 1: 'Development in Human Context.'

26. *Daily News*, 7 December 1992, p. 17: 'Poverty Cannot Be Eradicated through Doles and Food Stamps, Says President'; *Daily News*, 15 September 1992, p. 17: 'Stress on development of Human Resources'; *Daily News*, 21 May 1992, p. 6: 'Manpower Our Most Abundant Resource.'

27. Examples of this kind of participation are to be found in nearly every television or newspaper account of a factory opening (cf. *Daily News*, 30 October 1992, p. 6: 'Mother, Father and Son in Garment Industry'; *Daily News*, 17 November 1992, p. 21, Advertisement: 'Today Dialtex Interweaves into Kuliyapitiya').

28. I might add here that this individual also implied that as an international donor institution, there were certain restrictions on the type of NGO they could fund. Not only did the funding of an NGO have to fit into the scheme of the international institution's development mission, but more importantly, the Sri Lankan government also had to approve the funding of any NGO. Thus the implication was that this individual was inclined to fund a wider range of 'participatory' activities but that there were limits on what could be done.

References

Ariyaratne, A.T. (1970), *Sarvodaya Shramadana: Growth of a People's Movement*, Moratuwa, Sri Lanka: Sarvodaya Press.

—— (1980), *Sarvodaya and Development*, Moratuwa, Sri Lanka: Sarvodaya Press.

—— (1982), *A Struggle to Awaken*, Moratuwa, Sri Lanka: Sarvodaya Press.

Brow, J. (1988), 'In Pursuit of Hegemony: Representations of Authority and Justice in a Sri Lankan Village', *American Ethnologist*, 15: 311–27.

—— (1990), 'The Incorporation of a Marginal Community within the Sinhalese Nation', *Anthropological Quarterly*, 63/1: 7–17.

Gramsci, A. (1971), *Selections from the Prison Notebooks of Antonio Gramsci*, New York: International Publishers.

Hall, S. (1977), 'Culture, Media, and the "Ideology Effect"', in J. Curran, M. Gurevitch and J. Woollacott (eds), *Mass Communication and Society*, Beverley Hills: Sage Publications.

Harvey, D. (1989), *The Condition of Postmodernity: An Inquiry into the Origins of Cultural Change*, Oxford: Basil Blackwell.

IRED (1991), *Development NGO's of Sri Lanka: A Directory*, Colombo: IRED-Development Innovations and Networks.

McNamara, R. (1987), 'Paupers of the World and How to Develop Them', in T. Shanin (ed.), *Peasants and Peasant Societies*, Oxford: Basil Blackwell.

Rahnema, M. (1992), 'Participation', in W. Sachs (ed.), *The Development Dictionary: A Guide to Knowledge as Power*, London: Zed Books.

Rupesinghe, K. (1983), 'Free Trade Zones to Agricultural Promotion Zones in Sri Lanka', *Social Science Review*, 3: 116–38.

Shanmugaratnam, N. (1985), 'Some Aspects of the Evolution and Implementation of the Policy of Peasant Resettlement', in C. Abeysekera (ed.), *Capital and Peasant Production: Studies in the Continuity and Discontinuity of Agrarian Structures in Sri Lanka*, Colombo: Social Scientist's Association.

Spencer, J. (1990), *A Sinhala Village in a Time of Trouble: Politics and Change in Rural Sri Lanka*, New Delhi: Oxford University Press.

—— (ed.) (1993), *Sri Lanka: History and Roots of the Conflict*, London: Routledge Chapman Hall.

Tennekoon, N.S. (1988), 'Rituals of Development: The Accelerated Mahaväli Development Programme of Sri Lanka', *American Ethnologist*, 15: 294–310.

Woost, M. (1990), 'Rural Awakenings: Grassroots Development and the Cultivation of a National Past in Rural Sri Lanka', in J. Spencer (ed.), *Sri Lanka: History and the Roots of the Conflict*, London: Routledge Chapman Hall.

—— (1993), 'Nationalizing the Local Past in Sri Lanka: Histories, Nation and Development in a Sinhalese Village', *American Ethnologist*, 20/3: 502–21.

Chapter 11

The Ideology and Politics of Community Participation: Tank Irrigation Development in Colonial and Contemporary Tamil Nadu

David Mosse

Introduction

This chapter examines some influential ideas about 'common property' and 'community management' which currently dominate policy thinking and programme design in an important area of natural resources development. I use the example of the 'rehabilitation' of indigenous irrigation systems in southern India to illustrate the way in which policy science, and particularly its theories of local collective action, is embedded in institutions and shaped by their prevailing interests as part of the way that they think (Douglas 1986). Underlying this is the acknowledgement that environmental and development discourse is never value free but uses arguments which 'elide empirical assertion and moral judgement'(Jacobs 1994: 81) to produce and validate particular constructions of rural society. The implication is that these often misrepresent development interventions in significant ways. My aim is to take a critical look at one specific development planning discourse and, following Foucault, to identify the historically specific interactions between knowledge and power which accord validity to particular images of rural society and to particular types of scientific knowledge or social theory to the exclusion of others (cf. Escobar 1992, 1995; Ferguson 1990; Sachs ed. 1992).

The broad policy argument with which I am concerned (and which exists in the policy documents of international aid donors, as well as in academic form[1]) can be stated as follows. Throughout the world, non-private land, forest and water resources are seriously degraded as a result of biotic pressure from growing local human and cattle populations, changed agricultural practices or growing national demand. At the same time, there has been a widespread failure by centralized state bureaucracies to protect and manage decentralized common properties. Indeed, state-managed systems are increasingly viewed (especially by international donors) as costly, over-subsidized, inefficient, and in deepening fiscal crisis. At the same time, the existence of many successful instances of locally managed resource systems challenges (and reverses) Hardin's thesis 'tragedy of the commons' (1968) on the unlikelihood of communal solutions to resource exploitation and the necessity of state control (or privatization). Where they are given unambiguous and secure rights of access and use, local communities are in fact better managers of the natural resources upon which they depend for their livelihoods than are state bureaucracies. Programmes for resource development should therefore work towards establishing community management regimes in which the state machinery (in this case departments of irrigation) transfers resource management responsibility to local users.

My primary aim is to understand this set of policy ideas, not so much to judge their validity as to examine the models of community they project, specifically in relation to contemporary irrigation development in south India. However, to understand how parts of the discourse on the community management of irrigation have taken shape, gained acceptance and exerted influence in south India today, it is necessary to trace their roots to the exigencies of colonial administration in the nineteenth century. I will also show how some of the ideas and assumptions built into community management policies seriously misrepresent both past and present forms of indigenous irrigation in Tamil Nadu and provide misleading models for change. This issue will take the discussion into the detail of a recent irrigation development experience in a Tamil village.

The 'Decline of Tradition'

Although communities are considered better managers of local resources, an important sub-theme in the prevailing discourse on common property is that present levels of degradation are in large measure the result of the 'dissolution of traditional institutional arrangements'for sustainable resource use (Bromley and Cernea 1989: iii). The real 'tragedy of the commons' is not inherent in common property systems – since under the right circumstances local institutions can and do manage community resources – but in the *collapse* of these community systems and the damaging shift towards uncontrolled 'open access' to non-private resources which results. Moreover, in some cases it is argued that it is the intervention of the state (especially the colonial state in India) and its assertion of proprietary rights over common property resources which is the principle cause of this demise of traditional systems of resource-use (Gadgil and Guha 1992). When linked to the idea of the dissolution of traditional systems, the policy objective of 'resources management transfer' (i.e. from state to community) becomes underlined by the powerful ideology of the *recovery* of lost tradition. The focus of discussion here is the development of tank irrigation systems in Tamil Nadu, where, as I will show, ideas of the recovery of lost tradition are extremely pervasive and deep-rooted and provide a powerful legitimizing idiom for policies of 'irrigation management transfer'and the promotion of new village institutions.

South Indian tank-irrigation systems are socially and hydro-logically complex, and there is no space to describe them here (see Mosse 1997a). Suffice it to say that tanks are man-made reservoirs formed (mostly from the fourteenth century) by putting up crescent-shaped earthen embankments across the drainage flow to capture and store heavy run-off from concentrated monsoonal rainfall. Some are fed by diverting water from rivers or streams, but many are rain-fed. In some areas tanks were constructed as interlinked local chains or 'cascades'. Tank water reaches fields by gravity flow through sluices. Beyond irrigation, tanks have functions in the recharge of ground water, flood control and silt capture, and they generate income from foreshore forestry and bricks from silt as well as irrigation water. The kinds of complex village and supra-village social systems which operate tank systems today (and which did so in the past) are discussed elsewhere (ibid.)

Until the 1970s tanks constituted the single largest form of irrigation in Tamil Nadu, but today the 36-39,000 tanks in the state have declined in importance, both relative to other forms of irrigation (especially irrigation from pumped groundwater) and absolutely. In all districts tanks are in disrepair, are silted up, encroached upon, their sluices damaged, their embankments and weirs broken. The picture of the degradation of tanks as a resource is variable and the reasons for it complex and regionally and historically specific. Factors include deforestation, changes in drainage, changing land-use and crop regimes, colonial revenue systems which penalized investment in irrigation, inadequate state investments and the privatization of water control through the use of individually owned wells.

Quite apart from this complex set of factors, probably the most pervasive popular diagnosis of the problem in official circles, as well as elsewhere, is that a traditional system of tank maintenance and management has collapsed and that traditional skills have been lost. As already mentioned, it is often the British colonial system which is seen as eroding traditional systems and 'weakening community spirit' (although, ironically, early nineteenth-century English East India Company officers saw decaying village tank systems as a sign of the administrative and moral disorder of the regimes which *they* had come to replace). Occasionally, however, the post-independence period is seen as the era of 'governmentalism'and the 'cult of dependency' so damaging to traditional tank systems (Narayanan 1995).

The understanding of traditional tank systems is often quite specific. Village tanks are widely believed to have been managed by specialist tank committees which formed part of elected village assemblies and to have been maintained through a system of voluntary labour referred to as *kudimaramat* ('villager repairs').[2] Traditional tank management was village-based, autonomous of outside influence and functionally specialist. The root of the problem facing tank systems is, as Vani puts it, that there has been an 'erosion of the *autonomous* functioning of *village* management systems'(1992: 9, emphasis added). Just as the operation of traditional tank systems evokes images of internal order and bounded domains, so the collapse of the system is seen as involving a 'breakdown of [the] system boundaries' and the intrusion of the *external*, whether other villagers (competing for water), absentee landlords, revenue officers, government engineers, contractors and middlemen, funding agencies, foreigners and forms of various 'political interference' (Narayanan 1995). Outsiders or external agents of any kind are viewed as the source of 'disorder in rural life, [of] the chaotic condition created by present day politics . . .' (Govindaiah 1995: 143). Corrective measures thus involve the re-establishment of the autonomy of the bounded village, the reduction of the responsibility of government and the generation of awareness to convince villagers that 'their ancestors themselves undertook "tank" repairs of their community asset . . . but they have come to depend upon the state' (ibid.: 145).

Kudimaramat: 'Villager Repairs'and the Colonial Construction of Community Management

The current flood of local interest in village institutions of tank management in Tamil Nadu (evident in workshops, conferences and publications as well as field programmes[3]) is only paralleled by the great volume of material produced on the subject in the late nineteenth century. I shall argue that this historical parallel is more than coincidental.

The Madras Public Works Commission of 1869–70 and successive commissions of enquiry during the remainder of the nineteenth century amassed a vast body of evidence to demonstrate the existence of autonomous village institutions of tank maintenance and communal labour, generally referred to as *kudimaramat*, 'villager repair or maintenance works'.[4] Three factors probably contributed to this unprecedented interest in documenting irrigation 'custom'. First was the increasing evidence (supported by reports from the districts) that a large proportion of tanks in many regions were in a state of disrepair. Secondly, a newly centralized Public Works Department insisted on its *right* to own and control water resources in the public interest, hence the origin of irrigation law in Madras. Thirdly, following the famine of 1877-8, the government was forced to abandon a narrow concern with protecting revenue sources and admit its moral *obligation* to maintain minor irrigation systems (Mosse 1997b). In other words, in asserting proprietorial rights over, and moral responsibility for, highly decentralized tank systems, the newly centralized and technically specialized Public Works Department (PWD) had created for itself an inestimably large administrative and financial burden. In the early part of the nineteenth century control over irrigation lay with the decentralized revenue establishment which, having settled into local structures of authority, had been able to command local labour for public works. Since the new centralized PWD experienced the loss of such local authority, handing over the responsibility of irrigation maintenance to village communities on the grounds that this was 'customary' promised a convenient solution.

The seriousness and urgency with which the Madras government addressed the problem of customary obligations and *kudimaramat* can be judged from its actions in the late nineteenth century. First, major new programmes, including the 'Tank Restoration Scheme'(begun in 1883 and continuing until very recently), were premised on villagers' maintenance of the majority of tanks 'according to the old custom of the country known as *kudi-maramat*' and the transfer of tanks to villagers for management.[5] Secondly, being also aware that these customary obligations were rapidly disappearing, the government decided to halt the loss of so valuable a custom by force of law.

The Commissioners of Public Works, Irrigation and Famine and the Board of Revenue were all convinced of the expediency of legislation 'to give permanence to existing organisations . . . [where the system of "Kudimaramat" is already in force] and of reviving it where it has fallen into desuetude'.[6] Indeed, more than anything else *kudimaramat* became a concept of legal obligation bound by the nineteenth-century British judicial 'norm of universal applicability' (Price 1991: 117). Beginning with the Madras Compulsory Labour Act of 1858 (known as the Kudimaramat Act) the government took a series of steps to enforce community maintenance of tanks and customary labour by law.[7] Not surprisingly the Act failed, and several Kudimaramat Bills (1869, 1883), drafted to underwrite custom with the force of law, foundered because enforcement of the law depended upon the impossible task of proving in court that *kudimaramat* was customary practice in any particular village.

Despite the failure of legislation, the policy debate on *kudimaramat* custom had some profound effects in shaping discourse on 'community management' in south Indian irrigation. In the course of its various commissions of enquiry the government recorded a diversity of reported practice and opinion from local Revenue and Public Works officials. However, the official understanding of *kudimaramat* was quite independent of this record. Rather, *kudimaramat* as a 'customary'institution was constituted firmly in the image of the Public Works Department and in terms of the engineering standards it employed. Thus, by 1882 an establishment existed to produce a centralized and uniform set of information which specified for each tank not only an engineering 'standard of efficiency', but also an officially approved standard for 'customary'community maintenance that must have existed to operate the system efficiently. This was to become part of the official village records and to stand as an authoritative guide in cases of dispute.[8] The idea of *kudimaramat* which has held sway for over a hundred years therefore does not derive from observations on some ancient social practice at all, but is rather a record of the *physical consequences* of the absence of this assumed custom (i.e. tank disrepair) against engineering standards of technical efficiency.[9]

The image of traditional tank management generated by the *kudimaramat* debate, that is, autonomous village-based systems independent of the state, is easily open to empirical and historical refutation. In a detailed study of tank systems in southern Tamil Nadu, I have shown that their operation (including the determination of rights to water and dispute arbitration) has long linked villages to supra-local networks, and that despite the persistence of sophisticated village-level systems of water allocation or distribution, tank maintenance and repair has long been viewed as 'government' work. Obligations of tank maintenance and repair are firmly linked to the rights of overlords to a fiscal share of the village produce (Mosse 1997a, 1997c). Having said that, it is also true that colonial rule itself (especially its revenue settlements) had the effect of fragmenting such overarching structures and isolating tank systems from the supra-village social relations and resource flows through which they had earlier been organised and sustained. In this sense, in some areas colonial government had the (unintended) effect of *producing* the very fragmented autonomous village systems which dominated the administrative imagination at the end of nineteenth century. Since these were village systems 'decapitated by colonial rule' (Dirks 1987: 8), their very autonomy was cause for their 'decline'. To the extent that tank systems were in decline, therefore, it was because of the wider political changes brought about by colonialism and the dismantling of earlier state forms (ibid.) rather than because the intrusion of the state into traditional village systems led to a dereliction of community obligations. It is clear, then, that the British administrative system did not undermine an autonomous village institution belonging to the people but rather defined, reified and invented a tradition consistent with its own organizational purposes.

These are admittedly rather crude generalizations on the complex transformations of common property systems under colonial government. However, my concern here is not with the history of tanks in Tamil Nadu, nor even with the disrupting impact of colonial administration on political relations and resource flows which sustained them. My intention is not to contradict the projections of *kudimaramat*, but to show how this idea emerged as part of an official colonial discourse on community irrigation management.

As officially constituted, the policy idea of *kudimaramat* had three effects. First, it fixed and rendered standard highly diverse irrigation maintenance practices. In the bureaucratic imagination, complex and regionally integrated tank systems were localized and traditionalized (cf. Washbrook 1988) in ways that made them amenable to administrative manipulation. Secondly, *kudimaramat* discourse legitimized the government's demands on village labour as 'custom'. Thirdly, by codifying community obligations, it extended government control over tank resources, creating a new (legal) accountability of villagers to government (Vani 1992: 55).[10]

In sum, *kudimaramat*, and the idea of traditional tank management it has come to stand for, is rooted in an ideological instrument enabling the assertion of the state's administrative control over minor irrigation while limiting state obligations. 'Community control' in this sense was not the inverse of the extension of state power (or the dominance of an engineering discourse), but a necessary corollary of it. However, the effect of the idea of *kudimaramat* was also precisely to conceal the interests and operations of a new centralized public works administration behind the veil of custom and tradition.

The *kudimaramat* policy debate is, in fact, one example of the way in which 'traditional village India' more generally was constituted, localized, ordered and statistically recorded as the basis of nineteenth-century colonial administration (Dirks 1987; Ludden 1993; Mayer 1993; Stein 1989). It illustrates the way in which the projects of colonial government were disguised behind 'orientalist' facades. But beyond this, the nineteenth-century policy regarding community custom is also relevant because it raises the question of the kinds of 'orientalist' constructions involved in development policy today and the institutional purposes they may serve. I would now like to turn to this question.

From 'Tradition' to Collective Action: Image and Action in Participatory Irrigation

Today, the idea of *kudimaramat* is part of the everyday knowledge of PWD engineers in Tamil Nadu. This is not surprising since, from the late nineteenth century, the state's minor irrigation policy has repeatedly evoked the idea of customary community obligations for maintenance. But since *kudimaramat* was an invented institution defined by engineering standards against which actual practice always failed to measure up, *kudimaramat* custom was in dissolution from the very moment it came into being (cf. Mayer 1993). Indeed, the same Western engineering science which required and defined *kudimaramat* custom also disregarded, limited and constantly interfered with local farmer-managed systems. This has contributed to the widespread perception that farmer involvement in irrigation management declined in colonial times (IIMI and IIMA 1995: 5). The more the government tried to capture this elusive tradition, the faster it appeared to dissolve. The notion of *kudimaramat* has truly always been inseparable from its decline and disappearance.

Although attempts to promote community involvement through the enforcement of custom by direct acts of law were abandoned in the twentieth century, the Public Works Department's institutional imperatives ensured continuing efforts to codify community contributions through a series of irrigation bills from 1906 to 1934–6 (Mukundam 1988: 15–18). However, the utility of attempting to justify claims on village labour and resources for irrigation maintenance in terms of custom declined and indeed was effectively abandoned when, in the 1930s, government began to levy a tax on irrigated land to cover tank maintenance. But the idea of traditional village self-management and its decline did not disappear from policy discourse. In fact it increased in importance as a justification for state intervention in a variety of new community-level initiatives from the late nineteenth century.[11] Within irrigation there was, however, a change in the way in which imagined 'tradition' was institutionalized into official thinking and programmes. In particular, in the twentieth century, 'community obligation' was no longer institutionalized in the form of law but of local organizations, in particular village *panchayats* (councils for village self-government), which were widely constituted after the 1920s. *Panchayat* law not only began to deal with tank maintenance but also to order certain activities related to tank irrigation, such as water *distribution*, which were hardly touched in *kudimaramat* Acts (Vani 1992).

Like *kudimaramat* law, *panchayats* were burdened with carrying the government's principles of resource management, that is, the extension of community *obligations* to share the costs of maintenance but the retention of state *rights*. Today, while the Public Works Department is responsible for repairs to tanks with larger irrigable areas (over 100 acres) the *panchayats* (now institutions of local government) deal with smaller tanks. Neither state nor local-level government have resources adequate to the task of carrying out the tank maintenance and repairs which are their legal responsibility, and both continue to attempt to transfer costs to farmers through some bureaucratically defined community obligation, and underline this by appeal to the need for the revival of *kudimaramat* (IIMI and IIMA 1995: 9–10).[12] The problem of commanding community involvement in state-directed programmes, and the bureaucratization of rural institutions which this commonly involves, is part of the more general development contradiction of state-directed community 'self-help', which has bedevilled the major post-Independence initiatives of Community Development and Panchayat Raj (see Hulme and Turner 1990: 197; Jain 1985).

As indicated at the outset, irrigation policy is again, in the 1990s, proposing the transfer of management from government to communities as a means of dealing with financially crippling demands on irrigation departments made by widely scattered small-scale tank systems (and which being unmet, result in serious neglect and disrepair) through enhancing farmer involvement in operations and maintenance (Maloney and Raju 1994; Meinzen-Dick, Mendoza and Sadoulet 1994; Svendsen and Gulati eds 1994). While in the nineteenth and early twentieth centuries community involvement was institutionalized in the form of legally enforced 'custom' or institutions of local government (i.e., *panchayats*), today it takes the form of specially constituted 'water-users' associations (WUAs) (IIMI and IIMA 1995).[13] If *kudimaramat* 'custom' served to determine the limits of government obligations for a newly extended colonial state in the late nineteenth century, then 'irrigation management transfer' (institutionalized in WUAs) has a parallel significance in allowing the 'rolling back' of a state bureaucracy weakened by performance deficiencies and fiscal crisis.

Unlike the situation in the colonial state, in the 1990s irrigation policy reform in Tamil Nadu is shaped by multiple institutions with different interests: international institutions (the World Bank and other donors), non-governmental organizations (NGOs), the state bureaucracy and elected government. This adds significantly to the complexity of interests underlying constructions of community. Among PWD officials, 'tradition' is still a legitimizing idiom, and new water users' associations are seen explicitly as a means of reviving the customary obligations of *kudimaramat* in order to solve the problem of irrigation maintenance (IMTI 1993b). Indeed, the official promotion of legally constituted WUAs is pervaded with the notion of lost tradition and the 'recovery', 'rehabilitation' or 'revival' of latent community capacities. This emphasis retains the colonial concern to legitimize the transfer of maintenance obligations and initiate cost recovery while retaining state rights and control over irrigation resources.

The institutions that are legitimized with reference to village tradition and custom are also no less defined and shaped by bureaucratic concerns than was *kudimaramat* 'customary' practice in the nineteenth century. The rhetoric of the revival of tradition co-exists with strong ideas about the superiority of modern organizational forms as well as engineering science. Water-users' associations have to meet expectations about the way in which Tamil farmers *ought* to organize themselves. Through their roles, procedures, records or membership criteria, these 'social technologies' attempt to impose quite *new* types of corporate groups, new tasks and accountabilities, and new ideas of procedural efficiency. Of course these meet organizational needs for a means of consulting with people, to harnessing local leadership and channeling development inputs, as well as persisting requirements for simplicity, orderliness and standardization, in short a need to recast the social organization of irrigation in manageable terms.[14] Arguably, in registered water-users' associations, the government has not only retained control over irrigation but also acquired a new mechanism to extend its influence in rural society.

Freed from its narrow use in colonial debates, irrigation

'tradition' (including *kudimaramat*) acquired new political meanings within nationalist and contemporary environmental
discourses. In non-governmental and environmentalist circles,
therefore, 'irrigation management transfer' forms part of a separate
discourse in which community rights and control are asserted *vis-
à-vis* the state. Community traditions are part of a critique of the
modernizing development strategies of the centralized state and
the dominance of 'Western' technical over indigenous community
perspectives (Sengupta 1993; Shankari and Shah 1993). This
perspective has also contributed to recent international policies
on community management of irrigation. For example, clear rights
and legal authority to manage tank resources are now widely
accepted as correlates of successful local irrigation management.
Secondly, it is pointed out that community institutions need *support*
from government in the form of funds, technical skills and training.
Thirdly, new principles of democracy and equity (caste and
gender) are introduced. Water-users' associations are expected to
manage tank resources and distribute the benefits proportionately
to all 'stake-holders': large and small farmers, tenants, landless
labourers, women and members of different castes.

While images of community tradition have long provided the
main way in which external agencies (governmental and NGO)
have conceived of and sought to mobilize farmer involvement in
irrigation, an alternative view, provided by institutional-economic
models, is now gaining popularity within international development agencies. This seeks to understand community action in
terms of the costs and benefits to individual actors. The focus is
not on values and social norms but on the context-specific structure
of incentives which determines the collective provision of rules
for irrigation use and which motivate strategizing *individuals* to
commit themselves to follow them (Ostrom 1990, 1992; Tang
1992).[15]

This reformulation of old communal ideas in terms of individual
costs/benefits and rule-following involves a new language which
changes the way things look in some fundamental ways. Farmers
(or *ryots*: colonial tenants or subjects) become 'users' or 'appro-
priators', their customs are 'social capital' and village organizations
are *'management* associations' (Malony and Raju 1994;[16] Ostrom
1990). Irrigation itself becomes less part of 'a nexus of community
and land which [link] local society to the state' (Gilmartin 1994:
1133) and more a business in which commercial arrangements link

clients and supply agents. This discourse, which strips irrigation of its social and political content, is gaining ascendancy precisely at a time when the Indian state is under pressure from ideologies of privatization and a renewed emphasis on the free market (linked to international capital). This is the language of international policy reform, intended not only to turn government into a reliable and commercially viable supply agent (e.g. by removing state subsidies), but also to incorporate villagers into the management of, and financial liability for, local irrigation systems.

Clearly, current policy on tank management transfer contains conflicting points of view. The policy concerns of NGOs and international donors are not easily compatible with state government concerns. For example, the PWD is no more enthusiastic about the NGO demand for the transfer of government's rights over tanks to villagers than about the demand for accountability to users, the removal of subsidies or a shift to departmental self-financing. 'Community management' policy involves competing representations of locality and community, each being a 'simplification ridden with power' and institutional interests (Li 1996: 502, 508). As the case discussed below will show, depending upon the way in which these interests are represented locally, the idea of 'community management' either opens up possibilities for emancipatory change and new access to resources for the disadvantaged or affirms dominant structures and interests.

Different though these representations of community are, they also produce some common images of community resources management. I have already indicated the way in which ideas of community derived from *kudimaramat* generate models of tank systems which are standardized and timeless, and in which the village is isolated from external influences. Institutional-economic theory adds to this the model of local resource-use systems as equilibrium outcomes of a structure of incentives which takes little account of external influence and change. Moreover, implicit assumptions about the sufficiency of economic modelling of resource systems isolates these other aspects (symbolic and political) of social life.

It is true that recent institutional work is critical of earlier unrealistic assumptions about people as self-interested economic maximizers. Ostrom, for example, employing a more open-ended set of 'situational variables', proposes a 'framework for analysing institutional choice' rather than a particular (restrictive) model

(1990: 214). This qualifies but does not question the basic idea that community institutions of resource use can be analysed in terms of economic behaviour and material benefits – that institutions of tank management can be understood, not as embedded in cultural institutions of caste and religion, but as special purpose organizational solutions to the problems of efficient maintenance, allocation, and conflict management associated with water common property, 'with benefits from better water supply as the motive for organizing' (Meinzen-Dick 1984: 46). The operation of irrigation organizations is determined by the nature of the resource (its boundedess, seasonality, visibility etc.), the tasks to be performed (water acquisition, allocation etc.) and the distribution of benefits within the group, rather than by wider social variables (see also Bagadion and Korten 1991; Uphoff 1986; Wade 1987).

I will return to the question of why this particular social theory has gained a commanding position within agency discourse on resources management. But first I want to shift focus to the detail of a local development setting in order to show clearly the selective emphasis which the discourse on community management brings to bear on tank development and the reasons why this is inadequate. In brief, I will be suggesting that tank systems have to be viewed not simply as an economic resource, but as forming part of the village 'public domain' through which social relations are articulated, reproduced and challenge. Only from this perspective can the processes of irrigation development be adequately understood.

The Politics and Meaning of Local Institution Development[17]

During the 1980s and 1990s, major investments in Tamil Nadu tanks have been made under an EEC-funded Public Works Department (PWD) programme of 'tank modernization'. As an experiment, and modelled on successful work in the Philippines, the Ford Foundation supported a programme undertaken by the Centre for Water Resources (CWR) of Anna University (Madras) aimed at promoting new water-users' associations (WUAs) in selected tanks under the modernization programme.[18] WUAs were to take contracts for tank development, organize construction work and manage the improved systems using resources generated from new community rights over trees, fish, silt and other income-generating tank resources (CWR 1990: 125–32). These associations were facilitated and supported by field-based teams.[19] Since 1989 the CWR approach has been included in the wider PWD-managed tank-rehabilitation effort in Tamil Nadu (IIMI and IIMA 1995: 17).

Discussion here focuses on the tactical manipulation of competing representations of community (Li 1996) involved in the evolution of a WUA in the village of Nallaneri (a pseudonym) between 1988 and 1993. Not only did the government (PWD) and the NGO (CWR) understand the process of tank development in different ways, but the two castes who composed the village, upper-caste Mudaliars (40 percent) and low-caste (untouchable) Harijans (60 percent), evoked and manipulated images of community associated with the tank in pursuit of their own separate strategies for social change. What is of particular significance in terms of the conflicting meanings of 'community management' is that the formation of the WUA involved the use and transformation of an existing 'traditional' tank management system.

The crux of the existing irrigation management system in Nallaneri village was a 'share'- (*panku-*) based rationing of tank water at times of shortage. There were six time-based 'shares' with a total entitlement of twelve hours' irrigation from the tank. The order in which the different 'shareholders' drew water from the tank was determined by drawing lots, and the distribution of water was overseen by a paid 'water guide'. These shares were held by leading Mudaliar families (and named after their former lineage heads). Through this system of *pankus* Mudaliars exercised privileged rights over scarce water to the exclusion of others. Mudaliar shareholders also had defined rights in the worship of the village temple.[20] This *panku* system probably represents the vestige of an earlier system, characteristic of the area, in which all village resources (rights in land, water, labour and temples) were controlled by share-holding collectivities (termed *mirasi* by the British).[21] The gradual consolidation of individual private property rights over agricultural land during the nineteenth century broke up these land-holding collectivities and introduced a distinction between farm land, now subject to private rights, and irrigation water (as well as trees, wasteland and temples), which remained in the 'public domain' (Ludden 1985: 198, 188). In recent times, *pankus* have had a much reduced proprietary significance, limited in practice to certain rights in 'public' or common village resources, namely rights to shares in tank water,[22] and rights in the temple. However, these *pankus* (shares in the tank) have a symbolic as well as a proprietary significance. They are not only entitlement to water at times of scarcity, but also symbols of the status and social position of leading Mudaliar families of Nallaneri village. Moreover, they suggest that the tank, while at one level an irrigation structure, is at another level (like the temple) a 'public institution' expressive of the village social order (Mosse 1997a). Such significance is often overlooked in popular views of 'traditional' tank systems as embodiments of indigenous 'technical knowledge'.

Traditional systems are also attributed characteristics of equity, efficiency and adaptability which they often do not possess. Indeed, when the CWR project began work in Nallaneri the *panku* system was virtually moribund as a mechanism for water distribution. It had failed to adapt to social change. In particular the 'shares' bore little relation to current wet-land ownership owing, first, to a change in the area of the tank command (irrigated area), and secondly, to the increased proportion of wet land held by Harijans (25.8 percent by mid-1993).[23] Because of the inequity of the system and the disputes between Mudaliars and Harijans that this generated, the *panku* system had largely been replaced by a procedure to distribute water in turn through different branch channels. This too gave rise to irresolvable conflicts (CWR 1990: 23).[24] As well as being inflexible and inequitable, the *panku* system was technically inefficient in that it had to distribute water to widely scattered field plots within the command area. In addition to a defunct water-management system, the tank had many physical symptoms of neglect, including encroached feeder channels and a silted tank bed.[25]

Despite these problems, and believing the *panku* system to be a platform for 'common village activities', the project staff agreed to re-establish the system as a basis not only for water distribution but also for representation on the Executive Committee of a new water-users' association (referred to as 'the Society'). To achieve this the number of *pankus* was first increased from six to ten so as to include *all* landholders (including Harijans) as shareholders. However, despite its significant practical benefits, the Society and its newly constituted rules (e.g., on labour contributions for maintenance, on water distribution or fines for cattle grazing crops) was not, as the project had hoped, accepted as a self-evident public good. One reason for this was that the practical functions of the Society were not, in the eyes of villagers, isolated from its wider social and symbolic significance.

When, in 1988, project staff sought to 'solve the prevailing caste conflict and establish traditional amity among the villagers' (CWR 1990: 47), they had in mind the development of the tank society as a basis for the project's strategy to promote farmer control of community resources. This carried the implicit assumption that the advantages of collective resource management would provide sufficient motivation for organizing. However, from another perspective, in promoting a water users' association the project had began to build a new and publicly avowable means by which Mudaliars and Harijans were able to pursue their respective and opposed strategies of caste dominance and social protest. Social meanings other than water resource management came into play. While its discourse was framed in terms of the development model of collective action for utilitarian outcomes, the Society was also built upon a prevailing cultural understanding of 'public' activity as a context for the expression of social hierarchy and protest. While for Mudaliars 'public service' (of which the new tank development programme was an instance) was an appropriate means to demonstrate leadership and social pre-eminence, for Harijans 'public service' had always been indicative of social subordination and dependence. Both parties articulated and validated their respective points of view in terms of the publicly avowable project ideas of community management and the common good and accused the other of 'non-cooperation'. But, interestingly, neither Mudaliars not Harijans appear to have seriously considered the Society as a basis for achieving a equitable access to common resources. This scenario can be explained by illustration.

Harijan Resistance to the WUA as a 'Public Good'

From a range of incidents, it is clear that for Mudaliars and Harijans the new WUA had a quite different significance. In brief, for Mudaliar leaders, the tank Society and its idiom of public service provided a means for their caste to reassert its claims to social superiority at a time when older hierarchical relations of dominance and subordination were being eroded. For example, as

Harijans acquired greater economic independence from Mudaliar landlords (based on increased land-ownership), they began withdrawing from their customary 'public services' and labour obligations, which were also indicative of social inferiority. Harijans refused labour to Mudaliar landlords and sought better paid contractual labour arrangements outside the village in place of secure but low-status work within it. They withdrew from ignominious public service roles at Mudaliar funerals and village festivals and refused to provide voluntary labour for the laying of a village road.[26] Ironically, the new Society provided just about the only public context controlled by Mudaliars in which Harijans could be incorporated in a position which was subordinate – for example, in terms of Harijan exclusion from leadership roles, their limited control of land-based *pankus* (which effectively denied the political importance of Harijan numbers) and in the seating arrangements in the office building (at least as I witnessed it: Harijans on the floor, Mudaliars on chairs or cots).

Harijans, for their part, perceived and experienced the tank Society as a Mudaliar organisation in which their own participation was heavily circumscribed. From the outset, Harijan farmers were sceptical of an association (the Society) so obviously founded on an institution of Mudaliar caste dominance (the *panku* system), albeit extended to include their minority interests. Their reluctance to be included in the 'moral economy' of the new 'Society' was expressed in various ways.

In the first place, Harijan leaders objected to the *panku* system as a criterion of Executive Committee membership on the grounds that, being based on wet-land ownership, it gave no recognition to Harijan numbers and social position in the village. In fact, Harijan membership of the executive was eventually increased from two to three (two representing their *panku* and one extra). They also objected to the inequity of a water distribution system which, being based on time, disadvantaged Harijans, who mostly owned small plots at the tail end of the irrigation distributary.[27]

A second issue was Harijan labour. Despite appeals to 'serve the common good', Mudaliar Society leaders were frustrated by Harijan members' persistent refusal to forgo the opportunity to bargain with 'their own' Society for higher wages, since this was seriously reducing the opportunity for profit from the PWD contract.[28] The Society failed to pre-empt wage-bargaining by persuading Harijan members to take over its Labour Sub-

Committee and handle the labour component of the PWD works on sub-contract. Relations between Mudaliar and Harijan society members became increasingly confrontational. As colony Harijans continued to bargain for higher wages from the Society, Mudaliars organised labour to undercut Harijan wage claims.[29] Under financial and time pressures, collective action ideals were gradually abandoned and private labour contractors engaged.

It was precisely the experience of the new Society as a manifestation of the hierarchical moral order from which they had recently asserted independence that underlay Harijan resistance to full participation. The 'community action' ideal compromised a newly acquired right to bargain not just wages but also social position. However, as an expression of an alternative democratic notion of community, articulated and supported by powerful outsiders,[30] the Society also offered unprecedented access to political support and resources. At various points, Harijan members tactically manipulated contacts with outsiders and their understanding of community in bargaining the terms of their 'participation' in the new tank institution and to gain material and symbolic resources. For example, Harijans sought to regain customary rights to resources, such as the usufruct of palmyra trees on the tank bund, which had previously been held in recognition of their public (or village) service but which had been denied them once they began to withdraw labour and services. They also bargained better representation in the Society, and treatment with respect at association meetings. The Harijans' achievement of position within a 'public' institution was in itself a significant symbolic acquisition. Nonetheless, Harijans ultimately accepted persistent inequalities in the Society because they were committed to a longer term strategy of social and economic advancement based on increasing their share of the village wet land.[31]

The Tank Society as a Challenge to 'Institutional Leadership'

The project-promoted tank Society did not just embody the ideal of co-operative action, it also institutionalized this in the form of new procedures and participatory conventions (e.g. new membership criteria, a system of office-bearers and duties, by-laws, records and registers, mediated public meetings, and task-oriented

274 *David Mosse*

committees requiring the representation of all castes). Not only were old antagonisms articulated in a new language of community, these also took place in new public contexts and involved new institutional resources, rights and entitlements. The Society was not only a vehicle for articulating changing caste relations (or being shaped by them), it also altered the terms of public engagement themselves. It created an alternative village public with new meanings which, over five years (and with the influence of the project staff and resources), gained some ascendancy. Indeed, the creation of new roles and the mediation of old disputes relied on this.

To the extent that the project involved the symbolic making of a new 'community of project participants', it also challenged established interests and disrupted existing structures of authority and styles of leadership. On the one hand the Society's work (the implementation of a PWD works contract) threatened the *material* acquisitions of contractors, officials and key village leaders. On the other hand, as its own procedures (e.g. those relating to purchasing and finance) became formalized and removed from the hands of dominant families, the society was itself less accessible as a *political* resource to village leaders.

As Mines and Gourishankar argue (1990: 762), in South Asia leadership is characteristically exerted through institutions. The south Indian 'big-man' is an '*institutional* big-man' defined by the institutions which he controls and which publicly establish his credibility as a trustworthy individual and a generous and altruistic benefactor of the public good. The wide range of institutions through which leadership is enacted include temples, charities, schools, loan societies, political parties, labour unions and NGOs. Arguably, individuals *need* institutions to head in order to become or remain leaders (ibid.: 764).

The tank Society offered a means to re-assert traditional leadership in Nallaneri, but only to the extent that the institution could be 'personalized', which was less and less as procedures were formalized. More than the loss of private contracts, it was the loss of the right to leadership of the Society as an important public institution and the damage to family honour which this implied that provoked major factional division and the obstruction of project work by key village leaders. Among other things, this was manifest in the substitution of private contracts for Society work, direct action to halt construction work, the damaging of components of irrigation structures, police complaints and counter complaints, telegrams to the senior officials including the Secretary PWD, allegations of riot, a case against the project in the consumer court, and other protracted litigation which halted all project work for one and a half years.

What was at stake was the control of an institution which, by virtue of its 'development' purposes, had increased resources, increased visibility and therefore increased political significance. The linkages involved in this international development setting had enormously raised the stakes and widened the canvas of a village dispute, such that the aggrieved family, having mobilized a wide network of individuals, could be found defending their status and honour even in the chambers of the Secretary of the PWD in Madras.

By 1991, the tank Society had become the focus of a bewildering variety of individual disputes, personal grievances and the settlement of old scores (Mosse, forthcoming a). The project did, however, eventually manage to mediate an enduring resolution, largely because prolonged litigation had eroded support for the 'dissident' group while new 'bureaucratic' Society leaders had won over Harijan members through new concessions. Ultimately, therefore, the emergence of the Society as a new type of public institution ensured the failure of 'institutional big-man' leadership just as it constrained the reproduction of Mudaliar caste dominance.

From its beginning, the Society brought together competing representations of community and meanings of 'public action'. Its early structure was a fragile negotiated compromise between Mudaliar assertions of social dominance, Harijan resistance and the distinctive aims and values of the project team (i.e. its principles of equity and participation). On the one hand the WUA was (and remained) only weakly legitimized by its function in irrigation management. Its *panku* system was socially inequitable, technically inefficient (irrigating widely scattered plots) and marginal to an increasing number of Mudaliar families, who were diverting economic interests from wet land cultivation to urban employment and business in nearby Chengalpattu town.

Ironically, on the other hand, the tank Society seemed uniquely placed to articulate caste and factional conflict. As a vehicle for social honour and political ambition, the tank's influence extended way beyond wet-land agriculture to urban-based kin (residents of Chengapattu and Madras) who had no interest in cultivation at all. The very fact that far more funds were mobilized for litigation than for tank repairs suggests that this water-users' association was as much a political institution dealing in the symbolic resources of honour and status as a functional body managing irrigation (or PWD contracts).[32] The question is, why should so much caste and factional conflict focus on the activities of an institution of tank development? I want to offer one general and one rather more specific answer to this.

At a general level, all development is about power as well as resources. When an agricultural development worker introduces new crop varieties to experimenting farmers, s/he distributes not only seeds, but also power.[33] Indeed, all development projects provide symbolic resources in the local competition over power. Taking a ride in the project jeep or sitting near prestigious visitors are examples of the many signs and symbols of power and status provided at the 'interface' between projects and communities. New village structures and societies certainly help institutionalize existing relations of power. But projects also bring their own agendas, which offer new opportunities to validate challenges or to redefine existing relationships.

Development action is invariably *public* action, particularly when participatory styles and strategies are adopted, and the public is the domain of power and authority. Discussions, meetings and participatory research events are all public activities. As I have argued elsewhere in connection with methods of Participatory Rural Appraisal (Mosse 1994), development action involves public social events in which communities act in front of a wider audience. Between 1988 and 1993, Nallaneri received an enormous number of outside and foreign visitors, including representatives of state and national departments, the EEC, Ford Foundation, independent researchers, PhD students, local NGOs and national research institutes. In these circumstances much was at stake in controlling or gaining prominence in the village 'development' institution (in this case a WUA) which came to represent the village to influential outsiders. But if through development interventions natural resources also become political resources, they do so in culturally and historically specific ways. To understand the symbolic significance of the tank as a 'common property resource', we need to understand it as part of the village 'public domain', the domain of public service and public action as defined through culturally specific Tamil conceptions and social practice.

Briefly, the village public domain is the domain of authority, rank and caste status. This makes tank work eminently political action. The public affairs of the tank articulate positions of power and social standing and conversely provide opportunities to challenge authority, canvass political support and articulate factional affiliation or caste protest. The Nallaneri tank Society was clearly a status institution through which changing inter-caste relations were articulated and social position and honour contested. In other Tamil tank systems too, rights in the tank, rights to water at times of shortage, rights to a share of fish caught or to usufruct on trees on the tank embankment and obligations of service all continue to express caste and social status. In consequence these rights and obligations (whose material significance may be no more than a handful of fish) are often subject to dispute out of proportion to their economic significance (Mosse 1997a, 1997c). Shares in the tank are similar to the more clearly symbolic shares in village temple worship. In fact, throughout Tamil Nadu, the language of rights and entitlement (e.g. *pankus*) embraces both material and symbolic types of common property or public resource.

The development project, through its new resources and external linkages, greatly enlarged the public domain and the symbolic (as well as material) resources at stake. At the same time, through new resources, procedures and values, it changed the local politics of common property. The project introduced, and by degrees enforced, its own notion of the 'public'or 'common good' – drawn from a contemporary development discourse which emphasizes equal rights, social justice, gender equality, participation and democracy – and its own conception of the tank Society as a task-focused corporate organization capable of increasing the accountability of the bureaucracy and asserting villager rights *vis-à-vis* the state.[34] The project therefore successively (and simultaneously) amplified *and* undermined the political significance of tank common property. The tension between local structures of authority and the project's development values, a tension exploited by caste and factional groups and mediated by project staff, is a more general feature of processes of local institutional development.

Conclusions

The purpose of this diversion into the detail of a local development experience is not only to bring to light the complex cultural dynamics of tank development, but also to throw critical light on the theories of collective action involved. Both colonial and contemporary irrigation sociology, both *kudimaramat* and institutional theory, divert the interest of planners away from social actors and their wider interests and take little notice of the contests of power in resource use and development. In this sense they are part of development as an 'anti-politics machine' (Ferguson 1990). By focusing on a narrow understanding of economic interest, the institutional models used in planning tend to render local, historical and social factors as, at best, of secondary importance and, at worst, as unanalysable random occurrences of marginal relevance to planning. They also endorse earlier constructions of water-users' associations as autonomous, self-managed, spontaneous institutions, influenced by external factors but basically sustained internally by a structure of incentives in relation to resource use.

But – and this is the point – it is precisely by this denial of power and history that models of custom or collective action are able to provide the generalizing and predictive models of rural society which are evidently *required* as a basis for rural administration or programme planning. Development projects are invariably conceived as closed and controllable systems which isolate hypothesized causal links in order to determine predictable outcomes from planned inputs (Mosse, forthcoming b). They necessarily project static or 'steady state', ahistorical and apolitical representations of rural society. These projections are also normative and ideological in the sense, for example, that newly theorized 'community management' ideas have emerged within a (global) discourse (policy and programme practice) oriented towards finding community solutions to the perceived problems of state and market-based water control and management. As Palmer-Jones has suggested (1995), internationally supported irrigation development programmes employ notions of community management which can quickly become self-fulfilling. Where 'success' is defined in terms of the prescriptions of the model itself (e.g. association membership, rule conformity) programme experience, policy and theory become mutually validating. In such a discourse, there is little capacity to embrace local complexity, such as that of the Nallaneri tank. Indeed, simplified models can leave out precisely those elements which account for local success and failure (see Mosse, forthcoming b).

Community management models not only ignore the *local* politics of resources development, they also serve to mask the significant role of *external* resources and actors, 'institutional organizers', agency representatives, government officials and the financial and political resources they command. As Nallaneri shows, outsiders have a critical role in negotiating structures and rules, enforcing sanctions, mediating conflict and acquiring resources. In Nallaneri, the 'incentives' of contractors, PWD engineers, political leaders, NGO workers and donor representatives proved to be as important as the incentives of farmer water-users in the operation of the tank Society. Indeed, community management models (like *kudimaramat*) 'construct as spontaneous and self-sustaining, institutional solutions which are in reality conceived, imposed and in most cases sustained by substantial external authority and resources' (Mosse 1997b). Moreover, the often exceptional allocations of financial and human resources put into well-publicized and innovative pilot projects (and agency interest in success stories) give a misleading picture of the performance and sustainability of 'community management' in the longer term or on a larger scale (Palmer-Jones 1995).

The Nallaneri story also makes it clear that farmers themselves do not perceive (or desire) community management institutions as autonomous village institutions. The central meaning and purpose of the new WUA has to do with linkage to external authority and with mediating access to external resources. In part, it is this purpose and orientation which makes water-users' associations so fundamentally political.

These comments are not to be taken as a broad criticism of community management approaches to natural resources development. In many respects these offer the most hopeful solution to resource degradation of common property resources. However, these approaches do imply a need for some more complex and locationally specific models of collective action if they are to provide useful operational guides for development. Equally, institutional economic approaches can contribute powerful explanatory frameworks in which to set community management efforts. My point is simply that these development strategies and the social theory which underlies them are strongly ideological in the same way that ideas on *kudimaramat* were in the nineteenth century. They can therefore misrepresent as well as guide local institutional development.

The final issue I want to return to concerns not the constraints of dominant models of community management in irrigation development, but the question of *why* these come to hold the influence that they do. The point is that in different ways both *kudimaramat* and more recent models of farmer 'participation' closely match the concerns of the administrative or development regimes within which they exist and from which they derive their legitimacy.

As Mary Douglas points out, our policy problems are posed and solutions found within institutions which 'systematically . . . channel our perceptions into forms compatible with the relations they authorize. They fix processes that are essentially dynamic, they hide their influence . . . they endow themselves with right-ness . . .' (1986: 92). Douglas reminds us that irrigation policy ideas such as *kudimaramat* tradition and self-governing local institutions are socially constructed: they are social facts, and part of policy-making as a collective enterprise.

However, policy ideas are rarely plainly stated as normative regional operational strategies. They need the wider authority gained through being linked to theorized bodies of knowledge about rural society and the way it works. Models of 'community management' are themselves 'substantiated according to the scientific standards of the day', whether these be the voices of authorized European officers speaking on *kudimaramat* in the pages of the commissions of enquiry in 'the Enlightenment rubric of objective science' (Ludden 1993: 252) or observations on collective action 'solutions' substantiated by the game theoretical models of economic behaviour which dominate contemporary development discourse. I am not suggesting that development institutions (irrigation bureaucracies or donor agencies) are the creators of social theory, merely that they constrain and select theory, nudge the thinking of their members in particular directions and impose particular interpretations (ascribe motivations etc.) on observed behaviours.

Furthermore (and conversely) this social theory has direct operational implications in shaping development interventions (or colonial administration). As Breckenridge and van de Veer say of 'orientalism' – the hegemonic form of knowing the 'other' explored by Said (1978): 'orientalism . . .is not just a way of thinking . . . [but] a way of conceptualizing the landscape of the colonial world that makes it susceptible to certain kinds of management' (1993: 6). The concordance of 'colonial government constructed between empirical evidence and social theory by weaving orientalism as a body of knowledge into the fabric of administration and law' (Ludden 1993: 266) is well illustrated by the thirty-year long *kudimaramat* debate. It is also evident in contemporary development discourse, which in its own way is also 'orientalist' (Palmer-Jones 1995).

Finally, development policy ideas engage with already contested domains of power and meaning (Li 1996: 515). These encounters produce a multiplicity of social and political effects. But these processes and outcomes cannot be predicted or identified within normal planning models or project monitoring systems. These are precisely the things which are excluded from development projects by management tools such as 'logical framework analysis' which are oriented towards identifying expected changes against pre-defined indicators. Yet the incorporation of analysis of local social processes and power relations is especially crucial to the implementation of community irrigation. The means to do this have only recently begun to be addressed, for example, in evolving methods for process documentation and monitoring (Mosse, Farrington and Rew, forthcoming; Uphoff 1992; Veneracion 1989).

Notes

1. This summary statement extracts from a very large literature. In connection with water resources, see especially IIMI and WUHEE 1994; Ostrom 1990, 1992; Uphoff 1986; see also Curtis 1991.
2. This picture is commonly supported by a rather selective use of historical material. Records of village assemblies and tank committees, for example, are found in some early (tenth-century) inscriptions. These mostly relate to settled Brahman communities (*brahmadeyas*) in fertile riverine or river-fed tank

irrigated tracts. Such assemblies do not appear to have been universal and were not a feature of the drier plains areas where tank irrigation dominated. Even where they did exist, after 1300 local assemblies were increasingly subsumed under new hierarchical political forms dominated by warrior castes (Dirks 1987). Even where it is recognized that supra-local authorities had a role in tank systems, attention invariably focuses on the village-level organizations rather than on the links to the wider structures of which they were a part.

3. For example, CWR 1990, 1991, 1993; DRDA and PRADAN 1994; IMTI 1993a; Janakarajan 1989, 1991; Malony and Raju 1994; MIDS 1983; Mukundan 1988; Pundarikanthan and Jayasekhar 1995; Sengupta 1991, 1993.

4. The term *kudimaramat* is a composite of the Tamil *kuti* 'inhabitant, subject', and the Arabic *maramat* 'repairs'. It appears in the records only after the 1860s, and remains, even today, largely unknown in rural areas. The deliberations on *kudimaramat* which occupied the major Commissions on Public Works (1869–70), Famine (1880) and Irrigation (1901–3) and filled the proceedings of the Board of Revenue and Public Works for over thirty years are reviewed and analysed in Mosse in preparation-a. For comparable colonial debates in north Indian canal irrigation maintenance, see Gilmartin 1994: 1134, 1137.

5. Report of the Indian Famine Commission, Part II 'Measures of Protection and Prevention . Parliamentary Papers Vol. LII, 1880 (India Office Library).

6. Proceedings of the Board of Revenue No. 1,192, 6 May 1876.

7. The government was undecided as to whether *kudimaramat* was essentially a system of voluntary or forced labour (Matthai 1915: 9–125), although the Compulsory Labour Act of 1858 undoubtedly put into place the practice of corvée labour (Ambler 1993: 4). This coercion of labour in public works was at times justified with reference to traditional village or high-caste rights over untouchable labour (Ludden 1985: 174). Ironically, the officers 'extrapolated from the village to the government' rights over labour formerly held by the dominant land-owning castes, but which had been rendered illegal by anti-slavery legislation (Ludden ibid.; Mayer 1993: 363).

8. 'Bill for the Enforcement of Kudimaramat in the Presidency of Madras', Appendix E. Public Works Commission 1870 (Tamil Nadu State Archives).

9. The British civil engineers from the military assigned to the Public Works Department in the mid-eighteenth century strongly emphasized technical efficiency and gave little if any attention to management issues in irrigation (IIMI and IIMA 1995).

10. The central bureaucratic invention of tradition described here is to be distinguished from the earlier 'social scientific discourse which underpinned British revenue settlement and administration in the early nineteenth century (cf. Gilmartin 1994). Through the latter, revenue officials explicitly recognized (or established) local rights and authority in tank systems. *Kudimaramat* was a quite different 'tradition, which, in fact, met with much opposition from district revenue officers (Mosse, in preparation).

11. For example, 'The Report of the Local Self Government Committee in Madras' (1882) (India Office Library).

12. *Kudimaramat* has tended to be conceived of officially as farmer contributions to government-initiated works. In a government order of 1963 *kudimaramat* implied a 40/60 sharing of maintenance costs between government and farmers, by 1974 this had changed to 4/3 apportionment, and in 1976 the Panchayat Unions were to undertake *kudimaramat* and recover the cost of these customary works from the farmers (IIMI/IIMA 1995: 10).

13. In canal irrigation, the turnover of operation and maintenance to user groups has recently been advanced officially throughout the state by government order under the World Bank-assisted Water Resources Consolidation Project. A Public Works Department Government Order (Ms. No. 1184, dated 23.11.94) directs the turnover of distributory level operations and maintenance on canal systems from the Public Works Department to Farmer Councils. Such an order for tank systems is awaited. What is ultimately proposed is a state-wide 'irrigation extension bureaucracy to support farmers organizations' (IMTI 1993b: 18 c–9).

14. I have elsewhere examined the specific and significant ways in which institutions in indigenous tank systems depart from the functionally focused corporate asset-holding organizations promoted under tank development programmes. For example, indigenous systems rarely involve *corporate* specialized organizations. Their procedures are informal and geared

towards minimizing social conflict and enhancing the position of local leadership as much as to maximizing utility or accountability (Mosse 1997b).

15. Institutional economic analysis uses formal models derived from the theory of repeated games to demonstrate the economic rationality of cooperation (e.g., in the use of common water resources) and the possibility of co-operative equilibrium outcomes from competitive games (Ostrom, Gardner and Walker 1994; Sengupta 1991).

16. Reporting on the National Workshop on Farmers' Management in Indian Irrigation Systems, Hyderabad, February 1992.

17. The following account of the formation and functioning of a formal WUA draws on process documentation records kept by the Centre for Water Resources (Anna University, Madras) project team from September 1988 until April 1993, as well as my own brief visits during 1993.

18. The complexity of this multi-agency project is quite typical of a number of programmes seeking to validate new approaches and influence wider government policy (in this case on irrigation management transfer) through innovative components added on to conventional programmes.

19. Each site-based team included a technical assistant, an institutional organizer and a process documenter, on whose monthly reports this account draws.

20. The annual festival of the goddess was celebrated on three days, the right to organize each day being held by two *pankus*.

21. As a Tamil principle of property right, *panku* or share is historically mostly associated with the wet zone of the Tamil country, where it was customary for an irrigated village 'to be owned by a group of family shareholders, each endowed with a portion of the village's collective assets expressed as a fixed number of shares (*pankus*)' (Ludden 1985: 85, 165). Mudaliars of Nallaneri probably emulated the pattern established in better endowed and high-status Brahman villages such as Uttiramerur. This latter was (from the tenth century) an established *brahmadeya* or Brahman settlement, whose elaborate set of functional committees, including that for the management of the large tank, are well known from the unusually rich inscriptional record (Stein 1980: 146–72).

22. Strictly speaking, since individual land title is a tax receipt

for wet land, it also includes rights to irrigation. For this reason in Nallaneri, the *panku* system is restricted to priority distribution in times of shortage.

23. Figures from my own rapid survey of wet-land ownership among Harijans (August 1993).
24. 'Nallaneri' monthly Process Documentation Reports (henceforth, PDR) September 1988, p. 4.
25. PDR September 1988, pp. 5–8.
26. PDR October 1988, pp. 5–7.
27. A point emphasized by the project's Community Development consultant P. Vasimalai. PDR May 1989.
28. Initially Harijans bargained on a daily wage rates, but were subsequently persuaded to accept a piece rate basis. PDR July 1990, PDR August 1990, PDR January 1991.
29. For example, PDR August 1990, PDR September 1990.
30. Including foreign visitors who insisted variously that tenants, the landless and women be adequately represented in the new Society. PDR March 1990, p. 42; PDR April 1990, p. 5.
31. Harijans openly accept that Mudaliars will attempt to employ the new institution to confirm priority access to benefits or to erode existing Harijan privileges. In the earliest public meetings, for example, Mudaliars expressed a preference for limited channel-lining and the diversion of resources into a community well to be sunk on land donated by a Mudaliar temple. Harijans, whose share of wet land in the tank command is disproportionately located in the middle and end reaches, stood to gain most from extension of the channel-lining (on farm work) and were sceptical of their chances of getting water from the new common well. Moreover, Harijans had to counter repeated claims that the tank-bund palm-leaves, to which they held established usufruct rights, should be auctioned to raise *common* society funds.
32. The relevance of Bourdieu's theory of 'symbolic capital' (Bourdieu 1977) to an analysis of these common property resource systems in Tamil Nadu is discussed elsewhere (Mosse 1997c).
33. Anil Bhatt's illustration from a training session in a project in western India.
34. The project's idea of the society as a common good is perhaps drawn from a distinctively European experience of the 'public sphere', which (as characterized in the analysis of Jurgen

Habermas) 'functions as an intermediary realm between "the state" and "the people"', rather than, as in Tamil society, as a domain of local authority and status (Price 1991).

References

Ambler, J. (1993), 'Financial and Institutional Challenges for Tank Sustainability: Some Historical Lessons', Keynote address, 'Think Tank Seminar' Madras, July 1993.

Bagadion, B.U. and F.F. Korten (1991), 'Developing Irrigators' Organisations: A Learning Process Approach', in *Putting People First: Sociological Variables in Rural Development*, Washington and Oxford: Oxford University Press for the World Bank.

Bourdieu, P. (1977), *Outline of a Theory of Practice*, Cambridge: Cambridge University Press.

Breckenridge, C. and P. van der Veer (eds) (1993), *Orientalism and the Post Colonial Predicament: Perspectives on South Asia*, Philadelphia: University of Pennsylvania Press.

Bromley, D.W. and M.M. Cernea (1989), *The Management of Common Property Natural Recources: Some Conceptual and Operational Fallacies*, Washington: The World Bank (World Bank Discussion Paper, No. 57).

Curtis, D. 1991 *Beyond Government: Organisations for Common Benefit*. London & Basingstoke: Macmillan:

CWR (1990), *Alternative Approaches to Tank Rehabilitation and Management: A Proposed Experiment. Annual Report 1988–89*, Madras: Centre for Water Resources, Anna University.

—— (1991), *Alternative Approaches to Tank Rehabilitation and Management: A Proposed Experiment. Annual Report 1989–90*, Madras: Centre for Water Resources, Anna University.

—— (1993), *Alternative Approaches to Tank Rehabilitation and Management: A Proposed Experiment. Bi-annual Report 1991–92*, Madras: Centre for Water Resources, Anna University.

Dirks, N. (1987), *The Hollow Crown: Ethnohistory of a South Indian Little Kingdom*, Cambridge: Cambridge University Press.

Douglas, M. (1986), *How Institutions Think*, London: Routledge & Kegan Paul.

DRDA & PRADAN (1994), *Discussion Papers: Seminar on 'Regeneration of Farmers' Management of Tank Irrigation Systems'*, *March 1–2 1994*, Madurai: District Rural Development Agency (DRDA) and Professional Assistance for Development Action (PRADAN).

Escobar, A. (1992), 'Planning', in W. Sachs (ed.), *The Development Dictionary*, London: Zed Books.

—— (1995), *Encountering Development: The Making and Unmaking of the Third World*, Princeton: Princeton University Press.

Ferguson, J. (1990), *The Anti-politics Machine: 'Development', Depolitization, and Bureaucratic Power in Lesotho*, Minneapolis: University of Minnesota Press.

Gadgil, M. and R. Guha (1992), *This Fissured Land: An Ecological History of India*, New Delhi: Oxford University Press.

Gilmartin, D. (1994), 'Scientific Empire and Imperial Science: Colonialism and Irrigation Technology in the Indus Basin', *Journal of Asian Studies*, 53: 1127–49.

Govindaiah, T. (1995), 'The Role of Water Management Committees in the Rehabilitation and Management of Tanks: A Study', in N.V. Pundarikanthan and L. Jayasekhar (eds), *Proceedings of the National Workshop on Traditional Water Management for Tanks and Ponds (Madras 14–15 September)*, Madras: Centre for Water Recources and Ocean Management, Anna University.

Hardin, G. (1968), 'The Tragedy of the Commons', *Science*, 162: 1243–8.

Hulme, D. and M. Turner (1990), *Sociology and Development: Theories, Policies and Practices*, Hemel Hempstead: Harvester Wheatsheaf.

IIMI and IIMA (1995), *A Survey of Irrigation Management Transfer Policies and Activities in Tamil Nadu*, Ahmedabad: International Irrigation Management Institute and Indian Institute of Management (Draft).

—— and WUHEE (1994), *International Conference on Irrigation Management Transfer: Draft Conference Papers, Vols. 1–3, 20–24 September 1994*, Wuhan: International Irrigation Management Institute and Wuhan University of Hydraulic and Electrical Engineering, Hubei Province, People's Republic of China.

IMTI (1993a), *Seminar on EC assisted Tank Modernisation Project Phase 2 Extension: Alternative Strategies and New Initiatives, 6–7 December 1993 (collected papers)*, Tiruchirappali, Tamil Nadu:

David Mosse

December 1993 (collected papers), Tiruchirappali, Tamil Nadu: Irrigation Management Training Institute.

IMTI (1993b), *Working Paper on Organising Farmers' Associations*, Water Resources Consolidation Project (World Bank), Tiruchirappali, Tamil Nadu: Irrigation Management Training Institute.

Jacobs, M. (1994), 'The Limits to Neoclassicism: Towards an Institutional Environmental Economics', in M. Redclift and T. Benton (eds), *Social Theory and the Global Environment*, London and New York: Routledge.

Jain, L.C. (1985), *Grass without Roots: Rural Development under Government Auspices*, New Delhi: Sage Publications.

Janakarajan, S. (1989), 'Characteristics and Functioning of Traditional Irrigation Institutions', *Bulletin, Madras Development Seminar Series*, 19/12: 81–101.

—— (1991), *In Search of Tanks: Some Hidden Facts*, Madras: Madras Institute of Development Studies (Working paper No. 97).

Li, T.M. (1996), 'Images of Community: Discourse and Strategy in Property Relations', *Development and Change*, 27: 501–27.

Ludden, D. (1985), *Peasant History in South India*, Princeton: Princeton University Press.

—— (1993), 'Orientalist Empiricism: Transformations of Colonial Knowledge', in C.A. Breckenridge and P. van der Veer (eds), *Orientalism and the Post Colonial Predicament*, Philadelphia: University of Pennsylvania Press.

Malony, C. and K.V. Raju (1994), *Managing Irrigation Together: Practice and Policy in India*, New Delhi: Sage Publications.

Mattai, J. (1915), *Village Government in British India*, London: T. Fisher Unwin.

Mayer, P. (1993), 'Inventing Village Tradition: The Late 19th Century Origins of the North Indian "Jajmani-system"', *Modern Asian Studies*, 27: 357–95.

Meinzen-Dick, R. (1984), *Local Management of Tank Irrigation in South India: Organisation and Operation*, New York: Cornell University (Cornell Studies in Irrigation, No. 3).

—— M. Mendoza and L. Sadoulet (1994), 'Sustainable Water Users Associations: Lessons from a Literature Review', Paper prepared for World Bank Resource Seminar, 13–15 December.

MIDS (1983), *Tank Irrigation in Tamil Nadu: Some Macro and Micro Perspectives*, Madras: Madras Institute of Development Studies.

Mines, M. and V. Gourishankar (1990), 'Leadership and Individuality in South Asia: The Case of the South Indian Big-man', *Journal of Asian Studies*, 49/4: 761–86.

Mosse, D. (1994), 'Idioms of Subordination and Styles of Protest among Christian and Hindu Harijan (Untouchable) Castes in Tamil Nadu', *Contributions to Indian Sociology*, 28/1: 67–106.

—— (1997a), 'Ecological zones and the culture of collective action: the history and social organisation of a tank irrigation system in Tamil Nadu', *South Indian Studies*, 3.

—— (1997b), 'Colonial and Contemporary Ideologies of Community Management: The Case of Tank Irrigation Development in South India', *Modern Asian Studies*, 13.

—— (1997c), 'The Symbolic Making of a Common Property Resource: History, Ecology and Locality in a Tank-irrigated Landscape in South India', *Development and Change*, 28(3).

—— (forthcoming a), 'Village Institutions, Resources and Power: The Ideology and Politics of Community Management in Tank Irrigation Development in South India', *Papers in International Development*.

—— (forthcoming b), 'Process-oriented Approaches to Development Practice and Social Research: an Introduction', in D. Mosse, J. Farrington and A. Rew (eds), *Development as Process: Concepts and Methods for Working with Complexity* [provisional title], London: Routledge, provisional publisher.

—— J. Farrington and A. Rew (eds) (forthcoming), *Development as Process: Concepts and Methods for Working with Complexity* [provisional title], London: Routledge, provisional publisher.

—— (in preparation), *The History and Social Organisation of Tank Irrigations System in Tamil Nadu*.

Mukundan, T.M. (1988), 'The "Ery" Systems of South India', *PPST Bulletin*, 16: 1–33.

Narayanan, L. (1995), 'Tank Management: Change and Continuity, Rejuvenation and Extension of Traditional Systems', in N.V. Pundarikanthan and L. Jayasekhar (eds), *Proceedings of the National Workshop on Traditional Water Management for Tanks and Ponds (Madras, 14–15 September)*, Madras: Centre for Water Recources and Ocean Management, Anna University.

Ostrom, E. (1990), *Governing the Commons: The Evolution of Institutions for Collective Action*, Cambridge: Cambridge University Press.

—— (1992), *Crafting Institutions for Self-governing Irrigation Systems*, San Francisco: Institute for Contemporary Studies Press.

Ostrom, E., R. Gardner and J. Walker (1994), *Rules, Games and Common-pool Recources*, Ann Arbor: University of Michigan Press.

Palmer-Jones (1995), 'Water Markets and Water Management in South Asia', Paper presented at the International Conference on the Political Economy of Water in South Asia. Joint Committee on South Asia Social Science Research Council, American Council of Learned Societies and Madras Institute of Development Studies (5–6 January 1995).

Price, P.G. (1991), 'Acting in Public versus Forming a Public: Conflict Processing and Political Mobilisation in Nineteenth Century South India', *South Asia*, 14: 91–121.

Pundarikanthan, N.V. and L. Jayasekhar (eds) (1995), *Proceedings of the National Workshop on Traditional Water Management for Tanks and Ponds (Madras, 14–15 September)*, Madras: Centre for Water Recources and Ocean Management, Anna University.

Sachs, W. (ed.) (1992), *The Development Dictionary: A guide to Knowledge and Power*, London: Zed Books.

Said, E. (1978), *Orientalism*, London: Routledge.

Sengupta, N. (1991), *Managing Common Property: Irrigation in India and the Philippines*, New Delhi: Sage Publications.

—— (1993), *User-friendly Irrigation Designs*, New Delhi: Sage Publications.

Shankari, U. and E. Shah (1993), *Water Management Traditions in India*, Madras: PPST Foundation.

Stein, B. (1980), *Peasant State Society in Medieval South India*, New Delhi: Oxford University Press.

—— (1989), *Thomas Munroe: The Origins of the Colonial State and his Vision of Empire*, New Delhi: Oxford University Press.

Svendsen, M. and A. Gulati (eds) (1994), *Strategic Change in Indian Irrigation*, New Delhi: Indian council of Agricultural Research, and Washington: International Food Policy Research Institute.

Tang, S.Y. (1992), *Institutions and Collective Action: Self-governance in Irrigation*, San Francisco: Institute for Contemporary Studies Press.

Uphoff, N.T. (1986), *Local Institutional Development*, West Hartford: Kumarian Press.

—— (1992), *Learning from Gal Oya: Possibilities for Participatory Development and Post-Newtonian Social Science*, Ithaca and London: Cornell University Press.

Vani, M.S. (1992), *Role of Panchayat Institutions in Irrigation*

Management: Law and Policy (Tamil Nadu and Karnataka), New Delhi: The Indian Law Institute.

Veneracion, C. (ed.) (1989), *A Decade of Process Documentation Research: Reflections and Synthesis*, Quezon City: Institute of Philippine Culture, Antenes de Manila University.

Wade, R. (1987), *Village Republics: Economic Conditions for Collective Action in South India*, Cambridge: Cambridge University Press.

Washbrook, D. (1988), 'Progress and Problems: South Asian Economic and Social History c.1720–1860', *Modern Asian Studies*, 22: 57–96.

Index

UNICEF (United Nations
  International Children's
  Fund), 163
United States, anthropology in
  the, 1–2, 5, 21
Unnithan, Maya, 9
USAID (United States Agency
  for International
  Development), 65

vegetation zones, 37
VHWs (Village Health
  Workers), 186
vikas, 26, 167
village-level studies, 27
village, traditional, in India,
  261–2

Wageningen approach, 3
Warren, M., 7
Werner, O., 7
WDP (Women's Development
  Programme), 157, 163
Western scientific knowledge,

13–14, 20, 24, 59, 68, 134
Westernization, 193
women
  empowerment of, 60, 97, 139
    158–9, 163
  in history, 71
  India, 21, 159–61, 163–80
    passim
  Kenya, 185
  Plantation Rehabilitation
    Project, 143
  see also gender
  Tanzania, 212
  Uganda, 209
  and work, 67, 70,
  Women in Development, 13
World Bank, 22, 63, 72, 92–3,
  97, 101

Zambia, 210
Zimbabwe, 68, 220–2
ZOPP (Zielorientierte
  Projektplanung), 99